A GUIDE TO RELIGIONS

TEF Study Guides

This series is sponsored and subsidized by the Theological Education Fund in response to requests from Africa, Asia, the Caribbean, and the Pacific. The books are prepared by and in consultation with theological teachers in those areas. Special attention is given to problems of interpretation and application arising there as well as in the west, and to the particular needs of students using English as a second language.

General Editor: Daphne Terry

TEF Study Guide 12

A GUIDE TO RELIGIONS

David A. Brown

WITH CONTRIBUTIONS FROM

Lynn de Silva, Joshua Kudadjie, Ruawai Rakena
Tongshik Ryu, and T. K. Thomas

PUBLISHED IN
ASSOCIATION WITH THE
UNITED SOCIETY FOR CHRISTIAN LITERATURE
FOR THE
THEOLOGICAL EDUCATION FUND

LONDON
SPCK

First published in 1975
by the S.P.C.K.
Holy Trinity Church
Marylebone Road, London, NW1 4DU

Reprinted 1977

Printed in Great Britain by
The Camelot Press Ltd, Southampton

COVER MOTIF

The 'praying hands' on the cover design are based on actual handprints dating from 20,000 years ago. They were made by men who left this mark on the walls of the caves they lived in near Santander in Spain.

ACKNOWLEDGEMENTS

The photographs in this book are reproduced by courtesy of the British Museum (p. 10), J. Allan Cash (p. 17), Miss Sophia D. Lokko (p. 30), Tongshik Ryu (p. 49), Methodist Missionary Society (p. 176[2]), Baptist Missionary Society (p. 176[3]), and Camera Press Ltd.

SBN 281 02849 4 (net edition)
SBN 281 02850 8 (non-net edition for Africa, Asia, S. Pacific and Caribbean)

Contents

Part 5   Religions in the Modern World

Preface

This book has been the major task in my study during the past five years and I have found the writing and editing of it both a privilege and a challenge. It has been a privilege to become familiar, at least a little, with some of the great religions in which human people reach out towards God in prayer and in worship. At the same time it has been a challenge to understand more clearly the relationship between the other religions of mankind and the faith in Jesus Christ which I share with other Christians. I do not yet understand it as clearly as I would like to do.

Two convictions have been strengthened during the writing of this book and they have sustained me in it. First, I believe that God intervened in human history in a unique and personal way in the birth, life, death, and resurrection of Jesus Christ. He is for me the Word of God who became man and who lived among us to reveal the glory of God and to renew God's purpose in the creation of mankind. I am deeply thankful to be a disciple of the Lord Jesus and to have heard His word of life.

Secondly, I believe that the God who is revealed to us in Jesus Christ is the Eternal Father who cares for the whole of His creation. The living God is neighbour to every human person, and is present in love in every happening. On this account, therefore, I honour and respect the religions of mankind, in all their great variety, as those activities in which people respond to God's presence with them. There are many falsehoods and weaknesses in these responses to the living God but they all express, in one way or another, the fundamental relationship which exists between the created universe and the Eternal Spirit who brought it into being. Even more, they express the relationship of love and dependence which there is between God and human beings who are called to be His children.

These two convictions do not correspond exactly with each other but they intermingle and support each other in my writing and my study. They both cause me to wonder and to worship, for they are intimately concerned with the things which make human life beautiful and good and joyous. They cause me to treat the whole of human history with sympathy and with reverence. They fill me with hope that God's purpose for the whole of humanity will come to fulfilment in and through Christ.

Most of this book explores the relationship between the Creator and the creation as it is expressed in the religions of mankind. The purpose of these chapters is to describe religions at their face value, not to criticize or evaluate them. In the last chapter, however, I have tried to relate this discussion to my belief that in Christ God intervened in our world in a unique and decisive way. I am grateful for the opportunity to add this last chapter to the book.

It might appear strange that Christianity, and to a lesser extent Judaism, find a place in the description of world religions, especially in a book intended in part for use in Christian schools of theology. Let it simply be said that just as Christ became incarnate in the world of men, so also the Christian faith is planted in the human community and is an integral part of the human story.

I wish at this point to express my indebtedness to the great study of Dinka religion made by Godfrey Lienhardt and published in his *Divinity and Experience, The Religion of the Dinka.* Although I am personally familiar with the Dinka countryside and have had personal friends among them, I could not have written this chapter without using his book, and, to a lesser extent, that of Professor and Mrs Seligman (see p. 252). The prayers and myth stories are all taken from one or other of these two books. Similarly, the Jewish prayers and hymns on pages 113 and 116 have been taken from W. W. Simpson's *Jewish Prayer and Worship,* a book which has been of great help to me.

I would like to thank my fellow authors who have so generously made their work available for this book, and have allowed me to edit their contributions to fit into its general pattern. I am very deeply indebted to them. I wish also to thank Daphne Terry, the Editor of this Series, whose unfailing encouragement and confidence have sustained me in writing this volume. I thank her for her stringent but courteous editing of every page, and especially for her acting as link-man between me and my fellow authors and for her work with the study suggestions and illustrations.

DAVID A. BROWN
Bishop of Guildford

About this Book

In this book we aim to introduce readers to the various religions which are practised by people who live in the world of our time. There are many such religions, and in a book of this size there is not space for a full discussion of every religion. We have, therefore, selected for study some representative religions, together with those which have followers all over the world. We have arranged these religions into groups in order to make their study more easy to follow.

Part 1 introduces readers to a discussion about God, and to the fact that there are many different religions in the world, through which people worship Him.

Part 2 describes four religions in which the priests and elders teach their beliefs and practices orally, by word of mouth. They are associated with communities which follow traditional rather than modern ways of life.

Part 3 describes five religions, each one of which is linked with the history of one particular group of peoples, or nation in the modern sense of the word. All of them, except Shintoism, have books which their followers respect as sacred Scriptures.

Part 4 describes three other religions. They also have written Scriptures but differ from the religions mentioned in Part 3 in one respect: they all have followers in many different nations. Their followers also feel a responsibility to win people from all nations to their faith. We call them, therefore, in this book 'international religions', but they might also be called 'missionary religions'.

Part 5 looks at our world as it is today in order to see what is happening to religions. We shall see that, in many societies, people are less religious than they were in the past. We shall also discuss the problems which arise when people from different religions live closer together than in the past, and begin to understand one another.

Students should note that this book only *describes* the religions mentioned in it. It only states what the people of a particular religion say they believe about God and the world, and does not attempt to say whether their beliefs are true or false. It only describes what people do when they pray or worship, and does not attempt to say whether they are right or wrong to do these things. Except in Part 5, this book makes no attempt to say whether any one religion is better or more true than another.

STUDY SUGGESTIONS

Suggestions for further study appear at the end of each chapter, or, in longer chapters, at the end of each main section. They are intended to help readers to understand more clearly what they have read, and to relate their studies to their own experience of life and work in the world. As in other books in this series, they are grouped under four different headings:

1. *Word Study*   These will help readers to check and deepen their understanding of any technical or other special terms which it has been necessary to use.

2. *Review Questions* on the content of the chapter. These will help readers to check their progress, and ensure that they have fully grasped and remembered the ideas discussed and the facts presented. The answers should be written down and then checked with the Key (p. 255).

3. *Bible Study*   These questions provide an opportunity to compare and contrast the beliefs and practices described, in the light of Bible teaching.

4. *Topics for Discussion and Research*   These not only indicate possible lines for further study, but will stimulate thoughtful readers to examine anew the basis of their own religious assumptions and their everyday relationships with people of other religions.

Some teachers may wish to use these Study Suggestions selectively or to substitute questions of their own. Some readers may not wish to follow them at all.

The *Key* (p. 255) will enable readers to check their own work on those questions which can be checked in this way. In most cases the Key does not give the answer; it shows where an answer can be found.

MAP

The map on p. xiv shows the main areas where the religions described are practised.

BIBLIOGRAPHY

Some books which readers may find useful for further study are listed, according to subject, on p. 252.

INDEX

The Index (p. 267) includes all the proper names of important people and places mentioned, and the main subjects dealt with.

BIBLE VERSIONS

The English translations of the Bible used and quoted in this book are the New English Bible (NEB) for the Old Testament, and the Revised Standard Version (RSV) for the New Testament (except in chapter 16 which also uses the NEB).

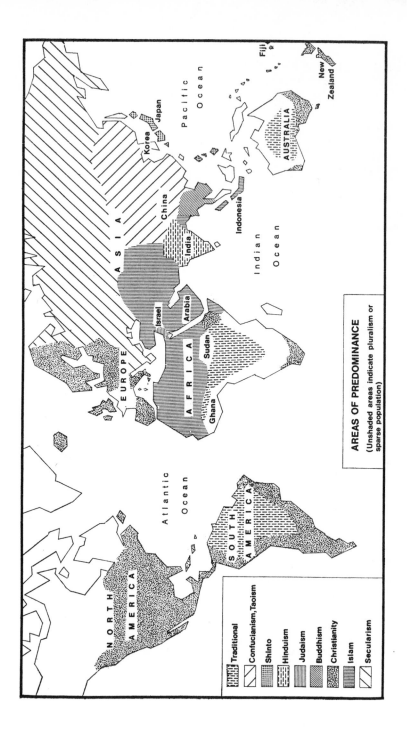

AREAS OF PREDOMINANCE
(Unshaded areas indicate pluralism or sparse population)

Traditional
Confucianism, Taoism
Shinto
Hinduism
Judaism
Buddhism
Christianity
Islam
Secularism

NORTH AMERICA
SOUTH AMERICA
EUROPE
AFRICA
ASIA
AUSTRALIA

Atlantic Ocean
Pacific Ocean
Indian Ocean

Korea
Japan
China
India
Israel
Arabia
Sudan
Ghana
Indonesia
New Zealand
Fiji

PART 1
RELIGION

Chapter 1
God

A. GOD

God is the living, eternal Being in whose presence all creatures 'live, and move, and have their being' (Acts 17.28). He has revealed Himself in many different ways, and human beings in particular have always felt His presence and responded to Him in worship. This living relationship between God and men is the basis of all religions.

But, as we shall see in this book, the peoples of the different religions think about God in different ways. Some believe that God is one personal Being for whom they use the word 'God' like a personal name. This is especially true of Jews and Muslims. Others believe that there are many different gods. Some Buddhists do not think of God as a personal Being at all. In the first two chapters of this book we do not use the word 'God' in any particular way, but as a convenient word by which to bring together the many different kinds of belief which people have. We are using the word *God* in a general way to mean 'the One whom people worship'. It is written, therefore, in these two chapters, in italics like this: *God*. In other chapters we shall use the word 'God' in the way in which the word is used in the religion which we are describing in each chapter.

God Himself is unchanging, always the same eternal Being who is beyond human power to describe in all His fullness. It is not surprising that people have different ideas about Him. Writing the word in italics, *God*, will help us to remember that *God* is a special word which describes the Eternal Creator whom we can never fully understand or speak about carelessly.

B. BEYOND AND WITHIN

In describing the relationship between *God* and the world, people say that *God* is *transcendent* and that He is *immanent*. These are two important words about *God*. They belong to each other as the two sides of one coin do.

Transcendent means that something is beyond what is natural and normal, and different from it. When people say that *God* is transcendent, they intend to make statements like the following:

(a) *God* is not limited to particular places and times as human beings are.

(b) *God* lives outside the natural world in which human beings live.

(c) Human beings can never fully know the will or the thoughts of *God*. He is beyond their understanding.

(d) *God* is always there first: He is the creator of all things and the initiator of all events.

(e) Human beings feel awe when they remember the presence of *God*. He is good and trustworthy in a way that they are not.

But human beings also feel the presence of *God* within their natural surroundings, and through what happens to them and their families. And so they believe that He is present within the natural world, although at the same time He transcends it. They express this belief by saying that *God* is *immanent*: *immanent* means 'dwelling within'. Immanence can, however, be a misleading word if we suppose that it means that *God* lives only within the created world. Some people think that it is better to say that *God* is in relationship with the world.

People of all religions think about *God* in these two ways, but different religions place different emphasis upon them. Muslims, for example, emphasize the transcendence of *God*. In Shintoism, believers worship the spirits who are everywhere in the world, and the Chinese religions teach that right conduct is of first importance. Christians say that Jesus of Nazareth reconciled the transcendence and the immanence of *God*, because he was both *God* and Man.

C. THE GREATNESS OF *GOD*

Many religious thinkers believe that *God* is in a living relationship with the whole universe at all times. For example, the great Muslim theologian al-Ghazzali (d. AD 1111) wrote:

His is the power and the kingdom and the glory and the majesty and to Him belongs creation and the rule over what He has created: He alone is the Giver of life, He is omniscient, for His knowledge encompasseth all things, from the deepest depths of the earth to the highest heights of the heavens. The smallest atom in the earth or the heavens is known unto Him. He is aware of how the ants creep upon the hard rock in the darkness of the night. He perceives the movement of specks of dust in the air. He beholds the thoughts which pass through the minds of men, and the range of their fancies and the secrets of their hearts, by His knowledge, which was from aforetime. (*Readings from the Mystics of Islam*, translated by Margaret Smith, p. 60)

2

Arjuna's Hymn of Praise to Krishna in the ancient Hindu *Gita*, written about 500–100 BC, expresses a similar belief about the relationship between *God* and the universe:

> Why should they not revere You? ... You are first Creator, Infinite, Lord of the gods, home of the universe. You are the Imperishable. You are what is and what is not and what is greater than both. ... You are the last prop-and-resting place of this universe. You are the knower and what is to be known. ... The whole universe was spun by You ... Your strength is infinite, your power is limitless. You bring all things to their fulfilment: hence You are All. ... You are the father of the world of moving and unmoving things.
> (From *The Bhagavadgita*, translated by R. C. Zaehner, pp. 85–86)

Some passages in the Bible also assert the close relationship between *God* and the natural universe. Here is a passage from the Wisdom Literature of the Old Testament, and another from one of the earliest prophetic books.

> By the words of the Lord his works are made. ... How beautiful is all that he has made, down to the smallest spark that can be seen! His works endure, all of them active for ever and all responsive to their various purposes! (Ecclus. 42.15, 22–23)

> He it is who forges the thunder and creates the wind,
> who showers abundant rain on the earth,
> who darkens the dawn with thick clouds
> and marches over the heights of the earth—
> his name is the Lord the God of Hosts. (Amos 4.13)

D. THE SIGNS OF *GOD*'S PRESENCE

In section C above we saw that many religions teach that *God* is in control of everything that happens in the whole universe. Most ordinary people, however, do not feel *God*'s presence in so wide and general a way. They usually feel *God*'s presence in special ways, or at special times and special places. In this section we consider the ways in which people see signs of *God*'s presence in their lives.

Human beings are always looking for ways by which to improve their relationship with the world around them. It is only by adjusting their lives to their surroundings that they are able to provide themselves and their families with the basic necessities of life: food, and shelter. Farmers must adjust their planting and sowing to the changes of the seasons. Fishermen and hunters must plan their work to fit in with the currents and movements of the seas, and with the habits of the fish and wild animals.

In some cases it is a hard task for people to adapt their lives to the conditions in which they live. They have to use many different skills as well as to be courageous and thoughtful. The Bedouin have to adapt their lives to the dry sandy deserts of Arabia, and the Eskimos to the ice and cold of the Arctic.

In trying to adjust their lives to their environment, people come into contact with powerful forces which appear to cause great changes in the natural world. They feel that these forces or powers are the ones which really control the world and the living creatures which inhabit it. They think of them as different from ordinary natural objects and living creatures. A child, for example, human or animal, is recognized as a natural creature, but the forces which cause conception, birth, and growth, are of another kind. Streams, rivers, and rain are natural things which human beings can to a certain extent control and use. But the succession of the seasons, the movement of the clouds, and the falling of rain appear to be controlled by forces which are beyond the merely natural. Unseen forces make people unite into groups such as families and tribes, while other unseen forces inspire them to battle and great deeds. Sometimes people are possessed by strange spirits. People call forces, powers, and spirits such as these *supernatural*: they are beyond the purely natural world and in some ways control it.

Experiences like these, repeated countless times through the centuries of human development, have helped human beings to feel the presence of *God*. They associate such forces and spirits with *God*, either as *God*'s servants or sometimes as living things which ought to be worshipped. We shall discuss examples of such beliefs later in this book.

Most developed religions teach that the relationship between *God* and the world is a universal one, and we considered this in Section C of this chapter. Even so, most religions teach that there are particular ways in which the relationship between *God* and the universe is expressed and strengthened, e.g.:

1. At the simplest level, particular natural objects are set apart as things through which the divine powers are able to work in human lives. Often these objects are stones, trees, or sources of water which people believe have special religious powers or significance. They often set aside the areas round such objects as sanctuaries or holy places. Sometimes they erect buildings near them for use as temples, mosques, or churches.

2. Particular people are called the ministers of *God*. They may be guardians of the sacred things, or leaders of the community's prayers and acts of sacrifice. Often they have an established position within the community as priests or temple-guardians. In some cases, however, individuals are associated with *God* almost against their will. People believe that such persons are compelled to speak on *God*'s behalf as

'Most developed religions teach that the relationship between *God* and the world is a universal one' (p. 4).

This belief is expressed today by many young people in many different parts of the world—like this couple in America.

In what ways is it chiefly expressed and taught in your country?

prophets or as seers. They are described as being possessed or inspired by *God*'s Spirit.

3. People also recognize *God*'s presence through the great events of nature. They think that great natural disasters or deliverances, floods, droughts, earthquakes, and the like, are acts of *God*. They may be either acts of His judgement or acts of His mercy.

4. In the same way, nations and tribes interpret the great events of their history as acts in which *God* intervenes on their behalf. Many books of the Old Testament and some chapters of the Qur'an recount history in this way.

5. In some religions, people treasure the records of great events and the words of the prophets and other inspired men as sacred Scriptures. People believe that these Scriptures have authority as revelations of *God*'s will and purpose.

In this book we shall discuss many ways in which people become aware of *God*'s presence through events in their lives or through special things which are close to them.

STUDY SUGGESTIONS

WORD STUDY

1. Look up the words 'transcendent' and 'immanent' in a dictionary. In what way, if any, do these words help you to talk about God?
2. In what ways does the word 'sacrament' help us to understand how God uses natural objects to help us feel His presence with us?

REVIEW OF CONTENT

3. Give four examples of beliefs about God which are held by people of all religions.
4. What are some of the forces which seem to cause changes in the natural world?
5. List three ways in which people of different religions try to strengthen the relationship between God and the universe.

BIBLE STUDY

6. According to the stories in Genesis, what were the different ways in which the Patriarchs, Abraham, Isaac, and Jacob, recognized the presence of God?
7. Read the following passages and say in each case whether the passage refers to (i) the transcendence of God, or (ii) His immanence, or (iii) both:
   (a) 1 Kings 8.27–30   (b) Isa. 55.6–11   (c) John 1.1–18   (d) Acts 17.24–29.

8. Read Matthew 5.43–48 and 6.25–34. What did Jesus teach in these verses, about the relationship between God and the created universe?

DISCUSSION AND RESEARCH

9. In what chief ways do you yourself recognize and experience the presence of God? Are these ways like or unlike the ways in which the Patriarchs recognized Him?
10. Which is more important to you, and why, God's transcendence or His immanence?
11. Find out as much as you can about:
    (a) The ways in which people of other religions in your country recognize the presence of God.
    (b) What they believe about the relationship between God and the universe.
12. Some people today say that God does not exist and that nothing is 'supernatural'. They believe that scientists will eventually discover and control even those forces which human beings do not yet understand and which seem to be beyond the natural world. What is your opinion of such beliefs? Give your reasons.

Chapter 2
Religions

A. WHAT IS A RELIGION?

In every community, big or small, the institutions of social life grow and develop in their own way. As time passes, the ways in which the community does things become fixed. So the rules which govern social behaviour become the laws of the community or of the nation, and the way in which a country is governed becomes a fixed political system. These institutions may, of course, be changed, sometimes quickly, sometimes slowly.

In a similar way, every community builds up its own religion. Most religions include the following elements:

1. The beliefs of the community about *God*.
2. The beliefs of the community about *God*'s relationship with the world.
3. The ways in which the people of the community worship *God* and pray to him.
4. The rules which the community follows because of their beliefs about *God*.
5. The places and people which the community believe to be holy and to belong to *God* in a special way.

B. THE VARIETY OF RELIGIONS

No human face is exactly the same as another human face, but it is like many others in having two eyes, a nose, two lips, and two ears. In the same way, no two people ever respond to *God*'s presence in exactly the same way. Each person's prayer is personal to himself, and each person's response to *God* has its own individual quality and characteristics. We should remember this whenever we discuss the religious practices of another person, especially when that person belongs to a different religion from our own. The relationship between *God* and every particular thing or living creature is unique, with an individual quality of its own.

Human beings, however, do not live entirely individual lives: a child is born into a family, and he or she grows up, marries, and brings up children within the family group. Family groups themselves are related to each other in the larger groupings of society: the clan, the tribe, the neighbourhood, the nation. Each individual has his own experience of *God*, but he or she can share it with others, and practise it with others in the community. Religion is both an individual and a social activity.

'Religion is both an individual and a social activity' (p. 8).

A Hindu sits alone by the river in Katmandu to pray. But he shares his faith with the hundreds of pilgrims who crowd the entrance to a cave temple of the god Shiva.

Which parts of your own faith are particular to you, and which do you share with others?

We should not be surprised by the great variety of religions in different parts of the world. Many different patterns of life have evolved in human society down through the ages, and many great civilizations and nations have been important at different times. It is not surprising, therefore, that the relationship between *God* and human people has taken many different forms. Each particular religion has a particular character because of the particular people who practise it. For example, Islam grew in the caravan cities of the Hijaz of Arabia, and Hinduism developed in the variegated life of India. American religions came to birth among those who lived in the swamps and forests and mountains and plains of America. The Dinka religion is close to the way of life of the cattle-owning Dinka of the Sudan, while Shintoism has many special qualities which fit the Japanese people who follow it.

C. THE RELIGIOUS ATTITUDE TO LIFE

We shall discuss many different religions in this book. Each religion is different from the others and has its own special characteristics. But there are certain ways of thinking and acting which occur in most religions: they show us that religion is a basic human activity which most people can understand and sympathize with.

1. People worship *God* as transcendent (See page 2)

In most religions, people believe that *God* is transcendent. He is independent of the world. Because of this they worship Him. They often see signs of His presence in extraordinary events and in the extraordinary powers which are at work in the natural world. These, however, are not the only ways in which they see signs of His presence. (See p. 3.)

2. People feel dependent upon *God*

Most religious people believe that *God* is closely related to the natural world, and they believe that He controls it. So they feel dependent upon *God*. They seek His help and protection and they fear His wrath. In most religions people believe that there are evil powers at work in the world which cause harm and illness. They seek *God*'s aid against them.

3. People feel that they owe a duty to *God*

Religious people feel that they have a duty to worship *God*. They do this by means of praise and gifts offered in religious ceremonies. In their daily lives they try to behave in ways which they believe will please *God*, and this helps them to decide what is right and wrong. They also link the more important events of human life with the worship of *God*, including those connected with birth, marriage, and death, or the planting and reaping of crops. When men fail to behave according to

10

their accepted ideas of right and wrong, they often feel that they have angered *God*. They use various means, especially sacrifice, in order to restore good relationships.

4. People pray with confidence

Religious people also believe that it is possible to gain the help of *God* by prayer, and they often accompany their prayers with sacrifice. The prayer of petition is, in some ways, the simplest and yet the most important of all religious acts. By praying, people express their dependence on *God*, and make their needs known to Him.

5. People think of *God* in personal terms

Human beings are *persons*. A person knows himself (or herself) to be a living being who exists as an individual. A person also has the power to think and to decide for himself. This self-consciousness and the power to choose make human beings into persons. Without these qualities human beings would be little more than animals. People think that *God* is a 'personal' being, like themselves. Another way to say this is to say that *God* is a 'he' and not an 'it'.

Most religions teach that human beings can have personal relationships of communion and fellowship with *God*. Many religious thinkers, however, teach that *God* transcends human life in this matter as well as in others. He is a personal being, but He is truly personal in a way in which human beings can never be because of their imperfections.

6. People see the universe as a whole and as related to the will of *God*

In the light of the relationship which people see exists between *God* and the natural universe, they work out for themselves a description or picture of how things fit together. By this picture, they are able to think of the different creatures and things which make up their world as related to each other according to the will of *God*. Such a picture is often called a 'world-view' or 'cosmology'.

In chapter 14, section B, we shall discuss some of the reasons why many people in our modern world have a world-view in which there is no belief in *God*.

7. People believe that *God* is the One who acts first in His relationship with them

The previous paragraphs have described the ways in which people practise their religions and what they believe about *God*. Many of the following chapters also will have much to say about the human side of the relationship between *God* and the world. But religious people believe that *God* is the one who acts first. He created the world, He gave them life, and He is the one who moves them to worship Him and to pray to Him.

STUDY SUGGESTIONS

WORD STUDY

1. 'People think that God is a "personal" being, like themselves' (p. 11).

    (a) In what ways do you believe it is correct to use the word 'personal' as a description of God?

    (b) Do you think the word 'transpersonal', i.e. beyond and above what is personal, would be more helpful? If so, describe some of the characteristics of God which are 'transpersonal'.

    (c) How do writers in the Bible describe God?

2. What is the meaning of the term 'world-view' or 'cosmology'?

REVIEW OF CONTENT

3. What seven elements do most religions include?

4. (a) What is meant by the statement that 'the relationship between God and every particular thing or living creature is unique, with an individual quality of its own' (p. 8)?

    (b) In what ways are the lives of human beings *not* unique and individual?

5. Give one reason for the great variety of different religions in different parts of the world.

6. 'People feel that they have a duty to worship God' (p. 10).

    (a) For what reasons do people feel this?

    (b) Give three examples of ways in which people try to fulfil this duty.

BIBLE STUDY

7. Read Genesis 1, and then describe in not more than 100 words the world-view expressed by the writer of that chapter.

8. Read Psalm 95.1–7. How does this Psalm illustrate the religious attitude to life?

DISCUSSION AND RESEARCH

9. A man born blind cannot understand colours, and a man born deaf cannot talk about music. Is it true that only a religious man can really understand religion? Or do you agree with those who say that religious people cannot speak truly about religion because they are prejudiced?

    Give reasons for your answer,

10. Discuss with your friends or fellow students in which ways your experience of God is like their experience. What, if anything, in your experience of God is unique, i.e. special to you, and not shared with others?

11. (a) Make a list of the different religions which people practise in your neighbourhood or in your country (ask your friends if they know of others).

(b) Add to your list the places or people which the followers of each religion believe to be holy, and the rules which they have laid down because of their beliefs about God.

12. Do you consider that the seven characteristics of religion listed on pp. 10, 11 are an adequate summary of the religion which you yourself follow? If not, what other characteristics can you suggest?

PART 2
FOUR TRADITIONAL RELIGIONS

Introduction

We have chosen four examples for study in Part 2, two from Africa, one from the South Pacific, and one from Asia. They are all different from each other, but they have one thing in common: they are all religions in which the prayers and the beliefs about God are handed down by word of mouth. They do not have any written Scriptures like the Bible or the Qur'an. They depend upon each generation of people handing on their traditions to the next.

There are many religions of this sort all over the world. In some their followers are few in number, often because they live in small and isolated communities. In others their followers number many thousands, and even millions. Each religion differs in some important ways from others, but each religion has important things to say about the way in which human beings have tried to worship God.

ONE GOD OR MANY GODS

The student will notice that in all the religions included in Part 2 people worship many different gods. Many of those who use this book will believe that God is one, and may find the mention of many gods difficult to understand. Perhaps the following points will help students to read these pages with sympathy and understanding.

1. God is present in the world even when human beings do not worship Him. He is present also when human beings have wrong ideas about Him. Humans have a very limited knowledge about God and often make mistakes in praying to Him. But God is loving and gentle: He hears prayers even when people pray badly, or use wrong words to address Him.

2. In many of the religions in which people worship many gods, they also believe that there is one supreme God who rules over all the others. In many cases they call this supreme God by names such as Father and Creator. (See pp. 18, 27, 40.)

3. Some of those who worship many gods recognize that these many gods are very closely united to each other. Some say that the different gods are 'all parts of one Divinity'. They believe that when they worship one particular god they worship Divinity as a whole. (When the word 'Divinity' is written like this with a capital letter, it means the whole group of divine powers and beings. When it is written without a capital

letter, 'divinity' can be used to mean one of the divine powers or a god.)

4. Many of the less important gods are personal names which people have given to the forces or powers which are at work in nature. Wind, Fire, and Rain, and similar natural forces, act sometimes as if they were living beings, and people treat them as such.

MYTHS

In religions which have no written Scriptures, people use *'myths'* instead. These are stories by which people express what they believe about the world in which they live. They are the fruit of people's thinking about the way life is, and why things happen as they do. In some religions they are written down by later generations.

Myths are usually about subjects like the following:

1. The creation of the world, both earth and sky.

2. The origin of man and woman, and the ways in which different tribes came into existence.

3. The entry of evil and death into the world.

4. The relationships between human beings and God.

5. The origin of different kinds of birds, animals, insects, and plants, and sometimes the reasons for their names.

6. The reasons why particular animals are associated with particular tribes or families.

Many of the myths have been handed down by many generations. They are often in old-fashioned language, and sometimes only the priests or elders are allowed to tell them, because they are among a community's most valued possessions. In the Bible, the myths of the Hebrews have been written down in the first chapters of Genesis.

Chapter 3
The Religion of the Dinka in Sudan

A. THE DINKA

The Dinka are a group of tribes living in southern Sudan. They are nearly a million people in number. They speak different dialects of a common language. They live in the swamps and flat country near to the White Nile and the rivers which flow into it from the west.

Most Dinka spend their lives looking after cattle. The cattle are their wealth, and are precious to them. Young men, in particular, become closely attached to the bulls with which they are associated. The flow of water in the streams and rivers varies very greatly during the course of the year, and because of this the Dinka often have to set up their cattle camps many miles from their homesteads. They spend long periods in the tribal cattle camps in the dry season, camping out in the open. The men are absent from home caring for the cattle at other times as well. In the rainy season the Dinka stable their cattle in large huts near their homesteads.

Most Dinka grow crops of grain and vegetables. Sowing takes place after the first rains in March or April, and harvest comes in October at the end of the rainy season. Some poor tribes have no cattle and little cultivation: they depend upon fishing and hunting.

Up to the present time, their way of life has been a simple rural one. Dinka homes are made of mud and wattle, with grass roofs. Each family has a few pots, gourds, household utensils, and spears. Like most cattle-owning peoples they make good use of skins, e.g. as leather vessels for holding milk and water, for bed-mats, and as garments for the women.

Not all Dinka share the religious beliefs described in this chapter. Many thousands have become Christians or Muslims.

B. BELIEFS OF THE DINKA ABOUT GOD

1. THE POWERS

The Dinka believe that there are superhuman Powers in the world, which affect their lives for good or ill. These Powers are able to act in ways which are beyond ordinary human ability. They are unseen, and their strength is more than human. The Dinka call these Powers 'jok', which may be translated as 'spirit' or as 'power'. Sometimes the Dinka refer to the Powers as *Nhialic*, which means 'that which is above

'Most Dinka grow crops of grain and vegetables. . . . They believe that *Nhialic* is the power who gives rain from the sky' (pp. 16, 18).

A Dinka girl working on a United Nations food-growing scheme helps to winnow the new year's rice crop.

What is the Dinka's chief purpose in praising their divinities? Do you think that a Christian Dinka has the same purpose in praising God at a harvest festival?

17

(in the sky)'. The Dinka treat these Powers in a religious way, praying to them, and offering sacrifices to them. They believe that the Powers are closely related to the Dinka. Some tribes believe that their first ancestor was one of these Powers.

2. NHIALIC

Nhialic means 'that which is above (in the sky)'. Dinkas use the word as a general term for all the Powers which they worship. At other times, they use it when speaking of the sky. Dinkas also use it, however, as a personal name for the greatest of the Powers. They address prayers to *Nhialic*, and refer to him as 'creator' and 'father'. In particular, they believe that he is the one who gives rain from the sky which is his home. Christian Dinka use *Nhialic* to translate the word 'God' in the Bible.

3. CLAN-DIVINITIES (for 'divinity' see p. 14)

Each clan has its own clan-divinity or divinities. Individual people may also respect the clan-divinity of other clans if they are related to them by marriage or in other ways. The Dinka associate a great number of different emblems with the clan-divinities. They believe that the divinities are present in these emblems, or are linked with them in a special way. These emblems include many kinds of animals, birds, insects, and trees, and also larger objects like the forest, the rain, the river Nile, and the planet Venus. (See p. 4.)

Dinka treat the emblems of their own clan-divinity with great respect. Members of the lion or hyaena clan, for example, leave portions of sacrifices for these animals to eat, and those who are associated with the river throw sacrifices into it.

4. 'FREE' DIVINITIES

These are not connected with particular clans. The Dinka know them by personal names, but not all Dinka know them all. Some of the most important are:

Deng or Dengdit: the name means 'rain', and Deng is particularly associated with rain, thunder, and lightning.

Garang: this free-divinity is associated with red-brown, and with red and brown colours in association with white. Men possessed by the power of Garang are believed to be able to cure sickness. 'Garang' was also the name of the first man.

Abuk: Abuk is a kindly divinity and thought to be female. The Dinka associate Abuk particularly with women.

Macardit: 'the great, black one' is a harmful Power. The Dinka associate Macardit with the evil influences which hurt men. They try to cool his anger by sacrifice.

The Dinka do not generally imagine the divinities or *Nhialic* to have human forms. They know them as the Powers which operate in Nature, and associate them with emblems which they take from the great variety of natural objects. (See p. 4.)

5. THE SPIRITS OF THE DEAD

The Dinka believe that every human being has within him a soul or spirit, called *atiep* or *tiep*. This word also means 'shadow'. When a person dies, his *atiep* jumps from the body and remains near the house or place of burial. Sometimes a person dreams that an *atiep* asks for food: he then prepares food and leaves it in a bowl until evening. The *atiep* has power to hurt its relatives by causing sickness.

Dinka sacrifice animals as offerings to their dead. They also observe periods of mourning after a burial, when they do not cut their hair, or wash, and they refrain from sexual intercourse. The *atiep* become weaker as time passes. After a few generations they may be forgotten without harmful results.

The spirits of more important dead people are called *jok*, and are associated with the divinities. They include the ancestors of particular clans, whether they are believed to be men or animals. These remain strong and powerful. The Dinka pray to them for help, especially in times of stress or danger. When a Dinka throws a spear at a hippopotamus, for example, he cries out *'jongawa'*, 'O spirit (*jok*) of my father'. On important occasions, for example in illness, the Dinka sacrifice to the *jok* of their ancestors, as well as to the divinities.

Sometimes the Dinka build small shrines as 'houses' for the spirits of important people who have died. These are usually low mounds of clay in which they erect bull's horns or small trees. The people place offerings near them.

THE PRESENCE OF THE POWERS

The Powers of various sorts which the Dinka worship make their presence known in various ways (see p. 3):

(a) They show their presence through rain, thunder, and lightning, and the changes of the seasons.

(b) They show their presence in strange or unusual events. For example, a Dinka who noticed a very large pumpkin in his garden said 'the spirit has fallen': he would not eat it until he had sacrificed a goat.

(c) They show their presence by causing sickness.

(d) They show their presence by dreams, or by causing feelings of remorse or guilt.

(e) They show their presence by taking possession of human beings and speaking through their mouths.

C. SOME DINKA MYTHS

The Dinka believe that earth, the home of men, and sky, the home of *Nhialic*, were at one time joined together. They believe that the earth and sky became separated because of human foolishness, and as a result death and suffering came to mankind. The Dinka express this belief in a myth which tells how a blue bird, *atoc*, cut the rope which linked heaven and earth. In some accounts, the bird did this because of a quarrel between the god Deng and his wife Abuk.

Many stories are told to explain the connection between Dinka clans and their particular clan-divinities and emblems. Here are a few examples.

1. The clan Maic have fire as their clan-divinity. Their ancestor Lual lived when there was no fire. Lual saw fire fall from heaven. He collected wood and grass to feed it. At night he dreamed that the spirit (*jok*) of fire came to him and said, 'My name is Maic: I will be your *jok*.' Lual soon realized that food could be cooked by fire. This myth expresses men's dependence upon fire.

2. The Boweng clan are associated with the river. Long ago members of the clan came to the river and saw a beautiful girl called Alek coming up out of the water. She came with them to the village, but when they laid hands on her she became as water. The villagers escorted her back to the river. They sacrificed bullocks and cows. The girl disappeared into the river, and took a calf with her. The Boweng clan still sacrifice a bullock on the bank of the river at the end of the rains. They also throw a cow and calf alive into the river. These actions and the myth express their dependence upon the river for life itself.

3. The Gol e Luel clan-divinity is associated with the crocodile. Long ago Luel found the eggs of a crocodile. He put them in his canoe, and when he reached home buried them under the floor of his hut. One night, as the eggs were hatching, the old crocodile came and scratched them up and then led the young to the river. Before leaving the hut, the crocodile said to Luel: 'Do not hurt us, and we will not hurt you. If any of you see a man from another tribe kill a crocodile, wear mourning on your head and stomach for it.' A man of this clan will not hesitate to swim in the river, even at night, for the crocodile will not hurt him.

D. WAYS OF WORSHIP

The Dinka believe that life and health, strength and vitality are the gifts of *Nhialic* and the *jok*. They seek these gifts by prayer and sacrifice.

1. SACRIFICE

The Dinka offer sacrifices for a variety of reasons, for example:
   for the coming of rain in the spring-time;
   for protection of the people in the cattle camps of the dry season;
   for recovery from illness;
   for relief from famine;
   for good hunting.

Normally they offer bulls and oxen, sometimes sheep and chickens, sometimes beer and milk. They offer them to one or more of the divinities, and to the spirits of their ancestors.

2. PRAYER

The Dinka accompany their sacrifices with spoken prayers. They use short phrases which they repeat again and again.

Those who say the prayers often hold a fishing-spear in their hands. They emphasize the separate phrases with thrusts of the spear at the animals which are to be sacrificed. All through the prayer the spectators take up the words of the speaker and repeat them, like a chorus, in short phrases. The following example illustrates how this is done:

Speaker: Repeat this son of my sister. You of my father!
Chorus: You of my father!
Speaker: I call upon you because my child is ill.
Chorus: I call upon you because my child is ill.
Speaker: And I do not want words of sickness.
Chorus: And I do not want words of sickness.
Speaker: And I do not want words of fever.
Chorus: And I do not want words of fever.

The repetition of the words and phrases has a powerful effect upon those who are present. The leaders often show signs of deep feeling and ecstasy. As the ceremony continues, the speakers express their prayers more and more strongly, and the others who are present become more and more drawn in to what is happening.

The Dinka invoke their clan-divinities and their own ancestors by name. They also call upon *Nhialic* and sometimes one or other of the free-divinities. Here is an example (the words in italics are the divinities of particular clans):

'You Earth, you are called by my words, and you Nhialic you are called by my words, because you look after all people. You are greater than anyone and all people are your children. And if evil has befallen them, then you are called to come and join with them in it also. And you

21

are not now called for good, you are called for evil (i.e., a specific case of disease), come, help. O you *Flesh*, divinity of Pagong, if you are called then you will indeed hear me, and you, *Awar grass*, you will hear. And you, *Flesh* of my father, and *Fig-tree* of my father, and *Head carrying-ring* of my father, you will hear.'

On important occasions the act of prayer and sacrifice may continue for a number of hours. The act will probably include the following stages, but not always in this order.

(a) *Description of the trouble.* The speakers describe the things which are causing anxiety. For example, here a man who has no brothers or sisters is seriously ill (his name is Akol Agany):

'Why is it, O *Nhialic*, that when one son is left alive alone out of all the children his mother bore, you do not help him, that he may be in health? You, *Nhialic*, if you have left Akol Agany behind to beget children, and he now becomes ill, we have refused (to accept) this illness in him.

For Akol Agany has no sister born with him, and no brother born with him, and if *Nhialic* does not help him to bear his children, then the children will become the children of the mother. And you, *Nhialic*, you are the great person, father of all people, and if a man has called upon you you will strengthen his arm, that no evil may befall him.'

(b) *Confession.* Those who are present confess past acts of evil in case they are the cause of the sickness or other evil. For example:

'And you (divinity) of my father, if you are called, then you will help me and join yourself with my words. And I did not speak (in the past) that my children should become ill; that quarrel is an old matter.'

(c) *Praise.* They offer praise to the divinities, in the hope that this will make them listen. These acts of praise are like the hymns of honour they sing to visitors and like the ox-songs of the young men. The language of these praises is very difficult for people who are not Dinka to understand.

(d) *Expulsion of the misfortune.* The Dinka identify the misfortune with the animal which is being sacrificed. This frees its victim from the misfortune and sends the misfortune out of Dinka territory. For example, this is a prayer said on one particular occasion before an ox was sacrificed:

'And you, ox, it is not for nothing that we have tethered you in the midday sun, but because of sickness, to exchange your life for the man, and for the man to stay on earth and for your life to go with the illness. You, *Nhialic*, hear my speech, and you, clan-divinity, hear my

22

speech, and you, illness, I have separated you from the man. I have spoken thus: "You leave the man alone, you have been given the ox called *malith*." '

Often the Dinka add other prayers which describe the good life which they are seeking. Here is an example:

'You, *Nhialic*, we shall kill your ox (bull), . . . that you should be pleased with us. You will let us walk in health, and we have made a feast (a ceremony) so that there should be no fever, and that no other illness should seize people, that they may all be well. And if my clansman travels, then let him complete his journey without sickness, and let no evil befall him or anybody. And you, *Nhialic*, do not bring evil upon us, and I shall be pleased. You, women, clap your hands, and sing and *wuu* away the fever, that nothing may be wrong with us. You, tribe of my father, walk in health, nothing shall harm us, and *Nhialic* will be pleased with us, and we will pray to *Nhialic* that there may be no bad thing, and sing . . .'

The previous sections describe how Dinka pray together at times of crisis and on important occasions. They pray most frequently in this way. They do not often pray as individuals. But at moments of difficulty or danger, a Dinka may make a short petition to his clan-divinity or to *Nhialic*.

E. PRIESTS

The men who lead the prayers are known as 'masters of the fishing-spear'. They are the ones who use the sacred spears in killing the sacrifices. They speak the prayers. They preside at the rain-prayer ceremonies. They pray for victory before fighting. They settle quarrels and make peace between enemies. They are the ones who stand between men and the divinities. They do not use magic, but address their prayers to *Nhialic* and the spirits.

The well-being of the tribe depends upon the spear-masters and their vitality. They take certain of the vital organs from the animals which are sacrificed. In earlier times they may have consented to being buried alive when they felt themselves becoming weak through old age or illness, so that their heirs could take over their work.

The spear-masters watch over the well-being of the community. One of their main tasks is to pray at night in the cattle camps. They ask protection for their people and their herds. Here is a verse from a Dinka song in which a master of the fishing-spear says at night:

'Let the cattle move, let the cattle move across the river,
Which becomes dry, which is not to be deep.
I have released the cattle (by prayer).'

Dinka clans also recognize 'cattle-chiefs', but the masters of the fishing-spear are the most important men in the tribe. The office is a hereditary one.

Sometimes a spirit or divinity may take possession of an individual and speak through him or her. The Dinka believe that this has happened when the person concerned has fits of trembling and unconsciousness.

Such persons answer questions about sickness, and they give advice about lost cattle and other such matters.

The Dinka erect forked sticks in their homesteads or cattle camps, and place small offerings of flesh or of beer and milk near them. They place similar sticks in the homesteads of the 'masters of the fishing-spear'. We have already referred to the clay-mounds associated with the spirits of important dead people (p. 19).

There are also a number of buildings, like the cattle byres, which belong to the divinity Deng. They contain sacred spears and other objects. Dinka in special need visit such sanctuaries to offer sacrifice.

STUDY SUGGESTIONS

WORD STUDY

1. What are the two chief meanings of the word 'Divinity' or 'divinity' as used in this book?
2. (a) Which two of the following words are nearest in meaning to 'myths'?
   histories fables statements reports legends records
   (b) In what ways are myths different from the two words you chose as answer to (a)?
   (c) Give two examples of myths from the Bible, and at least one example, if you can, of a myth from some other source.

REVIEW OF CONTENT

3. (a) Describe four different sorts of superhuman powers believed in by the Dinka.
   (b) List some of the ways in which the Dinka believe that these powers show their presence.
4. Give examples of the ways in which Dinka religion illustrates:
   (a) the transcendence of God (note the word *Nhialic*),
   (b) the way in which natural forces help people to think about God,
   (c) the religious attitude to life.
5. Give an example of the stories by which the Dinka explain the connection between clans and their particular clan-divinities and emblems.
6. What four stages are usually included in a Dinka act of prayer and sacrifice?

7. Compare the way in which the Dinka use sacrifices to carry away sickness with the Jewish ceremonies on the Day of Atonement, as described in Leviticus 16.1–28.
8. Read the story of Samuel in 1 Samuel 4—8. In what ways are the actions of the 'spear-masters' among the Dinka like those of Samuel for his people?

DISCUSSION AND RESEARCH

9. In what ways, if any, does this account of the Dinka's religion help you to understand Part 1 of this book?
10. Do any of the religious leaders in your own community or country act in a similar way to the 'spear-masters' among the Dinka?
11. What chief likenesses and differences do you see, between the Dinka acts of (a) Confession, and (b) Praise as described on p. 22, and Christians' acts of confession and praise of God?

Chapter 4
The Religion of the Ga in Ghana

From material contributed by
J. N. Kudadjie

A. THE GA

The Ga live in Accra, the capital of Ghana, and its surrounding towns and villages. Ga land stretches from Accra about twenty-two miles to the north, about twenty miles to the east, and about seventeen miles to the west. The Atlantic Ocean is its southern boundary. The whole area is about 480 square miles. There are nearly three hundred thousand Ga-speaking people. The Ga belong to a larger tribe called the Ga-Adangme.

According to Ga-Adangme traditions, which are preserved in old songs associated with the senior deities of the tribe, the Ga-Adangme came from a far-distant land. Some traditions mention Chad as their original home, but most traditions say that Benin was the original home. (See section on Myths, p. 20.) It is said that they were driven out by invasions of the Fulani Tribe under a chief named Dafoleo, and wandered through Nigeria, Yorubaland, and Dahomey. Finally they settled at Ayawaso, a forest some ten miles from Ga Mashi, the seat of the modern Ga state. This was about seven hundred years ago.

Later, the Ga-speaking section broke away and spread across what we now call the Accra plain, up to and along the coast. The main occupations of the Ga were fishing and farming. A good many of the Ga people continue to be fishers and farmers today. But there are Ga people in the other occupations of modern society.

Ga society was at first ruled by the *Nae Wulomo*, that is, the priest of the sea-god called *Nae*. He was also the Chief Priest of the Ga. Their present system of rule by *mantse* was borrowed from the Akan tribes near whom the Ga settled. *Mantse* literally means 'father of the town'; it is now translated 'chief'. When the Ga-Adangme tribes arrived, they had to fight many wars with the Akan tribes. It became necessary to appoint war captains to lead in the wars. *Nae Wulomo* had to stay at home and look after the religious interests of the people, and so, in course of time, the *Wulomo* lost his political powers to the chiefs and war captains. The first known *Ga Mantse* was Nii Ayi Kushi, who ruled from about 1483 to about 1519. In modern Ga society, there are many chiefs for the various Ga towns and clans. The *Ga Mantse* is the official political and administrative head of the Ga people; and the Chief Priest *Nae Wulomo* is the spiritual head. He installs the *Ga Mantse*, and sits in his Council. He advises on various matters affecting the religious and spiritual life of the Ga community. He leads in prayers and rites at ceremonies which affect the whole of the Ga community.

B. OBJECTS OF WORSHIP

The Ga have their own traditional religion. Even though many Ga now follow other religions like Christianity and Islam, the traditional beliefs and worship remain.

1. NAA NYONMO

The Ga believe in the existence and power of numerous spirit-powers who influence nature and the affairs of men. But they do not worship all these spirit-powers. They believe that the most powerful spirit is *Naa Nyonmo*. *Naa Nyonmo* is believed to live in the sky. He created everything. First, he created the Heavens, and then the Earth, together with the waters and other things on earth. With the waters, *Naa Nyonmo* created the Sea. These are the three great creations. Nothing can be done successfully without their help. Therefore, in everything, the traditional Ga calls on Heaven, then Earth, then the Sea. *Naa Nyonmo* himself has no priest or shrine. The Ga believe that he is too far away from men, but they invoke his name and power whenever they make a libation or sacrifice to the other spirit-powers.

2. THE GA GODS

The Ga believe that *Naa Nyonmo* has many sons and daughters: these are known as *dzemawodzi* (that is, 'the gods of the world'). The *dzemawodzi* walk about the world, though they have their own abodes in the sea, lagoons, mountains, and other natural objects. They are powerful and intelligent. *Naa Nyonmo* has handed over his authority to them. They are in active contact with the world of nature and of men. Each Ga clan has its own *dzemawon*, or divinity.

The gods are not all of the same rank, some are more senior than others. The senior gods are the original Ga gods. Some of them are: *Nae*, the Sea-god; *Sakumo*, a River-god, who is also the god who leads in war; and *La Kpa*, a Lagoon-god. The most senior god is *Nae*. *Afiyee* is his wife. He has many children, two of whom are *Koole*, a Lagoon-goddess, and *Ashi Akle*, a Sea-goddess. The Priest of *Nae* is also the Chief Priest of the Ga, and he is called the *Nae Wulomo*. The Ga offer worship to these gods and goddesses.

3. OTHER GODS

In addition there are numerous other gods, such as the *Akan* gods which are associated with natural objects like trees and mountains. There are also gods which are not associated with any natural objects; for example, the *Otu* group of gods are man-made. These other gods are gods which the Ga have adopted from other tribes, like the Fante, the Akwapim, and the Ewe.

4. OTHER SPIRIT-POWERS

Apart from the gods described above, the Ga believe that there are several other spirit-powers in the world. There are, for instance, the spirits of dead people. The Ga believe that everyone has *susuma* and *mumo* (soul and spirit). It is the *mumo* that keeps him alive, and the *susuma* gives him his personality. When the *mumo* leaves his body, a man dies. But his *susuma* becomes a *sisa* (ghost). They live in 'the land of ghosts' which is distinct from this physical world. But the life in that world is a continuation of life in this world, and is like this one. The spirits of the departed influence the life of people still living in the flesh, for both good and ill. The Ga, therefore, fear the ghosts; when they know their wishes, they carry them out with care, to avoid the punishments and misfortunes which the ghosts can inflict on offenders. The punishments they inflict are usually sudden death, chronic diseases, or poverty.

In spite of the respect and fear which the Ga have for departed spirits, they do not worship these spirits. But a person, such as the dead person's child, may invoke a departed spirit if he feels he is being neglected or cheated by the people administering the property left by the dead person. It is believed that the spirits promptly answer such appeals, and severely punish the cheat.

The Ga also believe that dwarfs, fairies, and suchlike spirits inhabit rivers, forests, certain trees, and other natural objects. But as a people, the Ga do not worship these spirits, though some individuals do.

C. MEDICINE, MAGIC, WITCHCRAFT

Among the Ga there are people called *tsofatsemei* (literally, 'people of tree roots'). These are usually medicine-men or herbalists who heal diseases. The Ga believe that man is both body and spirit (or soul). Therefore, disease is not healed physically only; the soul of the diseased person must also be healed at the same time as the body. For this purpose, the herbalists are also spiritual men. They invoke all kinds of spirit-powers to heal the spiritual side of their patients. Some medicine-men have shrines, while others have only sacred objects—like the horn of some animal, or an empty clay pot—placed somewhere in their rooms.

Others use magic or witchcraft to achieve their purposes. The nature gods are usually invoked for the protection and well-being of the community, but the other spirit-powers are often used for destructive purposes. Therefore, in Ga society, medicine-men, magicians, and witches are held in contempt; they are also suspected of, and often actually accused of, being the cause of accidents, sudden deaths, and failure in business. Some of these persons are mediums. They also act as 'witch-doctors', and perform rituals to free victims from the spells of other witches, magicians, and sorcerers.

D. PRIESTS

In Ga society, the public do not take much part in the worship of the gods. It is the priests who worship on behalf of the people, and their aim is to promote the well-being of the community.

1. THE WULOMO

The *Wulomo* (the priest) is the spokesman of the god. He is usually referred to by the name of his god. So the priest of the god *Dantu* is called *Dantu Wulomo*. The *Wulomo* is never possessed by the spirit of the god. His function consists in performing rites, in praying and sacrificing to the god in the shrine on behalf of the people, and in interpreting messages from the god which come through other people. He may authorize one of his assistants to perform some of his functions.

The functions of the priest bring him into direct contact with the god, and, for this reason, it is necessary that he should be different from ordinary people. For example, he must be morally outstanding, and so also must be his wife or wives. (It is customary to give a newly ordained priest a wife who is a priestess.)

The *Wulomo* also observes certain taboos which keep him from being contaminated with *mudzi* (literally, 'dirt'). He must not see a dead person. If by 'accident' he sees one, rituals are immediately performed to cleanse him. He must not speak while eating, and some Ga priests will not eat until the sun is seen in the sky. The *Nae Wulomo* is forbidden to eat salt, but he may eat food cooked with sea-water. Certain types of food, prescribed by the gods themselves, are taboo for their servants. (For the meaning of the word 'taboo' see p. 43.)

2. THE WOYEI

After the *Wulomo* come the *Woyei* ('god's women'). There are many of them, and they help the *Wulomo* in carrying out his work. A *Woyoo* (singular of Woyei) may help to purify the shrine by burning incense. She also prepares the food that is offered to the god on his holy day. One important function of a *Woyoo* is to act as the medium through which the god speaks. When possessed, she may become wild, or fall into a trance. Often, she speaks in a tongue different from her normal language, perhaps even in a language she has never learnt. The message from the

'In Ga society the priests worship on behalf of the people. The gods are normally worshipped in their shrines' (pp. 29 and 32).

The *Nae Wulomo* (bearded and holding cup) pours a libation during the 1974 *Homowo* Festival, assisted by a *Woyoo* (his wife) and an elder. Below is one of the shrines of the lagoon god, *La Kpa*.

How does the role of women in Ga worship compare with their role in the worship of your own Church?

god may be one of goodwill and joy, or it may be a reminder or warning to do something or refrain from doing something. Care is taken to do whatever the god says.

3. THE AGBAAYEI AND AGBAAHII

The *Agbaayei* and *Agbaahii* are below the rank of *Woyei*. They are servants who serve at the shrine in various ways. They can perform some of the work of the *Wulomo* or *Woyoo*.

E. RELIGIOUS FEASTS

The Ga hold feasts which have important religious aspects. The most popular of their feasts is the annual *Homowo* festival. '*Homowo*' literally means 'hunger hooting'. The festival is a harvest festival and lasts for several weeks. It starts from the first or second Monday in May and ends sometime in September. The various Ga towns take turns to celebrate the festival, sometimes at weekly intervals. The different religious groups perform ceremonies throughout the festival. At the beginning of the festival period there is a ceremony in which the priests till a garden plot which is sacred to the gods. The priests of the participating gods, with the help of their assistants, lift a hoe and point it to the sky in turn. The *Wulomo* addresses the following prayer three times to *Naa Nyonmo* (see p. 27).

> 'Lend ears, lend ears, lend ears!
> Lord God, we beseech Thee,
> Let there be rain, let there be dew,
> That the Earth may be fertile,
> That grain may grow,
> That there may be plenty for all.
> Life! Life!
> We are praying life for all.
> Let one year go and another year come to meet us alive!'

Members of the public may attend the religious ceremonies, but it is the social aspects which are of greatest importance to most people. During the celebrations, the towns are full of 'strangers': those who have travelled to live and work in distant villages and towns. The feast is a time of family reunion. The dead are mourned. Disputes are settled. There is general jubilation as the beginning of a new year is marked. In all homes, people prepare the traditional food called *kpekple*, made from corn-dough and served with palm-nut soup and fish, and eat it with great joy.

The purpose of the rites is to thank the gods and to ask for their blessing, to ensure the fertility of the soil and the increase of the family, and to guard against misfortune.

F. WORSHIP AT THE SHRINE OF *NAE*

There is a Ga proverb which says that the bitter nut will still be bitter no matter where you chew it. The gods can be called on in any part of the world, and they will respond. However, the gods are normally worshipped in their own shrines. Let us take a look at what happens in the shrine of the most senior Ga god, *Nae* the Sea-god.

The shrine of *Nae* is located in a room in a clean, ordinary homestead about two hundred yards from the sea. The homestead is painted in white. The *Wulomo*, or priest, of *Nae* lives in the house with his wife, children, and other members of the extended family.

1. REGULAR WORSHIP IN THE SHRINE

In addition to public rituals and annual ceremonies at feast time, there are regular services of worship in the shrine on days holy to *Nae*. These holy days are Tuesday, Friday, and Sunday. On the night before a holy day, the whole of the homestead in which the shrine is located is purified. This is done by burning a particular product of the oil palm tree. This incense-burning is repeated on the dawn of the holy day, to ensure that no *mudzi* ('dirt') remains in the house when the god visits the shrine. *Mudzi* can be caused, for instance, by persons who have seen or touched dead bodies, or by menstruating women, coming to the house. The purification is done by the *Wulomo* and one of the *Woyei*, usually his wife.

After the incense-burning at dawn, both the *Wulomo* and the *Woyoo* have a ritual bath. The bath is ordinary water in which two kinds of leaves have been put. The water and the leaves are consecrated by the *Wulomo*. The water is now 'holy water', and some of it is used for the ritual bath. The couple, as well as their assistants, dress in white calico.

The *Wulomo* then pours a libation with gin. He invokes *Nwei*, *Asase Afia*, and *Nae* three times. With *Nae*'s presence assured, the *Wulomo* then addresses petitions to him on behalf of various groups of people who reside in Ga territory: fishermen, farmers, traders, government officials, the sick, and so on. He also prays for the good things of life: health, grain, fish, money, children, and so on. He repeats the prayer three times.

After the prayer, the officiating priestess prepares food for the god, *kpekple* mixed with red and white palm oil. She sprinkles the food at the shrine, in the yard, and in the precincts of the homestead. Any left-over is eaten by members of the household, or by any outsider who wishes to do so.

Members of the clan and the general public are free to take away some of the 'holy water' to use in bathing or to wash their faces. It is believed that this will cleanse them and rid them of any ailments, especially ailments of a mental and spiritual kind.

2. RITES OF EXPIATION

The *Nae Wulomo* also performs special rites and prayers for people when they come to him to make some request to *Nae*, or to thank him for granting some request.

Among the people who come for special prayers of thanksgiving or intercession are those who have offended the god and have come for pardon. These are very solemn occasions. A person may offend against the god in many ways. For example, he may have sworn in the name of *Nae* and failed to carry out his vow, or he may have cursed in *Nae*'s name. Such offences cannot be pardoned without the taking of life. Curses are particularly offensive, because they hinder every effort and hope of the people for the increase and well-being of society. They are also against the wishes of the god himself.

When an offender confesses to the offence and admits his guilt, he is made to bring various sacrifices. These vary according to the nature of the offence. Often, he is made to bring a goat and two fowls (one male and the other female).

On the appointed day, the *Wulomo* and others taking part in the ritual purify and cleanse themselves. The *Wulomo* invokes *Naa Nyonmo*, *Asase Afia*, *Nae*, and other gods and spirits affected by the offence. He describes the offence to them. He pleads with them on behalf of the offender to accept the sacrifice and to pardon the offender and restore his life to him. He then very carefully brushes the offender from head to toe with the fowls. This takes away the offence.

Next, the *Wulomo* strangles and tears off the head of one of the fowls with his hands or toes. The dead fowl is thrown away. As this is done, there is absolute silence. If the fowl falls with its breast up, this is a good sign, for it means that the offence has been pardoned. If not, the offence has not been pardoned. This may mean many things: perhaps, the offender has not confessed something; perhaps some of the gods and spirits affected have not been invoked; perhaps some part of the ritual has been faulty. Care is taken to find out what it is that is wrong. When it is discovered, it is put right at once. The strangling is repeated until a fowl lies breast up.

When all are satisfied that the divinities are pleased, there comes the final stage. The goat which represents the offender is slaughtered. The life of the offender is restored to him as the goat dies. Some of its blood is drained into a big round wooden bowl containing 'holy water'. The pardoned offender is given a ritual bath with the 'holy water' into which the blood has been dripped. He has now been completely pardoned and purified. He is free, and the blessing of the gods rests on him.

The carcass of the goat is skinned and cut up. One of the limbs is given to the sacrificer. But he himself must not eat of the meat; he may give it to his relations. The rest of the meat is either cooked and eaten by those present, or it is distributed among the servants of the gods and other persons attending the ceremony.

3. ARBITRATIONS

The *Nae Wulomo* does not only stand between his people and their god. He also stands between individual members of society. As a religious duty, he settles disputes and cases of all sorts, ranging from disputes over custom and tradition, to refusal by debtors to settle their debts, quarrels between husbands and wives, illicit sexual relations, and so on. He imposes fines where necessary. In this function, also, the *Wulomo*'s sole aim is to ensure peace, harmony, and well-being among his people.

STUDY SUGGESTIONS

WORD STUDY

1. (a) The word 'spirit' is used in this chapter to mean at least four different things. What are they?
   (b) What other meanings can the word 'spirit' have, in your understanding?
2. Look up the word 'taboo' in a dictionary. Give at least two examples from everyday life, of taboos which are observed by people in your country.

REVIEW OF CONTENT

3. (a) What do the Ga people believe about the creation of the universe?
   (b) What is their 'world-view'?
4. (a) What do the Ga people believe about the spirits of dead people?
   (b) What is their attitude towards such spirits?
5. What is the attitude of the Ga people towards medicine-men, magicians, and witches?
6. Describe in your own words the following religious observances among the Ga:
   (a) the annual *Homowo* festival,
   (b) regular worship services in the shrine of *Nae*.

BIBLE STUDY

7. Compare the Ga beliefs about the *dzemawodzi* (p. 27) with the Jewish belief about *Nephilim* as described in Genesis 6.1–4.

8. What part do the priests play in both Dinka religion and Ga religion? In which religion do the ordinary people have the greatest share in the prayers?

9. Make a list of the chief gods in the Ga religion and another list of the chief gods in the Dinka religion. Compare these lists. Can you tell from the description of the gods listed which people live on the coast of Africa and which live in the interior of the continent?

10. 'The *Wulomo* observes certain taboos . . .' (p. 29).
(a) Do you yourself observe any taboos, and if so, for what reasons? Are they all religious reasons?
(b) What taboos, if any, should Christians observe, and for what reasons? (Romans 14.1—15.6 may be helpful in thinking about this question.)

Chapter 5
The Maori

From material contributed by
Ruawai Rakena

A. THE MAORI

The people who live on the islands in the south Pacific Ocean are called Polynesians, and the area between New Zealand (in the south), and Hawaii (in the north), and Easter Island (in the east) is sometimes called 'The Polynesian Triangle'.

It is said that many thousands of years ago, the ancestors of the Polynesians all lived together on one group of islands. As their population multiplied some had to sail away in canoes and live on other islands. This happened many times. When at sea, strong winds and storms blew some of the canoes off course. People from these canoes landed and lived on islands which they did not previously know existed. In these ways Polynesians came to live on all the islands within the Polynesian Triangle.

One group of Polynesians are the Maori. They are a group of forty-two tribes who now live on the two large islands called New Zealand, and they number over 250,000 people. They began to arrive in New Zealand in about AD 950 and the first to do so was a man named Kupe.

The Maori settled in villages close to the bush, the river outlets, and the sea. These were the places where they got most of their food. They brought with them in their canoes, from other islands, the *kumara*, or sweet potato, *taro* for making flour, and some birds.

The Maori built their houses from branches and leaves, with a bare earth floor. They built their houses in different ways for different purposes. The meeting-house was the place where tribes welcomed visitors, mourned their dead, and discussed tribal affairs. The Maori made some meeting-houses fine and beautiful, with decorations in wood, and they placed carved images of tribal ancestors around the inside walls. Much talking was done on the ground in front of the meeting-house.

Both men and women shared in the work of the village. Men usually did the heavier work, built the larger houses, made the canoes, and did the fishing from them. The men also had to be ready for fighting, and the Maori built some villages on hill-tops and fortified them for protection.

Europeans settled in New Zealand from 1800 onwards, and they brought with them many new ideas, and new ways of making and doing things. Many Maori have become Christians and there have been marriages between Maori and other people. Not all Maori, therefore, now share the religion which is described in this chapter, although many still honour and respect these beliefs and practices. This chapter describes the Maori religion as it was before the changes of the last hundred years.

The journeys of the Polynesians to new islands in the south Pacific took place over thousands of years. Gradually the way of life, the customs, and language of the Polynesians living on one island changed from the way of life, customs, and language of Polynesians living on other islands. Today there are many differences between different groups of Polynesians, but there are still many things which remain the same among them all. The divinities, religious beliefs, practices, and myths that will be mentioned in this chapter about the Maori, are some of the things which the Polynesians of an earlier time shared in common, and which some Polynesians still share today.

B. THE MAORI'S BELIEFS ABOUT GOD

1. THE POWERS: *Atua*

The Maori believed that there were powers at work throughout the whole of life. These powers could not be seen, and they were stronger than any power that the Maori had themselves. The Maori called these powers *atua*.

The Maori believed that the *atua* affected their lives in both good ways and bad ways. Sometimes the *atua* provided plenty of food, sometimes they provided very little food. The Maori believed that the *atua* could bring them good things, or cause bad things to happen.

The *atua* gave greatness or 'power' to a person, a family, or a tribe. For this reason, the Maori believed it was very important to respect the *atua* and try to please them all the time.

The Maori thought about the *atua* in much the same way as they thought about themselves. They believed the *atua* were invisible people. More important, they believed the *atua* were ancestors.

The Maori divided the *atua* into three main groups. *Atua* of the first group had more 'power' than those in the second group. *Atua* of the second group had more 'power' than those of the third group. We use 'power' in this chapter to translate the Maori word *mana*. We could also translate it by 'strength' or 'greatness'.

(a) *Atua of the first group:* All tribes worshipped these. Some of the most important were the following:

Tane: the word means 'man' or 'married man'. *Tane* was father of the trees, birds, and animals. He also created human beings and gave them life. *Tane* had the most 'power' of all *atua*.

Tu: the *atua* of warfare. In Maori life a brave and skilful warrior was highly praised. His power was great. The Maori dedicated male babies to *Tu* soon after birth and prayed that *Tu* would make them brave. Before and during warfare, opposing tribes offered their prayers and sacrifices to *Tu*. They hoped that *Tu* would support and protect them.

Rongo: the word means 'peace'. Rongo was the *atua* of peace and agriculture. When war ceased the tribes who had fought would say their prayers and make their offerings to *Rongo*. The Maori also offered prayers and offerings to *Rongo* during the planting, cultivation, and harvesting of such crops as the sweet potato and *taro* (a root from which flour is made). The first sweet potato or *taro* from a new harvest was offered to *Rongo*.

Tangaroa: the *atua* that controlled everything to do with the sea. Like all other *atua*, *Tangaroa* was the father of many children. Some of his children were fish and shellfish. One kind of fish decided to leave the sea and live on land. This fish became the ancestor of lizards.

Tawhirimatea: the *atua* of the winds and storms. The Maori often prayed for *Tawhirimatea*'s help to calm storms and bring fine weather.

Whiro: the *atua* of darkness and evil. *Whiro* caused disease and sickness, even death. He was the father of those powers that tried to harm people.

(b) *Atua of the second group:* Only some of the tribes worshipped these. Here are some of them:

Maru: an *atua* of warfare.

Kahukura: an *atua* of warfare.

Uenuku: an *atua* of warfare. Some tribes believed that both *Kahukura* and *Uenuku* revealed their presence in the rainbow. If a rainbow appeared in front of a war party, the party was advised to return home. If a rainbow appeared behind a war party then they were encouraged to go on because *Kahukura* or *Uenuku* had shown their support.

(c) *Atua of the third group:* only families worshipped these. The Maori believed in a variety of family *atua*. This third group included many *atua* which tried to harm people and bring about sickness and death. The Maori asked their family *atua*:

to protect the family, or certain members of the family;

to perform certain tasks for the family, such as taking a message to another person;

to guard family treasures and sacred places and things.

The Maori found it easier to think about and to understand their divinities through the things which they could see with their eyes or touch with their hands. For this reason, they associated a star or comet in the sky, a rock, a tree, a spring of water, a bird, or an animal, with particular divinities. The Maori believed that the divinity's 'power' entered such things. They called them the divinity's *aria*, 'visible representative'. Such things were very sacred (see p. 4).

'The Maori (like other Polynesians) believed that there were powers at work throughout the whole of life. Among the most important were *Tangaroa*, controlling the
sea, and *Tawhirimatea*, the *atua* of winds and storms' (p. 38).

This boat-skipper in the Pacific is becalmed so he calls for the *atua*'s help by blowing
for a wind, on a conch shell.

If you know any sailors or fishermen, find out what they believe about the power of
winds and storms.

2. SPIRITS OF THE DEAD

The Maori believed that human beings have a spirit (*wairua*) as well
as a physical body which can be seen and touched. They believed that
when a person died, his or her *wairua* lived on and went on a long

journey. First of all the *wairua* went to the top of New Zealand, to a place called *Te Rerenga Wairua*, which means 'The Flying-off-place of Spirits'. From there it made its way back across the sea to the island of *Hawaiiki*, which is where the Maori believed their ancestors first sailed from, and then on to *Hine-nui-te-po*, the *atua* of death.

During ceremonies for a deceased man, woman, or child, the Maori farewelled the *wairua* with such words as:

'Farewell, O kinsman,
return to the world beyond:
return to distant *Hawaiiki* whence you came:
return to your ancestress *Hine-nui-te-po*:
farewell, O kinsman, farewell, farewell, farewell!'

Such words were spoken many times. The Maori hoped that the *wairua* would return quickly to *Hawaiiki* and *Hine-nui-te-po* and remain there. This did not always happen. Sometimes the *wairua* came back to visit living kinsmen. The visits of some *wairua* were good visits. Visits from other *wairua* were bad, and people were afraid of being visited by such *wairua*.

The Maori included *wairua* who visited them among the family *atua*. They believed that the *wairua* made such visits through a particular member of the family, or through a bird, an animal, or other object. The *wairua* often visited through an owl.

Family priests sometimes used the harmful *wairua* to cause harm to those whom they or their families hated. Tribal priests, however, whose *atua* were stronger than the *atua* of family priests, could send all *wairua* back to *Hawaiiki*.

3. THE 'HIGH GOD'

The Maori called their 'High God' *Io*, which means 'the innermost part'. They thought of *Io* as the supreme *atua* or power. *Io* lived before anything else lived. *Io* was the innermost part of everything that was living in the sky and on the earth. The Maori added other names to the name of *Io*. These tell us what the Maori believed about *Io*. The following are some of *Io*'s full names:

Io Matua: the parent father,
Io Matua-kore: having no parents,
Io Mata-ngaro: face that cannot be seen,
Io Wananga: source of all knowledge,
Io Te Waiora: the spring-water of life.

The Maori held the 'High God' *Io* in great awe. He was the most sacred of all the Maori divinities. Only priests with great 'power' were allowed to know anything about *Io*, and to say his name.

C. MYTHS

The Maori passed down many myth stories from one generation to another. The stories told how things came into being, and they helped to keep alive the beliefs, the traditions, and the customs of the Maori. Myths also helped to keep alive the names of the divinities which the Maori worshipped and depended upon.

1. The most important Maori myth tells how the world came into being. It is the story of *Rangi* and *Papa*, the father and mother of all divinities and all living things. Rangi and Papa were, however, less important than *Io*.

Rangi lay on top of *Papa*. They were so closely joined together that they looked like one person. Their children were squeezed in the middle, and found it difficult to move about. It was also very dark, although light sometimes appeared between *Rangi* and *Papa*'s bodies. One day, the children of *Rangi* and *Papa* decided to separate their parents. Two of *Rangi* and *Papa*'s many children disagreed with the decision. One after another the elder brothers tried to push *Rangi* and *Papa* apart, but each failed. Then another brother called *Tane* tried and was successful. *Tane* was successful because he turned upside down and pushed with his shoulders and feet. *Rangi* was pushed upwards to become the sky, and *Papa* remained to become the earth. Their separation brought light into the world of their children, and allowed them to grow and move about all over the earth.

The children of *Rangi* and *Papa* were the *atua* which the Maori worshipped. *Tane* was the most important. *Tane* created human beings and gave them their breath of life.

2. Another important myth tells how one of the islands of New Zealand came into being. The hero of the story is called *Maui*. *Maui* came into being as the result of a miscarriage from his mother's womb. *Maui* was the spirit of an embryo, and a very mischievous spirit. *Maui* liked playing tricks on other people. By a very clever trick *Maui* managed to get his grandmother's lower jaw-bone. The jaw-bone helped him to do great things. *Maui* used his grandmother's jaw-bone to hit the sun and make it go slower across the sky and give people longer days. One day, *Maui* went fishing with his brothers and used the jaw-bone for a fish-hook. *Maui*'s brother scoffed at him. When *Maui* pulled in his fishing line his brothers saw that *Maui* had caught the biggest fish their eyes had ever seen. The fish was named *Te-Ika-Roa-a-Maui*, which means 'The Big Long Fish of Maui'. The Maori today still call the North Island of New Zealand by this name.

D. WORSHIP

1. PRAYER

The Maori talked to their divinities through special prayers, called *karakia*. The priests composed most of these prayers and chanted them. The Maori had prayers for every kind of occasion and purpose. They did not have a written language, and they learned these prayers and other sayings or songs by memory at special schools. The schools for priests were very sacred, because the prayers had to be learnt and chanted correctly. When a prayer was not chanted correctly the Maori believed that the *atua* would be angry, and cause something bad to happen.

Prayers were put together and chanted for such occasions and purposes as the following:

> to help woo or court a lover,
> to help kill a bird,
> to help a person to run quickly or to make his opponent run slow,
> to help mend a broken bone,
> to remove harmful spirits from a house,
> to give strength and accuracy to a war spear,
> to help fix things in the memory,
> to dedicate babies and help them grow up to become good adults.

This is an example of a dedication prayer for a new-born baby girl:

> Sprinkle with the water of *Tu*.
> Proceed, navel cord,
>   to prepare food for yourself;
>   to weave garments for yourself;
>   to weave fine cloaks for yourself;
>   to welcome visitors;
>   to carry firewood on the back for yourself;
>   to dig for shellfish for yourself;
>
> Give these to help growth
> For this first-born girl.

2. SACRIFICE

The Maori did not offer any sacrifice to their 'High God' *Io*. They offered sacrifices with prayers to nearly all the other divinities. The priest made the sacrifice by raising the offering above his head with both hands and then, with words like 'To you, O *Tane*', he placed the offering on the ground by the sacred tree or object.

The sacrifice was usually some kind of food, a bird, a fish, or some small animal. The first fish that was caught on a fishing expedition was killed and offered to the divinity of the sea, *Tangaroa*.

On rare and very sacred occasions, or in times of warfare, the Maori offered a human being as a sacrifice. They often chose people who had been captured and enslaved in warfare to be human sacrifices. Human sacrifices were usually offered to the divinity of warfare *Tu*. The Maori offered the sacrifice to gain *Tu*'s help and favour, or to thank *Tu* for giving success to the warriors.

3. THE SACRED

The Maori word for sacred is *tapu*, and something *tapu* was something associated with the *atua*. It is from this word that the English word 'taboo' is derived. 'Taboo' is chiefly used to describe something which is forbidden because it is sacred.

(a) *Sacred People:* The most sacred people were priests. The Maori set them apart and treated them in very special ways because they were sacred. The priests talked to the *atua* on behalf of the people, and the *atua* talked to the people through the priests. Some priests were more sacred than others, and received greater respect. People avoided touching such a priest, and often another person had to put the food in his mouth. Even his shadow was believed to be sacred. The priests of the family *atua* were treated with less respect, and often tried to make up for their weakness by practising witchcraft and magic.

(b) *Sacred Things and Places:* Any thing or any place could become sacred. A tree, a stone, a piece of human hair, a walking stick, a spring of water, a clump of flax, a part of the sea, or a piece of land, could become sacred. By making things sacred the Maori helped members of the tribe to behave in such a way that they did not offend other members of the tribe. By making special things *tapu*, they prevented the greedy families from using up all the shellfish, or killing off all the birds in the bush, or digging up sweet potatoes before they were ready to cook and eat. The birth of a baby, sickness, warfare, and especially death, were associated with the *atua* and therefore sacred.

The Maori had no temples or special houses in which they worshipped their divinities. They carried out their religious ceremonies at such places as the following:

Sacred places, where the dead or their scraped bones were buried. Many were caves.

Sacred waters, springs or rivers where important dedications took place. Some places were believed to be able to cure sickness.

A pile of stones, a rock, or twigs of wood stuck into the ground by a priest to serve as an altar. It was a temporary place of worship where a priest chanted his prayer and offered a sacrifice.

Wooden beams in village latrines, which the priests sometimes used like an altar. They were most often used in ceremonies to give strength to warriors about to go to war.

E. WITCHCRAFT AND MAGIC

Among the Maori, only the priests who acted for families and family *atua*, and the spirits of the dead, practised witchcraft and magic. Their 'power' was not so great as that of other priests. Witchcraft and magic were always associated with evil intentions, disease, and death.

The Maori believed in many divinities, both good and bad, but they believed that the divinities that made daily life good were greater and stronger than the divinities which made daily life bad.

STUDY SUGGESTIONS

WORD STUDY

1. In describing the gods of the Dinka and the Ga we have chiefly used the word 'divinities', in describing the gods of the Maori we have used the word 'powers'.

   (a) Which of these two words most emphasizes the idea of 'immanence' and which emphasizes the idea of 'transcendence'?

   (b) Which of the following qualities would you associate more with the word 'divinities', and which with the word 'powers'?

   strong   holy   sacred   potent   mighty   forceful   heavenly almighty   great

2. Write a short paragraph to illustrate the meaning of the Maori word *tapu*.

   What English word would it also serve to illustrate?

REVIEW OF CONTENT

3. (a) To what larger group of people do the Maori belong?

   (b) In what sort of geographical surroundings have they mostly lived?

4. Into what three main groups do the Maori divide the 'powers', and by whom was each group worshipped?

5. Re-tell in your own words the Maori myths about the creation of the universe.

6. In what way was the Maori's worship of their 'High God' *Io* different from their worship of other powers?

7. 'The Maori had no temples or special houses in which they worshipped' (p. 43). List four different sorts of places where the Maori did carry out their religious ceremonies.

8. What was the Maori attitude towards witchcraft and magic?

BIBLE STUDY

9. 'The Maori talked to their divinities through special prayers called *karakia*' (p. 42).
   Read Psalm 144. Which of the 'blessings' for which the Psalmist was praying or praising God are like the occasions and purposes for which the Maori priest composed *karakia*?

DISCUSSION AND RESEARCH

10. *Nhialic*, *Naa Nyonmo*, and *Io* are the names which the Dinka, the Ga, and the Maori give to the most important of their gods. Make a list of those things which all three peoples say about them. If you were translating the Bible into these languages, would you think it right to translate 'God' by all or any of these names?

11. All three peoples, the Dinka, the Ga, and the Maori, associate the spirits of the dead with the divinities. Which of the three offer sacrifice to the spirits of the dead? Compare these beliefs with the Christian belief in the 'communion of saints'. In what ways, if any, is the Christian belief about the dead like that of the Dinka (or the Ga or the Maori); in what ways is it different?

Chapter 6
Shamanism in Korea
From material contributed by Tongshik Ryu

A. THE KOREANS

The Korean peninsula extends due south of Manchuria and Siberia. Korea is about the same size as Britain. Koreans are descendants of several Mongol tribal groups who migrated from the north in prehistoric times. Their language belongs to the group of languages which are spoken throughout northern Asia and north-eastern Europe.

Korean civilization dates from the fifth century BC, when the tribal nations began to emerge in Korea, although the written history of Korea only reaches back to the first century AD. By the fourth century AD, the early Korean Kingdoms had adopted Confucianism and Buddhism from China. Christianity was introduced into Korea in the eighteenth century, and Christians have become one of the largest religious groups in Korea today. Thus Buddhism, Confucianism, and Christianity are now the major religions which cover more than half of the total population of Korea.

There is, however, a folk religion in Korea which is still strong within Korean culture alongside the other religions, and is the ancient natural religion of Korea. It is called Shamanism. Other forms of Shamanism exist in Northern and Central Asia, Mongolia, and Manchuria.

B. THE BELIEFS OF SHAMANISM

At the heart of Shamanism is the belief that there is communion between gods and men. According to this faith it is not man or nature which rules over all things in the world, over life and death, over good fortune and bad. These things are the acts of the gods. Thus in order to control the world of nature, or his own destiny, a person needs to have the right relationship with the gods who are the source of power. A person must be able to persuade the gods to control all these things as he wishes. The Shaman religion tries to make this possible. Through their ceremonies of worship the Shamans invite the gods, entertain them, listen to their will or oracles, and obey them.

The ceremonies have three main aims:

1. First, there is the ceremony by which people try to eliminate all evil fortunes and bring forth blessings (*Kibok-che*).

2. Secondly, there is the ceremony by which people try to expel evil spirits and have diseases cured (*Pyong-kut*).

3. And third, there is the ceremony by which people try to comfort and purify the souls of the dead, in order to send them to the other world so that they may not cause disasters in this world (*Songryong-je*).

C. THE SHAMANS

At the centre of Shamanism are the Shamans, who are the priests. (The Korean word for Shaman is *Moodang*.)

There are two sorts of Shamans in Korea:

1. The Shamans by heredity or learning. These are most important in south Korea. They receive an education from the old master Shamans and pass through certain initiatory ordeals.

2. The Shamans by choice and gift of the gods. These are most important in central and north Korea. When a person is chosen by the gods to be a Shaman he experiences sickness, dreams, and ecstasies. In Shamanistic ritual, ecstasy comes through singing and dancing: people believe that this ecstasy repeats the experience of rebirth which the Shaman first experienced when the gods chose him to be a Shaman. (Literally, 'ecstasy' means 'standing outside'; a person in ecstasy stands outside normal everyday experience, or outside the physical world, and becomes aware of powers and truths which cannot be known through the ordinary working of his senses. Sometimes he appears to be in a dream, or he becomes either still and cold or very excited.)

The Shamans worship and serve the gods by singing and dancing in a ceremony of worship called a *Kut*. In this the Shamans attempt to create a happy new world by means of the power of the gods and spirits. They try to remove calamities and to bring forth blessings.

D. WAYS OF WORSHIP

The Shamanic ceremonies of worship, called *Kut*, are related to two cycles in human life: the cycle of human ageing, and the cycle of the year (i.e. the seasons).

1. THE CYCLE OF HUMAN AGEING

On the occasion of marriage, the Shamans hold the 'ceremony of detection' to get rid of misfortune and to pray to the gods for blessing on the couple, to start them in a happy new life. When a child is conceived, they hold a small ceremony to please the guardian of a new life, and to pray for a safe and easy birth for the baby and for security during its growth. They also hold ceremonies from time to time during a person's life, when they pray for a long happy life, without illness and with riches and honours in their fullness. After a person's death, they hold a ceremony to pray for a safe journey and entrance into the other world.

2. THE CYCLE OF THE YEAR

The Shamans hold various kinds of ceremonies in the spring, in order to pray that evil fortune may be eliminated for the year, and that an abundant harvest be given. For instance, all the villagers gather together at and around the time of the First Moon, to perform the rituals of 'treading on the earth God', or to prevent misfortune. As the crops are ripening, the villagers once again hold a ceremony for the agricultural gods, which is to pray for a rich harvest. The Eighth Moon, and the Tenth Moon, are seasons of thanksgiving, for which a ritual is held offering the new harvest to the heavenly god.

Large-scale rituals usually consist of twelve sequences. This does not mean that every ritual is divided into exactly twelve sections; but just as twelve months make a complete year, so it seems that twelve of these sequences make a complete ritual or, as one might say, a 'full course' of *kut*. Sometimes they consist of about fifteen sequences, and at other times of less than a dozen. Usually, however, they combine twelve independent fragmentary sequences into one complete full-scale ceremony. There are also simpler rituals aimed mainly at preventing calamities.

In each of the sequences, the Shamans call on a particular god with a particular function, and, in a complete ceremony, the different sequences follow a pattern like the following:

Sequences 1 and 2: Introductory sequences to purify the place of ritual and to call down a host of gods.

Sequence 3: A prayer for protection.

Sequence 4: Expulsion of evil spirits.

Sequence 5: The deity of richness, *Taegam-sin*, is invited and prayer made for the blessings of wealth.

Sequence 6: Chesok-sin, the Buddhist guardian god, is invited and prayer is made for long life.

Sequence 7: Prayer is made for peace.

Sequences 8 and 9: As 4 and 3.

Sequences 10, 11 and 12: The Shaman worships the guardian gods and offers sacrifices to all sorts of spirits in order that there may be no evil consequences.

Each of the sequences in a full ritual follows almost the same pattern. It is as follows. The Shamans call down first of all the god who is the object of the ritual. Ordinarily they start by singing an invitation to worship. Then the Shaman starts to sing and dance to a special tune and rhythm in order to please the god who has already been invited down. After he has sung and danced increasingly violently, he reaches a

'The Shamans hold various kinds of ceremonies' (p. 48).

Korean villagers crowd close to the Shamans as they worship the gods by singing and dancing.

What is good and what is bad about this sort of worship, in your opinion?

state of trance or ecstasy in which he is in communion with the god, and conveys the words of the god. He may utter warnings or commands, or promise blessings. Then the Shaman sends the gods back to their places by singing songs of praise to the god for his blessing, and by dancing.

E. SOME PRAYERS

The most important of the sequences are those which pray for blessings in positive terms. Here are some examples of the prayers for wealth, long life, and peace.

1. *Taegam-sin is the god of wealth.* Here are some of the prayers for wealth, uttered in Sequence 5 (p. 48 above):

'Thou art *Momju-daegam* (guardian god) and
Pomul-daegam (treasure god)
who gives us enough food to spare,
Enough goods to spare.'

'If you are blessed with enough food,
Enough goods to spare,
Know that our *Taegam-sin*
Helped you from high above.'

2. *Chesok-sin* is the Buddhist guardian god who gives blessings upon children and controls life (see Sequence 6, p. 48). Prayers which praise *Chesok-sin* are as follows:

'You helped to make our short lives long;
Long, long around and around in a coil.
You fastened our iron life with stone ropes;
Our rock-like life with iron ropes.
You helped and added more years
To our age of eighty.'

3. Prayers are offered directly for blessing to *Songju*, the guardian god who superintends and rules over the whole household:

'Please look after our household.
Help to make it rich and happy,
Achieve our wishes and aspirations.
Protect our household from all troubles,
And keep us away from all evil spirits.'

The aim of the ritual is to drive out all diseases and evil fortune, and to secure wealth, peace, and long life.

4. A Shaman who fled from North Korea during the Korean War of 1950–53, composed the following, which gives a very clear example

of the normal contents of prayers in ritual. Here is the song just as it was recorded:

(The Shaman invites people to worship.)

'Let us go, let us go to receive long life,
Let us go before *Chesok-num*,
To receive long life from him.
Rejoice!
Rejoice!

Let us go to earn money,
Let us go to make money.
Let us go to the pleasant places in the South-east.
Let us go to make money there.
Rejoice!
Rejoice!'

(The Shaman expresses the blessings of the gods.)

'Carry the blessings from above on the back,
Carry the blessings from below on the head.
Receive the blessings from in front in the arms.

Take the blessings from the sides by the arms.
Enough food to spare, enough goods to spare;
Enough so as to spoil and rot beneath.
Spoilt and rotted they turn into fertilizer,
From which new sprouts may put forth.'

(The Shaman invokes the help of the God of wealth.)

'Please help us, *Taegam-sin*.
Use strength and power
To help us become the richest among the rich,
So that may we outshine all other peoples,
Because we make the most abundant offering.
And make us popular throughout the country.'

(The Shaman sends the god back to his place.)

'*Sinryong* (another god) which stays around the mountain-shrines,
Enjoy yourself before you leave.
Enjoy yourself before you leave.
From where the national *Man-sin* (Shaman) stood,
May all the treasure spring up,
Silver, gold, and all precious stones.'

STUDY SUGGESTIONS

WORD STUDY

1. (a) What is the literal meaning of the word 'ecstasy'?

(b) What sort of experience does a person in ecstasy go through?
(c) How is ecstasy induced in Shamanistic ritual?
2. What is a 'sequence' in Shamanistic ritual?

3. (a) What three major religions are followed by more than half the population of Korea?
(b) In what other areas, besides Korea, does Shamanism exist?
4. (a) What is a 'Shaman', and what is his function?
(b) What are the two sorts of Shaman, and what are the differences between them?
5. What are the three chief purposes of Shamanistic ceremonies?
6. (a) In what way is the yearly cycle of the seasons important in Shamanism?
(b) What other cycle is similarly important?

7. Read Leviticus 23 and list some of the ways in which the spring and autumn ceremonies held by the Shamans are like and unlike the Jewish festivals.
8. Read Psalms 121, 122, and 128. For each of the petitions in the prayer to the guardian god *Songju* (p. 50), select a verse or verses from these Psalms which prays or praises God for the same blessing.

9. (a) What would you reply to someone who said: 'The Shamanistic rituals are meant to bring people into a right relationship with the gods, and Christian worship services are meant to bring people into a right relationship with God. I don't see much difference between them'?
(b) What is the chief difference between the teaching of Shamanism about the dead (p. 47), and Christian belief about the dead?
10. (a) What do you think is the most interesting *belief* in each of the four religions studied in part 2?
(b) What do you think is the most interesting *custom* in each of the four religions studied in part 2?
Give reasons for your answer in each case.
11. In chapter 2, section C (pp. 10, 11), we listed beliefs which are common to almost all religions. Write out the seven headings of this list and under each heading write the four names: Dinka, Ga, Maori, Shamanism. Underline each name in turn if you find the belief present in that particular religion.

PART 3

FIVE 'NATIONAL' RELIGIONS

Introduction

In this part we study five religions, each of which is associated with a particular nation. There are many differences between them.

We begin with Shintoism, which is the national religion of Japan. Shintoism is very similar to the religions which we studied in Part 2, but it is practised by a much greater number of people within a single country. Shintoism also has books which its followers honour, but not in the same way as Christians and Muslims honour the Bible and the Qur'an.

We next study Hinduism, which is the complex religion followed by very many of the different communities and tribes in modern India. Hinduism has followers from many different groups of people and with many different beliefs about God.

Shorter studies of two Chinese religions follow the one on Hinduism. These are teachings about right conduct more than teachings about God.

The last religion which we study in this part is Judaism. Many students already know about this religion through the Old Testament. We shall consider Judaism as it is practised today, as well as looking at its past.

All the religions in this part, except Shintoism, have sacred Scriptures which their followers honour as authoritative guides for what they believe and how they should live.

Chapter 7
Shintoism

From material contributed by
Tongshik Ryu

Shintoism is very closely related to the Japanese way of life and to Japanese tradition. The most concise statement of the meaning of Shinto is found in the meaning of the word itself. 'Shinto' is a term made up of two Chinese characters. The first, *Shin*, means 'god' or 'gods'. The second, *to*, means 'way'. Thus the word 'Shinto' is usually translated as 'the way of the gods'. Not all Japanese, however, share the Shinto religion. Many are Buddhists, while some are Christians, or belong to new religions.

A. THE HISTORY OF SHINTOISM

From the beginning, Shintoism was a part of the indigenous religion of the Japanese people. Its basis was a worship of the *kami* (spirits) in order to assure prosperity. Shintoism in this form was similar to the religions of other early agricultural communities.

In the fourth century AD, the Yamado clan assumed power as the ruling family in Japan. Shintoism became a national religion, and centred on the sun goddess Amaterasu Omikami. This goddess was regarded both as the guardian of agriculture and as the ancestress of the ruling family. The Emperor Jimmu, her great grandson, was supposed to have received from her three sacred articles: the mirror, the sword, and the jewel. The possession of these regalia has been the symbol of the emperor's authority. In that period the link between Shinto and the family of the Emperors began.

Buddhism (see chapter 11) came into Japan via the Korean peninsula about AD 552, and its influence was greatest in the eighth century. At that time it touched every part of Japanese religious thought and worship. In the ninth century a movement began whose purpose was to unite Shinto and Buddhism. This was known as *Ryobu Shinto*, or 'Two-Sided Shinto'. Adherents of this movement believed that the *kami* were manifestations or incarnations of the Buddha and the Bodhisattvas (see p. 139). The sun goddess, Amaterasu, was identified with Vairocana, the Great Sun, the central Buddha figure of Mahayana Buddhism (see p. 140). Buddhism became more and more part of all Shinto shrines and temples. Under Buddhist influence Shinto became more personal and practical, and acquired a philosophical framework which it had not previously possessed.

Confucianism (see chapter 9) also had an influence upon Shintoism.

It had entered Japan by way of Korea, in the fifth century, and gave to Shintoism a system of ethics. It also strengthened the traditional rites of ancestor worship.

Buddhism grew in influence in Japan and became more and more mixed with Shintoism during the following one thousand years.

In the eighteenth century there was a revival of Japanese Shinto, and this led to the declaration in 1868 that Shinto was Japan's official state religion. This event coincided with the accession of the Emperor Maiji to the throne as the descendant of the sun goddess Amaterasu. This revived the belief that the Emperor was divine. At the same time all connections with Buddhism were officially cut, though most ordinary Japanese continued to believe and practise as they always had done. They tended to think of Shinto as taking care of their needs in this present world, and to think of Buddhism as taking care of matters after death.

In the twentieth century the Japanese government compelled the people to participate in Shinto ceremonies as an expression of patriotism. Because of this many people suffered, particularly Christians. The greatest persecutions occurred during the time of World War II. After the defeat of Japan in 1945 the occupying Allied powers abolished Shinto, but it was not long before the old traditions were revived. Official statistics show an annual increase in the number of Shintoist worshippers, with the most recent count standing at a total of more than eighty million.

These are the main types of modern Shinto in Japan:

1. SHRINE SHINTO

This is the most popular and is the link between the Shinto of ancient times and the present day. Shinto shrines are considered to be the dwelling places of the *kami*, and they are also the buildings for their worship. Most shrines are located in rural settings—on mountains, near waterfalls, or on remote islands. These locations are thought of as sacred places. According to statistics compiled by the Japanese government in 1969, there are eighty thousand such shrines in Japan.

2. SHINTO OF THE IMPERIAL HOUSE

This is centred on the performance of rites on behalf of the spirits of the imperial ancestors. The Emperor himself performs these rites. They are not open to the public.

3. FOLK SHINTO

This is a term used to describe the mixture of superstition, magic, and other practices of the common people. Most Japanese accept Shinto customs and attitudes in their daily life.

4. SECT SHINTO

This term is used to describe thirteen religious groups which came into existence during the latter years of the nineteenth century. A common characteristic of these sects is their concern for human welfare in this present earthly life.

5. STATE SHINTO

This was a political creation developed in the nineteenth century in order to combine Shrine Shinto with the Shinto of the Imperial House. It continued in existence until 1945, when it was abolished by decree of the occupying Allied commanders in Japan.

B. SHINTO BELIEFS

Shinto worship centres around the *kami* or spirits. The concept of *kami* is very difficult to explain, and even Shinto believers themselves do not give a precise explanation of *kami*. One great Japanese scholar, Motoori Norinaga (1730–1801), has written, for example:

> I do not yet understand the meaning of the term, *kami*. Speaking in general, however, it may be said that *kami* signifies, in the first place, the deities of heaven and earth that appear in the ancient records, and also the spirits of the shrines where they are worshipped. It is hardly necessary to say that it includes human beings. It also includes such objects as birds, beasts, trees, plants, seas, mountains, and so forth. In ancient usage, whatever was outside the ordinary, or possessed superior power, or was awe-inspiring, was called *kami*.

Perhaps it would be accurate to say that *kami* is anything towards which the believer feels awe, or inferiority. Thus it is natural to call the emperor *kami* because of his great power. In addition to human beings, other things in the world which deserve to be feared or revered are called *kami*. But the deities of Shinto are not thought of as absolute supernatural beings, as deities may be in other religions. In the Shinto viewpoint all things which exist possess a spiritual nature, and so anything may be called *kami*. Thus Shinto is polytheistic. (*Polytheism* is a religion in which people worship many gods: *monotheism* is a religion in which people worship only one God.)

Shintoism teaches that man is a child of *kami*, because his life has come from the gods. In addition, man is a superior being, a potential *kami*, whose life on earth is destined to be one of blessing. In this respect Shinto is optimistic, and leads the believer to accept life as it is. ('Optimism' is the attitude to life which believes that everything is basically good and that things will become better in the future, not worse.)

There is no radical opposition between life and death in Shinto. Man is believed to live on after death, and to continue receiving the blessing of the *kami*. The only difference between the living and the dead is in the place where they are. The living are in the world of light, the dead are in the world of darkness. Even so, the dead are allowed to visit the world of light during the time of the Shinto festivals. The Shinto attitude towards death is optimistic and without anxiety.

Shinto has no ethical system, and offers no moral code, though it has absorbed the ethical system of Confucianism which is centred on filial piety (see p. 92). Shinto places its emphasis on quietly living out one's proper way of life. To live a natural and harmonious life is itself goodness, blessedness, and beauty. That which is bad is the lack of natural beauty. Shinto does not regard evil in a moral way, but in terms of pollution or contamination. The cause of evil is believed to lie outside the sphere of human activity, in the actions of evil spirits. Thus the cure of sin is not thought to be personal repentance, but participation in the ceremony of purification which is an act of cleansing. Accordingly, in Shinto there is no idea of a final judgement. The Japanese people are optimistic, believing that human beings are good, and that things will turn out well.

C. SHINTO SHRINES AND WORSHIP

Shintoism places great emphasis on the proper performance of rites and ceremonies at the shrines. There are many of these, and they are the dwelling-places of the *kami*. The followers of Shinto worship the *kami* (see above p. 56) in order to secure prosperity, and they try to obey the will of the *kami* in their daily lives.

There are three main sorts of ceremonies at the shrines:

1. PURIFICATION RITES

Examples of these are:

Misogi, or ablutions: These may be carried out privately with water and salt, or with water alone. Their purpose is to remove minor contaminations. These are very ancient ceremonies, and the oldest record of Japanese culture, written in China by a Chinese historian about AD 300, says about the Japanese: 'When the funeral ceremonies are over, all members of the family go into the water together to cleanse themselves in a bath of purification.'

Harai, or exorcisms: A priest usually performs these by swinging a purification wand over the people and the objects to be purified.

Imi, or abstentions: These are practices which protect against impurity.

'Shintoism places great emphasis on the proper performance of rites and ceremonies at the shrines—dwelling places of the spirits' (p. 57).

Believers announce their entry into the temple by sounding a gong to summon the spirits.

What is the chief difference between this custom and the Christian custom of ringing bells before—or during—a Church service?

2. OFFERINGS

Once the believer has been purified in body and in mind, he is ready to participate in the rites of offering and dedication. Rice, rice wine, and other foods are offered to the deities. Then follows the offering of festive foods and the presentation of music and dance.

3. PRAYER

The focal point of these rituals is prayer to the deities of the shrines. They take the form of praise of the *kami*, petitions for protection, and entreaty for blessings in this present life. The prayers are normally read.

SCRIPTURES

The most important books in Shintoism are two ancient books which tell stories about the *kami* of ancient times. These books are: the *Kojiki*, or *Record of Ancient Matters* (written in AD 712), and the *Nihon Shoki*, or *Written Chronicles of Japan* (AD 720). The Kojiki is written in Japanese; the Nihon Shoki was originally written in Chinese with the title *Nihongi*.

STUDY SUGGESTIONS

WORD STUDY

1. What is the meaning of the word *Shinto*, and where does it come from?
2. Examples of three different sorts of Shinto purification rite are mentioned in the chapter: (a) *ablution*, (b) *exorcism*, and (c) *abstention*. For each of these words choose one from the following list which you could use to explain the meaning of that particular practice:
   absolution wishing refraining washing exercising expulsion restraining

REVIEW OF CONTENT

3. Did Shintoism grow up traditionally within Japan, or was it imported by missionaries from outside?
4. At what period did Shintoism become a national religion, and how did this happen?
5. (a) At what periods and from which country were Confucianism and Buddhism brought into Japan?
   (b) What influence on the development of Shintoism did each of these religions have?
   (c) In what different ways have ordinary Japanese tended to think about Shintoism and Buddhism?
6. What connection is there between the Emperor Jimmu and the Emperor Maiji in Japanese religion and history?

7. Name four different sorts of Shinto practised today, and briefly describe each.

8. 'The deities of Shinto are not thought of as absolute supernatural beings, as they may be in other religions' (p. 56). Explain this statement. (If you use the word *kami* in your answer, explain its meaning also.)

9. (a) What is the chief teaching of Shintoism about human behaviour?
(b) What is the teaching of Shintoism about evil?

10. 'Shintoism places great emphasis on the proper performance of rites and ceremonies at the shrines' (p. 57). What are the three chief sorts of Shinto ceremonies and what are their aims?

BIBLE STUDY

11. 'The Japanese people are optimistic, believing that human beings are good, and that things will turn out well' (p. 57).
Read John 3.1–17, and also Romans 3.9–28, and then write in a short paragraph what you think a Japanese Christian might wish to say to a Shintoist neighbour.

12. Compare the offering of gifts in Shintoist worship with those made by the Maori. Read Exodus 23.14–19 and Deuteronomy 14.22–29, and list any similarities which you find. Do you offer similar offerings in your churches at harvest time?

DISCUSSION AND RESEARCH

13. 'Shinto does not regard evil in a moral way. . . . The cause of evil is believed to lie outside human activity. Thus the cure of sin is purification' (p. 57).
(a) Read Mark 7.1–23. Which verses in this passage show most clearly the difference between Christian belief and Shinto belief on the subject of evil?
(b) What effect do you think it would have on your own general behaviour and your relationships with other people, if you shared the Shinto belief that the cause of evil lies outside human activity?

14. What are the main differences between the attitude of Shintoists towards their relatives who have died, and the attitude of (a) the Dinka, and (b) the Maori?

15. In the fourth century AD, Shinto became a national religion. In 1868 it became Japan's official state religion.
(a) Explain the terms 'national' and 'state' as applied to religion.
(b) What connection, if any, is there between religion and the state in your own country?
(c) Find out which countries in the world today have an official state religion, and the ways in which heads of state or other political leaders are involved in these religions.

Chapter 8
Hinduism

From material contributed by
T. K. Thomas

A. WHAT IS HINDUISM?

1. A MAJOR RELIGION

Hinduism is among the most widely practised religions of the world. Over 400 million people follow the Hindu faith.

More than 80 per cent of Indian people are Hindus. There are followers of the Hindu faith in Pakistan, Bangladesh, Nepal, and Bali in Indonesia, and considerable numbers of Hindus in Fiji, Malaysia, Singapore, Sri Lanka, Mauritius, the West Indies, and a few of the African states. They are the descendants of Indian emigrants.

Unlike Christianity, Buddhism, and Islam, Hinduism was never a missionary religion. In recent years, however, Hindu missionaries have opened spiritual centres in several Western cities. Many people in the West are attracted to the Hindu way of life. Young people especially are increasingly drawn to it. But it is difficult to know how deep their interest is, or how permanent it will prove to be. It is too early to assess the influence of Hinduism in the West.

The influence of Hinduism on the culture of some of the East Asian countries, however, is much more evident. Buddhism was an offshoot of Hinduism, and Hindu elements are part of the Buddhist way of life. The spread of Buddhism, therefore, meant the spread of Hindu ideas as well.

2. THE OLDEST LIVING RELIGION

Hinduism is perhaps the oldest living religion in the world. The word *Hindu*, like the word *Indian*, is derived from the name of the river *Indus*, but the religion itself is older than the name. Hinduism was originally known as *Arya Dharma*, or the 'Aryan Way'.

Dharma is a key word in Hinduism and means duty, right, virtue, morality, law, truth, righteousness. *Dharma* is the way that leads to salvation or liberation (*Moksha*). In other words, it is religion in its broadest sense.

There was a flourishing civilization in India as early as 3000 BC, but we know very little about the religious beliefs of these pre-Aryan people. The Aryans came to India in about 2000 BC, but we do not know a great deal about their religion then. It is generally believed that Hinduism contains both Aryan and pre-Aryan elements.

'Hindu missionaries have opened spiritual centres in Western cities' (p. 61).

The Guru Maharaj Ji was successful in doing this when he was a young man. He is seen here at a rally in Delhi addressing followers, many of whom had flown in from European countries.

What should be the attitude of the Churches in 'Christian' countries to such missions?

3. AN ETHNIC RELIGION

Hinduism is the religion of a people and it developed through the long centuries of their life as a nation, giving rise to a great variety of beliefs and practices.

There are at least three important differences between Hinduism and the other great religions of the world:

1. Hinduism has no founder. We do not know how or when Hinduism came into being. It has no date of birth. It is the result of a process of gradual evolution through thousands of years.

2. Hinduism has no common creed. There is no generally accepted system of dogma or body of doctrines.

3. Hinduism is not institutionalized. There are Hindu institutions, but Hinduism itself is not an institution. It does not have a body of believers who follow one common pattern of worship, or live according to one common code of conduct.

4. A FAMILY OF RELIGIONS

There is such a variety of beliefs and practices within Hinduism that it is often described as a family of religions. It is difficult, in fact, to say who a Hindu is. To be a Hindu, a person may observe a complicated system of rules—or none at all. One may give up the world, or accept it; one may worship one god, or many gods. One may worship a man as god, as many do in India, or one may worship no god at all, and yet be a Hindu.

Thus Hinduism is a flexible faith. It is able to accept, and in course of time absorb, new ideas and beliefs. It is no wonder that Pandit Nehru, the first Prime Minister of independent India, described Hinduism in the following words:

Hinduism, as a faith, is vague, amorphous, many-sided: all things to all men. It is hardly possible to define it, or indeed to say definitely whether it is a religion or not, in the usual sense of the word. In its present form, and even in the past, it embraces many beliefs and practices, from the highest to the lowest, often opposed to or contradicting each other. Its essential spirit seems to be 'to live and let live'.

B. THE SCRIPTURES OF HINDUISM

1. SRUTI AND SMRITI

Hindu Scriptures are divided into two classes: *Sruti* and *Smriti*.

Literally *Sruti* means that which is heard. It is *truth as it was revealed* to the sages of old. The four *Vedas*, which are collections of ancient texts, together form the *Sruti*. They are the fundamental Scriptures of the Hindu faith. They are the primary sources and the authoritative texts of Hinduism.

Smriti means that which is remembered. It is *truth interpreted* by sages and scholars. If *Sruti* is like the Bible, then *Smriti* is like the teaching and tradition that are derived from the Bible. All Scriptures other than the Vedas are classified as *Smriti*. Most of them are of a sectarian nature, and only of secondary importance. These include many stories and legends, rules of conduct for individuals and communities, manuals of worship, and accounts of theological schools and philosophical systems. But a few of them, notably the two epics or *Puranas—The Ramayana* and *The Mahabharata*—are part of the common heritage of Hinduism.

2. VEDAS AND UPANISHADS

The four Vedas are the Rig-Veda, the Sama-Veda, the Yajur-Veda, and the Atharva-Veda. Each of them consists of four main parts.

(a) The *Mantras:* these are hymns and chants in praise of God.

(b) The *Brahmanas:* these are explanations of the Mantras, together with detailed descriptions of the sacrificial rites which are related to them.

(c) The *Aranyakas:* these are meditations which explain their meaning.

(d) The *Upanishads or secret teachings:* these go beyond the rituals to discuss the nature of the universe and man's relation to it. The teaching of the Upanishads is known as *Vedanta*—the *anta* or end of the Veda. It is full of profound spiritual truths. Much of Hindu literature through the centuries is comprised of commentaries on the Upanishads, and interpretations of the lofty thoughts contained in them.

3. RAMAYANA AND MAHABHARATA

These are the national epics of India. They are the common man's Scriptures and the masses of the Hindu people draw their values and ideals from them.

The *Ramayana* is the story of Rama who destroys the demon-king Ravana and re-establishes righteousness on earth. Rama and his consort Sita are considered to be the ideal man and woman. Rama is believed to be an *avatar* (i.e. 'incarnation') of God, and the repetition of his name is the most common devotional exercise in popular Hinduism. ('Incarnation' means the action in which a divine being or a spirit takes human form, and a human body.)

In the *Mahabharata* we have the story of a great war. The hundred *Kaurava* brothers, who represent Evil, are ranged against their five cousins, the *Pandavas*, who represent Good. With the help of Sri Krishna, another incarnation of God, Good triumphs over Evil.

These great epics contain much more than what we have outlined above. They abound in characters and episodes which illustrate human qualities and human situations. They teach values of courage, loyalty, devotion, truthfulness, and steadfastness. They have inspired men and women for many generations. They have shaped Indian art and literature, and they have left their stamp on Indian life.

4. BHAGAVAD GITA

The *Bhagavad Gita* or 'the Lord's Song' is the best-known book of Hindu Scripture. It is a part of the *Mahabharata*. On the eve of the great battle, Arjuna, one of the Pandava brothers, is beset with doubts. How can he wage war against his own people, even though his cause is just? On the battle-field the god Krishna expounds to him the moral and philosophical implications of human action.

The whole text may be considered as a long dialogue sermon. It teaches men to do their duty, their *dharma* (see p. 61), whatever that *dharma* may be, and whatever consequences it may have. The basic teaching of the Gita centres on the need for selfless action. Such action should take place, it tells us, as part of our unfailing devotion to God:

> He is the One from whom all beings proceed, and by whom all is pervaded. Man attains perfection by worshipping Him through the performance of his own duty.

This is typical of the teaching of the Gita. It is very practical. 'Do your duty,' it says. 'By doing your duty, whatever the duty may be in the given situation of your life, you are really worshipping God.'

The Gita is said to contain the essence of Hindu philosophy and it has been called the layman's *Upanishad* because it presents the difficult teachings of the *Upanishads* in a way that common people can understand.

The Gita has played a vital role in the revival of Hinduism in modern India. Gandhi, for instance, to whom modern India owes more than to any other single individual, valued the Gita as 'an infallible guide of conduct'. He wrote about it in his autobiography, *The Story of My Experiments with Truth*:

> Just as I turned to the English dictionary for the meanings of English words that I did not understand, I turned to this dictionary of conduct for a ready solution to all my troubles and trials.

Millions of Hindus read the Gita daily. Millions regularly listen to discourses on the Gita, sitting in the shade of village trees or in the big halls of cities. The Gita is today the most widely used among all Hindu sacred writings.

STUDY SUGGESTIONS

WORD STUDY

1. What is the origin of the word 'Hindu'?
2. Which are the key words in Hinduism that are used to express each of the following ideas?
   (a) liberation   (b) righteousness

REVIEW OF CONTENT

3. Which of the following statements are true and which are untrue?
   (a) Probably the oldest living religion in the world is Hinduism.
   (b) Hinduism has always been a missionary religion.
   (c) Hinduism has had no influence in the West.
   (d) Hinduism is not flexible enough to absorb new ideas.
   (e) Many Hindu ideas and practices are also part of the Buddhist way of life.
   (f) It is easy to recognize a Hindu by the way he worships.
4. List the three chief differences between Hinduism and the other great religions of the world.
5. 'Hindu Scriptures are divided into two classes: *Sruti* and *Smriti*' (p. 63).
   (a) Which of these two classes can be compared to the Scriptures in the Bible, and what does its name actually mean?
   (b) What does the name of the other class mean, and what does it include?
6. The basic Scriptures of Hinduism are the four *Vedas*. What four different sorts of writing does each *Veda* contain?
7. (a) What is the chief teaching of the *Bhagavad Gita*?
   (b) Why is the *Gita* sometimes called 'the layman's *Upanishad*'?

DISCUSSION AND RESEARCH

8. Could we divide the books of the Bible into *sruti* and *smriti*, as the Hindu holy books are divided?
9. Do you know of any Christian books, other than those in the Bible, which have influenced and inspired ordinary Christian people in the way that the *Ramayana* and *Mahabharata*, and the *Bhagavad Gita* have influenced and inspired Hindus? Are any of them used today in the way the *Gita* is used according to p. 65?

C. THE HISTORY OF HINDUISM

For centuries Hinduism was indifferent to time and history. The result is that there are no precise dates or definite evidences for the beginnings of Hinduism. When was the Gita written? When and where did a particular event take place or a movement begin? We do not know. There are no ancient records or chronicles that record stories of the lives of important people, or give the dates of great events.

Till we come to modern times we must, in the circumstances, study Hinduism without reference to Indian history. And we must be content with general observations on broad periods and on developments that took place through many centuries.

1. THE VEDIC AGE: 2000–600 BC

This was the formative period for Hindu faith. It is confusing in many ways, but Hinduism began to take a definite direction. There was immense variety, but there was also an underlying unity.

(a) *Vedic deities and rituals:* Vedic literature took shape during this period. The earliest of the Vedas, *Rig Veda*, contains a vast number of hymns addressed to such deities as the sky, the sun, the earth, the storm, and the fire. The gods of popular belief during this time were the forces of nature. Chief among them were Indra, the god of power, and Varuna, the god of righteousness. Rituals and sacrifices were performed to please the gods. It was believed that the order of the universe was maintained through sacrifice. The universe itself, according to one text, came out of a sacrifice performed by the gods.

But such ideas were too difficult for ordinary people to understand. They were content with the outward aspects of sacrifice. For them the rituals of worship were a kind of magic. Thus, in course of time, the rituals lost their meaning and became no more than religious routine. The priests who performed the rituals grew in importance and power. They were thought to be a superior class. They were considered to be the guardians of secret knowledge, and necessary to the well-being of the people.

(b) *The Search for Ultimate Reality:* The Vedic hymns show that, along with their worship of many gods, people were searching for the God behind the gods. They were groping towards 'monotheism', the belief that there is only one God. In the teaching of the *Upanishads* this search for Ultimate Reality became much more marked and much more advanced. Upanishadic teaching is often summarized in the text, 'That thou art'. This means that the Supreme Soul of the universe, or the Spirit which creates and sustains it, is the same as the individual soul or spirit of man. This teaching goes even further from the idea of one God above and beyond the created Universe to which man belongs. It claims that there is only one reality. *Brahman*, the Spirit of the Universe, and *atman*, the human soul, are not two but one and the same. This teaching is known as *advaita*, which literally means 'not-twoness'. This attempt to know God and to grow into

God was the religion of the few. The common people tried to please the gods by performing sacrifices.

(c) *The Caste System:* In every country people are divided into different groups depending on their relative wealth, the sort of work they do, or their family background. In India these divisions have been strongly emphasized by the system of caste. This fixed the position of each social group or caste within society as a whole. It laid down rules about how people belonging to one caste should behave towards those in others, and the homage and service due from those in lower castes to those in higher ones. The system of caste developed during the Vedic period. In the *Rig Veda* there is a mythical account of its origin: the *Brahmin* or priestly class came from the mouth of Brahma the Creator, the *Kshatriya* or ruling class came from the arm of Brahma, the *Vaisya* or merchant class came from the thigh of Brahma, and the *Sudra* or workmen were born from the foot of Brahma.

Originally, perhaps, the caste of a man was decided by his occupation. He could change his caste by changing his occupation. But later on caste became a matter of heredity, and a man's caste—and thus his occupation—was decided according to the caste of his parents. This led to a rigid social structure which preserved the privileges of the few and perpetuated the exploitation of the masses. At first, caste probably had a stabilizing effect on society, but its defects became greater than its merits. It controlled all social relationships, and denied individual freedom. Innumerable sub-castes arose within the main caste divisions, each with its own intricate rules. Outside these were the 'Untouchables', whose shadow, even, was believed to be polluting.

(d) *The Doctrine of Karma:* The law of *karma* is related to the caste system and is central to Hindu faith. What caste was in the sphere of practical life, *karma* was in the realm of spiritual life.

The aim of human life, according to ancient Hindu teaching, is to realize oneness with Ultimate Reality. This cannot be achieved in one life, so each soul goes through many lives. A soul is not born, nor does it die. As death follows birth, so rebirth follows death. The process continues, till the soul is purified and ready to merge into the Soul of the Universe, which is its destiny. The process itself is known as *samsara*, which means 'going through'. It is the ceaseless series of birth and rebirths, till at last the final release from the bonds of life takes place. The release is called *moksha*. It is the exit from this world of existence, and liberation from the series of births and rebirths. It is also the entry into real existence, the absorption into God, which is the state of supreme blessedness in the Hindu scheme. It is life in God.

This is where the law of *karma* comes in. What people are today, this law says, is the result of what they were yesterday. What they will be tomorrow, depends on what they are and how they live today. Every action is followed by another action or an event appropriate to it. This is the law of *karma*. It is an impersonal law, and involves no judgement whatever. There is neither reward nor punishment as we normally understand these words. The law of karma simply links this present life with the previous one and the following one. (See also p. 130.)

Summary: Thus, during the Vedic age, there was first the rise and then the decay of religious ritual. Philosophic speculation also developed in the *Upanishads*. Caste distinctions grew in importance, and the social structure became more and more rigid. The doctrine of karma was a good explanation for the changes and inequalities of earthly life. The basic beliefs of Hinduism thus came to birth. These beliefs went through many interpretations in succeeding centuries but Hinduism had become a clearly recognizable way of life by the end of the Vedic period.

2. THE AGE OF PROTESTS: 600–200 BC

Two movements of protest, *Jainism* and *Buddhism*, arose within Hinduism in the sixth century BC. Their founders rejected the authority of the priests, and wanted to liberate the masses of the people from the tyranny of religious rituals and sacrifices. They taught that the ultimate aim of man was to know himself—to fulfil himself—rather than to reach God. Man could achieve this aim, they said, through severe self-discipline and self-control.

It is important to remember, however, that both the Buddha and Mahavira, the founder of Jainism, were originally Hindus. This is particularly true about the Buddha, and at several points his teachings reflect the teaching of the *Upanishads*. (See p. 126.)

Jainism and Buddhism were only two of the many movements that arose, during the period, in opposition to Vedic orthodoxy. Most of the movements were short-lived. Buddhism flourished for a time, and then its popularity died down in India. It had its golden age under the emperor Ashoka, but even then it did not displace the Hindu faith. Some of the fundamental tenets of Hinduism were challenged, and many of its religious practices were called in question. But the foundations of Hinduism were not shaken. In fact Hindus later worshipped the Buddha as one of the gods.

The new movements, however, left their mark on Hinduism. There was a new emphasis on morality and good works. The protest against sacrifices resulted in a new respect for animal life. Monastic orders, which followed the Buddhist pattern, began to be popular.

The worship of images developed during this period. Belief in a personal God became more widespread. The old trends continued, but new elements also were creeping in.

3. THE AGE OF EPICS AND PURANAS: 200 BC–AD 1000

(a) *The Great Epics:* After a period of reaction and protest there came a revival. The *Ramayana* and the *Mahabharata* belong to an early part of this period, and they played a vital role in the development of Hinduism. The abstract ideas and principles expressed in the *Upanishads* were personified in the characters and stories of the two epic poems. These epics, and some of the later *Puranas* or ancient writings, became the Scriptures of popular Hinduism.

These writings reached the common people. They touched the hearts of men and fired their imaginations. In the *Upanishads* God is most often described as impersonal and without qualities. He is everything and He is nothing. He can only be described as 'not this, not that'. In the persons of Rama and Krishna, who are the heroes of these epic poems, this unknowable and impersonal Absolute becomes knowable and lovable.

(b) *Doctrine of Avatara:* In the *Bhagavad Gita* Krishna describes himself as the Absolute who is identified with all things that are. He is the light of the sun, the brightness of fire, life in all things, and the penance of the ascetics. In sacrifice he is the act of offering, the offering, the sacrificial fire, and the sacrificer.

But this Absolute has now appeared on the human scene, and Krishna tells Arjuna:

> I am unborn, the lord of all things. Yet I am born by entering nature through my mysterious power. . . . I incarnate myself from age to age, to save the righteous, to destroy the wicked, and to re-establish *Dharma*.

This is the doctrine of *avatara*, which means descent, especially the descent of a god from heaven. An *avatara* is an incarnation, but, unlike the incarnation of Christ, it does not signify a unique and final revelation. In fact, according to popular Hinduism, nine *avataras* have already happened, and a tenth one is yet to take place.

(c) *Cults of personal devotion:* The rise of the *avatara* doctrine was an important development. Popular belief had already begun to think of God as a person, and to describe Him in His threefold role of creator, preserver, and destroyer. Brahma was the creator, Vishnu the protector, and Siva the destroyer. Together they formed the *Trimurti*, the one God with three forms. Now the concept of *avatara* brought this God in a familiar form to the hearts and homes of men. It made personal devotion to God real and respectable. People learnt to express their religious faith in *bhakti* or devotion to the gods. *Bhakti* is a beautiful word. It means more than devotion. It is *loving devotion*. It stands for the soul's longing for God and clinging to God. The tradition of *bhakti* in Hinduism is long and rich. Philosophers like Shankara looked down upon it as an inferior path, but it was the warm glow of *bhakti* that lighted the path of common people through the gloom of centuries.

(d) *Puranas:* The religious poems known as *puranas* gave further encouragement to the *bhakti* movement. They tell the deeds of gods, the exploits of heroes, and the achievements of saints. There are eighteen principal *puranas*, and many secondary ones. Some are about Vishnu, some about Brahma, and the others about Siva. This meant that each god, in course of time, came to have his own devotees. For example, *Vaishnavites* are the devotees of Vishnu, and *Saivites* are the devotees of Siva.

Towards the close of this period the *Bhagavata Purana* appeared. It has a unique position in the devotional literature of Hinduism. It is a collection of edifying stories and devotional discourses which contains accounts of all the *avataras* (see p. 70) of Vishnu, and much else besides. The religious beliefs of the masses of the Indian people are derived chiefly from this work. It emphasizes the *bhakti* way of salvation, and has inspired innumerable plays and poems and pictures.

Along with the three chief gods, people worshipped *Shakti* (or power), as personified in the mother-goddess. The literature which it gave rise to is known as *Tantra* literature.

(e) *Darsanas:* The nine systems of Hindu philosophy were organized during this period. They are known as *darsanas*, which means world-views or systems. There are six orthodox systems; and three that are not orthodox which include Jainism and Buddhism. Some of them classify and interpret the truths contained in Vedic writings; others follow independent lines of enquiry, and cover many fields of knowledge. (For a definition of 'world-view' see p. 11.)

4. THE AGE OF BHAKTI: AD 1000–1750

This title can be misleading. It merely means that, during this long period, the chief element in the religious life of the common people was the element of personal devotion to God.

(a) *Ordinary Hinduism:* The common people belonged to one or another of the many sects that had developed within Hinduism. They worshipped their favourite gods in the many temples that had sprung up through the length and breadth of the country. They went on pilgrimages. They observed caste rules, which had by now become binding and intricate. Sometimes they kept an image of their favourite deity in their homes. They respected animal life, and recognized the sanctity of the cow. There were innumerable gods and goddesses,

'The religion of the ordinary people touches all aspects of their lives, and there are thousands of pilgrim centres, many connected with sacred rivers' (pp. 73, 82).

A Hindu family calls in holy men to offer sacrifices, hoping to drive out evil spirits which they believe are bringing misfortune to their home.
Pilgrims 'purify' themselves in the river Ganges at Benares.

Do you think people can avoid misfortune in this way? What is the teaching of your Church about evil spirits?

who had become familiar figures in popular imagination, but Vishnu, Siva, and Shakti continued to be the chief objects of devotion. The religion of the ordinary people was homely, and touched all aspects of their life.

(b) *Spread of Bhakti: Bhakti* movements were already active in the southern parts of the country. There were groups of poets and singers whose poems and songs expressed an intense personal devotion to God. At this time the Bhakti movements began to be supported by philosophic understanding. Rama and Krishna—*avatars* of Vishnu—and Siva and Shakti became the objects of popular devotion. In later centuries there were poets and sages like Kabir, Tulsidas, and Tukaram who contributed to the *bhakti* movement. In all of them we notice the fervour of personal piety and the belief that the way to salvation is the way of devotion.

(c) *Ramanuja:* Ramanuja lived in the early part of the twelfth century. He provided a philosophical foundation for *bhakti-marga*, the path of devotion to God. He stressed the importance of simple faith and complete surrender. According to him, God, the world, and the individual self are all real. The world and man's self, however, depend on God; they have no reality outside the Reality that is God. They are, in fact, God's body. Salvation comes through the realization of man's absolute dependence on God.

(d) *Impact of Islam:* During this period India was under Muslim rule, but the influence of Islam on the Hindu faith was not great. It did not weaken the caste system, nor the practice of idol worship. The Muslim Emperor Akbar tried to establish a new religion which included Hindu elements, but the experiment did not succeed. The weaver poet Kabir preached a universal religion, based on the personal realization that God dwells in the hearts of men. It is said that both Muslims and Hindus claimed his body when he died. Hindus wanted to cremate it, according to their custom, and Muslims wanted to bury it.

The presence of an entirely different religion in their midst, however, made Hindus more conscious of their Hinduism. They became more and more proud of their centuries-old religion and culture. They learned, for the first time in their long history, to fight for their faith. Hinduism did not become a proselytizing religion, but Hindus now learned to resist the zeal of missionary faiths. At the end of the Muslim era, Hindus were more consciously Hindu that they were at its beginning.

(e) *Sikhism:* During this period Sikhism arose as a new religion. Nanak, who founded the faith, was a simple and good man. He was inspired by a great love for his fellow men. His purpose was to reconcile Hindus and Muslims, and to realize a way of life and a system of beliefs which would make love real and brotherhood possible. What started as a reform movement, however, eventually developed into a new religion.

5. THE MODERN PERIOD: AD 1750 ONWARD

The modern period is the period of Western impact and Christian influence, and the rise of reform movements. Such movements owed much of their inspiration to the Western learning to which India became exposed. During this period, Indian nationalism came to life and, with it, a reaffirmation of the Hindu Way. The modern period is the period of reform. It is also the period of renaissance.

(a) *Reform Movements:* There were three major reform movements.

The *first* was the *Brahmo Samaj*—the Society of God—founded by Raja Ram Mohan Roy. The Samaj took up the cause of social and religious reform. It was a Puritan movement within Hinduism, and denounced social evils like child-marriage, and religious practices like idolatry. It took up causes like women's education and the re-marriage of widows. It was strongly monotheistic and did not teach belief in the *avataras*. It condemned caste distinctions. The Samaj owed a good deal to Christian influence, especially to the ethical teaching of the Gospels. One of its later leaders, Keshub Chander Sen, was deeply attracted to the person of Jesus Christ. He tried, through some of his experiments, to bridge the gulf between Christianity and Hinduism.

The *second* movement, the *Arya Samaj*, was a revivalist movement more than a reform movement. Its great leader was Swami Dayanand Sarasvati, who was a militant Hindu. The new movement challenged Hinduism to rediscover the riches of its own heritage. It was opposed to Islam and Christianity. It promoted religious nationalism, and taught Hindus to take their faith seriously.

The *third* is the *Ramakrishna Mission*, which was based on the teaching of Sri Ramakrishna Paramahamsa.

Ramakrishna was a simple, uneducated Brahmin with a great hunger for God. He was serving as a temple priest when he began to live a life of severe self-discipline and strenuous search for God. He meditated on the Mother-Goddess till she appeared to him in person. Later he had visions of other gods as well. He even had a vision of Christ. The essential unity of all religions became for Ramakrishna a matter of personal experience. He said:

I have practised all religions, Hinduism, Islam, Christianity; and I have also followed the paths of the different Hindu sects. . . . I have found that it is the same God towards whom all are directing their steps, though along different paths. Wherever I look I see men quarrelling in the name of religion . . . but they never reflect that he who is Krishna is also called Siva, and bears the name of Primitive Energy, Jesus and Allah as well—the same Rama with a thousand names. (T. M. P. Mahadevan, *Outlines of Hinduism*, p. 221)

Many young people gathered round Ramakrishna. They accepted him as their *guru*, or teacher. Ramakrishna himself did not write books or make formal statements of faith. We know of his teachings from the writings of his disciples. He taught them that the final purpose of human life is the realization of God. This goal is common to all religions, and it may be reached through devotion (*bhakti*). We must love the God whom we seek.

Ramakrishna was a saintly man. He was in the tradition of the great mystics of the world, but the religion he practised was a practical one. It did not depend on rituals, and it did not call for learning.

His disciple Vivekananda popularized the teaching of Ramakrishna. Vivekananda was a young university student when he first met Ramakrishna, and their meeting changed the whole direction of his life. He established the Ramakrishna Mission in order to propagate the teaching of his master. It has today developed into the missionary wing of Hindu religion. It is also a great social service agency. In India it runs a large number of educational, medical, and relief institutions. There are centres of the Mission in many Western cities. It has contributed enormously to the understanding of Hinduism outside India, as well as to its renaissance within the country.

(b) *Tagore:* The poet Rabindranath Tagore also played a decisive role in the renaissance of the Hindu faith. His songs and poems teach about God and man, and express the aspirations of the Indian people. He is thus the poet both of Indian nationalism and of renascent Hinduism. His poems sound a recurring note of deep personal devotion. For example:

Days come and ages pass, and it is ever He who moves my heart in many a name, in many a guise, in many a rapture of joy and of sorrow. (Tagore, *Gitanjali*, p. 72)

But God is not to be found in temples and holy places.

He is there where the tiller is tilling the hard ground and where the path-maker is breaking stones. He is with them in sun and in shower, and his garment is covered with dust.
God is not reached through renouncing the world, but by accepting it, for God has 'taken upon him the bonds of creation, he is bound with us all for ever'.

One of the beliefs of Hinduism is that man is God. Tagore sings of

God who is man, and his religion is the religion of man. This earth-bound vision of man's destiny, and this acceptance of life and the world, played a part in India's struggle for political freedom.

(c) *Gandhi:* The life and work of Mahatma Gandhi can be said to represent the best of Hinduism in our day. Gandhi is known to most people as the man who led India's struggle for independence, and successfully applied the principle of *ahimsa*, non-violence, in social and political struggles. He was a man of action. But action, in his case, was born out of faith. Gandhi was primarily a religious man, and he often claimed that it was because of his religious convictions that he took up politics. And his religion was Hinduism.

Gandhi also acknowledged his indebtedness to the teaching of Christ. The Sermon on the Mount was a formative influence in his life, and the story of the cross never failed to challenge him. But, in spite of all this, his deepest convictions came out of the Hindu Scriptures. He wrote:

> My religion is Hinduism which, for me, is the religion of humanity and includes the best of all the religions known to me.

'Truth is my God,' Gandhi used to say, 'and Non-violence is the way to reach Him.' Gandhi's God is not a person; rather it is a principle. But Gandhi would not quarrel with those who worshipped a personal God. He wrote:

> God is that indefinable something which we all feel but which we do not know. To me God is truth and love, God is ethics and morality, God is fearlessness—God is the source of light and life, and yet he is above and beyond all these. God is conscience. He is even the atheism of the atheist. He transcends speech and reason. He is a personal God to those who need his personal presence. He is embodied to those who need his touch. He is purest essence. He simply is to those who have faith. He is all things to all men. (*Young India*, 5 August 1925)

This is a typically Hindu view. Hinduism is never dogmatic. Hence the Hindu concept of the coexistence of religions. Gandhi believed, like other Hindus, that every religion is a legitimate way to God for the adherents of that religion. He saw no need for competition between religions, nor any need to change one's faith. He regarded conversion from one religion to another as pointless, and as disturbing to the harmony of social life. Gandhi had many Christian friends, but all through his life he disapproved of missionary work and conversion. We could call him the embodiment of the Hindu way of life for his time. He was both the embodiment of the Hindu renaissance, and its inspiration.

(d) *Radhakrishnan and Aurobindo:* Dr Radhakrishnan and Sri Aurobindo have been perhaps the most important exponents of Hinduism in our own day. Radhakrishnan, who was for a time President of the Indian Republic, believed that Hinduism could provide a solution to 'the problem of the conflict of religions', not in a common creed but in a common quest for 'God'. Sri Aurobindo has gone so far as to claim that:

> The Hindu religion is the universal religion which . . . can triumph over materialism by including and anticipating the discoveries of science and the speculations of philosophy . . . which embraces in its compass all the possible means by which man can approach God . . . and has utterly removed from us the reality of death.

STUDY SUGGESTIONS

WORD STUDY

1. What are the key words in Hinduism that are used to express each of the following ideas?
   (a) loving devotion   (b) consequences of action   (c) non-violence
   (d) incarnation
2. (a) What is an epic?
   (b) Name any epics you know of in the literature or traditions of your own country.
3. (a) What is the difference between *brahman* and *atman*?
   (b) Name an early Hindu doctrine about these two ideas, and briefly outline its teaching.

REVIEW OF CONTENT

4. What evidences are there for the early history of Hinduism?
5. Into what five main periods can the history of Hinduism be divided? Describe very briefly the chief characteristic of each period.
6. In the Vedic age Hindus worshipped the forces or powers of nature.
   (a) Make a list of the forces of nature which they worshipped.
   (b) Compare this list with the lists made for question 9, p. 35, and underline the gods or powers of nature which you have included in all three lists.
7. Name three other religions whose founders were first of all Hindus.
8. In what periods did the following Hindu doctrines first arise?
   (a) *bhakti*   (b) *avatara*   (c) *karma*
9. What was the effect of Islam on Hinduism during the period of Muslim rule?
10. (a) Name the reform movements founded and led by each of the following, and say briefly what each movement stood for:

(i) Sri Ramakrishna Paramahamsa   (ii) Raja Ram Mohan Roy
(iii) Swami Dayanand Sarasvati
(b) Name some important Hindu teachers who were influenced by Christianity.

11. 'The life and work of Mahatma Gandhi represents the best of Hinduism in our day' (p. 76).
Explain this statement.

12. Who or what are or were the following?
Puranas   Brahmins   Vishnu   gurus

DISCUSSION AND RESEARCH

13. 'Jainism and Buddhism were only two of the many movements that arose in opposition to Vedic orthodoxy' (p. 69).
(a) What elements in orthodox Hinduism led to the rise of these movements, and what new attitudes and practices resulted from them?
(b) What protest movements, if any, have arisen in the history of Christianity, or in the history of your own community, which can be compared to those which challenged orthodox Hinduism?

14. 'In every country people are divided into different groups depending on their wealth, the work they do, and their family background' (p. 68).
(a) Into what main groups are people divided in your country? Do these divisions have any connection with religion?
(b) What effect do the groupings you have listed under (a) have on people's relationships with other groups, or their political freedom, or on whether they are rich or poor?
(c) What difference, if any, would it make to you personally if the caste system existed in your country?

15. 'Rabindranath Tagore is the poet of Indian nationalism and renascent Hinduism' (p. 75). But many sincere Christians also find inspiration and comfort in his poetry. Find out all you can about Tagore's life and work, and then summarize (a) those of his beliefs which a Christian could share, and (b) those which a Christian could not share.

16. 'They were groping towards monotheism' (p. 67). 'The Brahmo-Samaj was strongly monotheistic' (p. 74). Can you think of reasons why people often come to believe in only one God?

D. HINDU BELIEFS

In tracing the evolution of Hinduism we have dealt with some of the important teachings and claims of the religion. We shall now try to explain a few of its major doctrines.

1. THE FOUR GOALS OF LIFE

According to Hinduism, there are four goals for life. They are *dharma* (righteousness), *artha* (worldly prosperity or material well-being), *kama* (enjoyment or pleasure), and *moksha* (liberation) (see p. 68). The final end is release from the bonds of flesh and the limitations of death-bound life. To progress towards liberation, one must live one's life here and now, and that means carrying out the responsibilities of social and family life, which is the pursuit of *artha*. That also means satisfying the demands of the flesh, which is the pursuit of *kama*. Both these are legitimate ends, but in their pursuit one should be guided by the overall goal of *dharma* (righteousness) and the ultimate goal of *moksha* (liberation).

2. THE FOUR STAGES OF LIFE

Traditional Hinduism divides the life of a man into four stages. The first stage is that of the student. The student is a bachelor. He lives in the house of the *guru* and, under his guidance, studies the sacred texts. The second stage is that of the householder. This is the important stage. It is the householder who maintains the fabric of society. He now lives with his wife. He discharges his debt to his ancestors by having children. He observes virtues like hospitality and industry, and contributes to the total well-being of society. During the third stage he retires to the forest with his wife, and meditates on the values of life. The fourth (i.e. last) stage is that of the holy sage. Now he renounces the world and all attachments.

It is interesting to note that the first three stages are said to be obligatory, i.e. all men experience them, while the last is only optional, not all men reach it.

3. THE THREE WAYS

The history of Hinduism is the history of man's search for reality. It is the story of a human quest—the quest for the truth of things. God, for the Hindu, is this reality or truth. There is a famous prayer in the *Upanishads* which reads:

From the unreal lead me to the real,
From darkness lead me to light,
From death lead me to immortality.

Hinduism, in its higher forms, expresses the human search for reality, light, and immortality. It recognizes three chief ways which the religious person may follow in order to reach this goal. He may follow any or all of them. These ways to God are also known as *yogas* or disciplines. The word *yoga* is related to the English word *yoke*. It signifies the yoking of our mind to God; it also means the disciplining of our mind and body.

1. The first way is the way of *good works*. It teaches unselfish service as the means of reaching God. Every man has his allotted duty or *dharma*. Right action consists in the discharging of this *dharma*. In the *Bhagavad Gita* Krishna tells Arjuna:

> You are entitled only to work, and not to its fruit. So never work for fruit, nor yet desist from work.

Renascent Hinduism rightly emphasizes this way of action. For a long time, Hinduism was considered to be an other-worldly religion. The ideal man, it was believed, is the holy sage, the man who has given up all possessions and all worldly attachments. Today it is action that is stressed, and not the giving up of action. A man like Gandhi, or an institution like the Ramakrishna Mission, is often held up as an example of involvement in the life of the world.

2. The second way is that of *devotion* (*bhakti*) (see p. 71).

3. The third way is the path of *knowledge*. Such knowledge is more than intellectual understanding, and it includes spiritual insight as well. It starts with the study of the Vedas and other Scriptures. This first stage is followed by a long period of reflection and meditation. The final stage in the growth of knowledge is that of self-realization, when a person becomes aware of his or her unity with God. When this stage is reached, one becomes a *jivan-mukta*, or liberated soul.

4. GOD AND MAN

Hinduism teaches, on the one hand, (a) that God is the impersonal Absolute, and, on the other, (b) that He is a personal God. Thus (a) He is above and beyond all that we see and know, but all that we see and know is a part of Him. He is eternally unchanging. But (b) He is also concerned about the human situation and He comes, periodically, into the world of men and matter in order to uphold righteousness (*dharma*) and root out unrighteousness.

Man's goal is God. His fulfilment consists in becoming one with the divine state of changeless bliss: that is liberation. It is earned through following one or more of the three Ways, and living through the four stages of life, and seeking the four goals of life. It is earned through many lives, accumulating credits in life after life, as an earnest student does through year after year of study.

E. POPULAR HINDUISM

So far in our study we have been dealing chiefly with the doctrines and theories of what is commonly called 'Higher Hinduism'. We have already seen that in 'Popular Hinduism', which is the religion of millions of ordinary Hindu people, there is no common pattern of devotion. Religious customs and practices vary from region to region and even from village to village. A person may choose his own favourite deity from the vast number of Hindu gods and goddesses. Each household worships its own god, and a village also often has its special deity.

At the local level Hinduism has many sects. The major sects worship Siva, Brahma, Vishnu, or Shakti, but in addition to these there are many minor sects worshipping their own gods. And between one local cult and another there are many differences. In this guide we can give only brief, general observations on certain common aspects of everyday Hindu religion.

1. WORSHIP

Hindus worship in their homes and in temples. Many wealthy people set apart a room, or part of a room, in their homes for *puja* (worship). It will have in it the image of the family deity, or at least a picture of the chosen god. During the time of worship, lamps are lit and incense is burned before the deity.

Worship for the Hindu is an individual act. It is not collective and congregational as in Christian churches. But the content of Hindu prayers is seldom personal, and has very little of the petitionary element. Prayer often consists in the repetition of the divine name, or the recitation of *mantras*, or sacred formulas. God is nameless, but He has nevertheless a thousand names, and the repetition of one name and the recitation of verses made up of many names are common acts of worship. There is an ancient story which relates how a very wicked man accidentally uttered the name of God during the last moments of his life, and thereby attained salvation. His son was called *Narayana*, which is a divine name. He called his son by name, and that saved him.

2. TEMPLES AND TEMPLE WORSHIP

India is famous for its temples. There are magnificent temples which dominate the life of whole cities, but practically every village has its own temple. In the big cities of India there are well-known temples which crowds of people visit regularly. There are also innumerable pavement shrines, humble structures which local people put up to house their chosen deity.

Temples differ widely in style and feeling. But each temple is dedicated to a particular deity, and worship centres round the image of the god or goddess. The temple priests bathe and dress and feed the image of the deity. Devotees come to gaze at the god, and to partake of the food which is offered to the god and then distributed among the devotees.

Hindu temples are often noisy and crowded. Amidst all the bustle, individual devotees move silently about, saying their prayers and making their offerings. Sometimes they process round and round the shrine in which is the image of the god or goddess.

3. FESTIVALS AND PILGRIMAGES

Hindus celebrate a great many festivals. There are national festivals like *Diwali*, the Festival of Lights, which commemorates the destruction of a demon king by Krishna, and there are also many local and regional festivals. Some of them are of a seasonal character. For example, *Onam* in Kerala and *Pongal* in Tamil Nadu are primarily harvest festivals. A number of festivals commemorate acts of liberation done by gods and goddesses. *Durga Puja*, the worship of the Mother Goddess, is the national festival in Bengal; it celebrates the triumph of good over evil. *Dasara*, another popular festival, commemorates Rama's victory over Ravana. Colourful processions and dramatic and dance performances mark the celebration of most festivals.

There are thousands of pilgrim centres in India. Most of them are connected with the exploits of gods and goddesses and those whose stories are told in Indian myths. Vrindaban in North India is honoured as the birth-place of Krishna. Some centres of pilgrimage, like Madurai and Rameshwaram in South India, are famous because of their temples. Others are connected with sacred rivers like the Ganges, and sacred hills like Thirupati and Sabarimalai. The Ganges is considered to be the most sacred river. Places close to its source are among the most popular centres of pilgrimage, and towns like Benares on the banks of the Ganges are considered to be among the holiest places in India.

People may undertake a pilgrimage at any time of life or at any time of the year. Usually, however, pilgrimages are made at certain seasons. This is partly because of the climate, and partly because of the belief that there is greater merit in a pilgrimage undertaken at the time of a festival.

Individuals, families, and large groups of people—rich and poor, educated and uneducated, from all walks of life and all strata of society—go periodically on such pilgrimages. They go by train and bus and bullock-cart. Often they cover long distances on foot, carrying their food and clothing with them. In some places pilgrims need only pay their respects to the deity and make their offerings. In others they are expected to undergo various austerities. Many pilgrims who go to Thirupati, for instance, have their heads shaven in the temple precincts.

'Sikhism arose as a new religion' (p. 73).

Ceremonial swords are raised at the inaugural service in a new Sikh temple near London, England.

Can you think of any 'new religions' which have derived from Christianity?

'Colourful processions mark the celebration of most festivals' (p. 82).

The State Elephant of Mysore is decorated and led out for the Dasara festival.

What do you think is the chief value of religious processions?

4. RITES AND CUSTOMS

The *Laws of Manu*, an ancient Hindu law book, lists twelve 'sacraments' for the Brahmin. The first of these 'sacraments' is a ceremony connected with conception. Not even orthodox Hindus observe all of them today. There are, however, many customs and rituals connected with birth, marriage, and death. These also vary a good deal from region to region. Each caste group has its own customs. Brahmins continue to observe the initiation ceremony at which boys are given the sacred thread, which they must wear all their life.

Astrology plays an important part in the life of a Hindu. Astrology is the forecasting of a person's character and life-experience from the position of the stars in the sky at the time of his birth. The position of the stars is known as a person's 'horoscope'. The time and the day of a child's birth are vitally important; it is on the basis of these that the child's horoscope must be prepared. There are auspicious hours and days—for buying and selling, sowing and reaping, starting on a journey and starting a business, and, of course, for marrying.

The parents of the bride and bridegroom normally arrange Hindu marriages. They study their horoscopes carefully, and only fix the marriage if these agree. The marriage ceremony itself may be extremely elaborate, lasting several days; but it can also be very simple. It may take place at home or in a temple.

As a rule Hindus cremate their dead. The eldest son should light the funeral pyre of the parent. This custom partly explains why Hindus value male children.

Notions of 'pure' and 'impure' play a large part in the daily life of the orthodox Hindu. There are ritual ablutions and food restrictions which are supposed to ensure purity.

Many Hindus do not eat meat, though vegetarianism is not obligatory. Even those who eat meat will not touch beef. The cow, from ancient times, was regarded as a symbol of the bounty of the earth, and Hindus hold it in special veneration. According to Gandhi, worship of the cow symbolized the Hindu's reverence for all life. It must be admitted, however, that many who worship the cow are no longer aware of such symbolism; they regard it as a fetish. But it is doubtful whether there are a great many people who worship the cow today in any real sense.

5. UNITY IN DIVERSITY

Hinduism holds within it an immense variety of religious experiences. Much of popular Hinduism is close to worship of nature spirits. At the other end of the Hindu spectrum are mysticism and a profound spirituality. The philosopher thinks of God as ultimate reality, the impersonal 'world-soul', and longs to become one with the divine state of eternal bliss. The illiterate villager thinks of God as a power to be propitiated, or a person to be loved and worshipped. Both are Hindus.

The swami who sits cross-legged and meditates on the mystery of God and the universe is clearly a Hindu. So is the old woman who stands in awe before the shining idol of Ganesha, the pot-bellied elephant-god. The people with caste marks on their foreheads are obviously Hindus. But there are thousands of people who never go to temples and never pray to gods, thousands of men and women who bear no external marks of Hinduism. They are nevertheless made what they are by the Hindu faith. They are Hindu in their thinking and attitude.

'As many minds, so many views'—that is a common Hindu saying. 'Truth is one; the wise call it by many names,' says the Rig Veda. It is this that provides for the resolution of the many contradictions within Hinduism. Krishna tells Arjuna in the Gita:

I make the devotee's faith steadfast in whatever form he seeks to worship by faith. . . . However men approach me, even so I accept them; for the path which men take on every side is mine.

F. THE FUTURE OF HINDUISM

INDIA AND HINDUISM

The renascent phase of Hinduism is not yet over, but the nationalist fervour of the struggle for freedom has ebbed. There were fanatical Hindus who wanted to establish a Hindu Raj in India, a theocratic Hindu state. But other counsels prevailed, and India today is a secular state. This does not mean that it is an irreligious state. It means that the state does not favour any particular religion more than others; the state is neutral in matters concerning the religious convictions and observances of the citizens. People of all faiths are free to follow, and to propagate, their religion.

But Hinduism continues to be the religion of the vast majority of the Indian people. The culture of the country is, by and large, Hindu culture. The ethos of the people is the Hindu ethos.

India as a nation has set for itself goals of development and modernization. It wants to secure better standards of life for its people. It wants to eliminate poverty. It seeks material prosperity. Its goals are the goals of developing nations all over the world. But the problems it faces are gigantic. There are many languages, many religions, and far too many people. There is grinding poverty. There are glaring inequalities.

So the question arises: How far do the teachings of traditional

Hinduism meet the needs and aspirations of independent India? Will Hinduism hinder, or will it help the process of modernization? Can it provide a basis for development and the energy needed for bold action? These are questions for which we cannot have easy answers.

TRADITION AND CHANGE

Hinduism faces a situation which other religions of the world are facing. There are Hindu thinkers who feel that Hinduism will go under, leaving only a few pieces of *bhakti* floating about on the surface. But there are others, as we have already seen, who think otherwise. They speak with a loud voice, and they sound confident. They are convinced that the forces of secularization will not overwhelm Hinduism. They believe that it has the inner resources to come to terms with new ideologies and fresh forces.

These defenders of Hinduism may well be right. Hinduism has survived similar situations of crisis in the past. It is a flexible faith. Its identity is not bound up with that of a person or a book. It can stand stresses and strains better than most other religions. It is resilient. It can tire out its opponent by its apparent tolerance!

Hinduism has rid itself of many of its social evils. In several areas it has submitted itself to social legislation introduced by the state. The caste system is no longer rigid. Untouchability has been banned. Women are free. Many of the old superstitious beliefs and anti-social practices—like *sati*, the cruel custom which demanded that a widow should burn herself on the funeral pyre of her husband, and child marriages—have disappeared from the Indian scene.

Rural economy has been disturbed by industrialization, and, with it, the rural way of life. The old family pattern has been disrupted by urbanization and similar forces. But traditional forces are still powerful. Village people continue to be fatalistic. Where the traditional values have disappeared, new values have not yet emerged to fill the vacuum. Caste is still a factor to be reckoned with. The external marks of caste are not very evident, but the caste mentality is still strong. The fact that even Christians practise caste in many places proves how strong its hold is.

There are a great many half-hearted Hindus, but this does not mean that the temples are deserted, or that festivals go unobserved. Far from it. Collections in the big temples have increased enormously. The old shrines in busy city corners and rural centres still have their worshippers. New shrines are coming up all the time. New cults make their appearance every now and then. People continue to go on pilgrimages. Saffron-clad *sadhus*—holy men—still roam about the streets. The fact that some of them wear wrist-watches and carry transistor sets does not necessarily make them less holy.

There are big publishing concerns, like Bharatiya Vidya Bhavan (the name means 'The Home of Indian Wisdom'), which brings out books and periodicals on Hindu religion and culture. The attempt to relate ancient teaching to modern life goes on all the time. Hinduism is still very much a living religion.

STUDY SUGGESTIONS

WORD STUDY

1. (a) From the following list of words choose one which gives the meaning of *dasara*, and one which gives the meaning of *darsana*:
   a goddess   a world-view   a pilgrimage   a demon   a festival
   a temple   a priesthood
   (b) What is the difference between *kama* and *karma*?

REVIEW OF CONTENT

2. Name the three gods who are chiefly worshipped by ordinary Hindus.
3. (a) What are the four goals of life, according to Hindu belief, and how are people expected to reach them?
   (b) What are the four stages of a man's life according to traditional Hinduism, and what sorts of activity belong to each stage?
4. 'The history of Hinduism is the history of man's search for reality' (p. 79). Describe the three chief ways in which a religious person carries on this search.
5. List three chief ways in which Hindu worship differs from Christian worship.
6. Describe briefly some Hindu customs relating to:
   (a) pilgrimage   (b) death and burial   (c) marriage
7. In what ways are the following important in Hinduism and for what reasons?
   (a) cows   (b) the town of Benares   (c) horoscopes
8. What is the Hindu teaching about the relationship between God and human beings? In what chief way does it differ from Christian teaching on this subject?

BIBLE STUDY

9. Read Matthew 11.28–30 and 28.16–20. Notice that the 'yoke' joins two together so that they help each other (Christ and the Christian). Contrast the promise of Christ with Hindu teaching about *yoga*.
10. Read Revelation 21.1—22.5 and 1 Corinthians 15.12–17.
    (a) What are the main differences between the Hindu hope for liberation (*moksha*), and the Christian hope for entrance into the

87

'City of God'? (b) In what ways does Paul's belief in the resurrection of the body differ from Hindu belief in the many rebirths of the soul (*samsara*)?

DISCUSSION AND RESEARCH

11. Hinduism is sometimes said to be a 'life-denying' religion, and to give little importance to ordinary human life. Why do you think people say this? Do the doctrines of *samsara* and *nirvana*, and the rules of caste, make human life seem to be of little importance? What other teachings in Hinduism, if any, suggest that life *is* important?

12. Can you suggest four hymns or songs in which Christians express *bhakti* towards God?

13. What is your opinion of the story on p. 81 about the wicked man who attained salvation?

14. In this chapter we have considered the future of Hinduism in the modern world.
(a) How far does the situation in your own country today resemble the 'modern situation' as we have described it?
(b) What effect, if any, is 'modernization' having on (i) the life of the Church, and (ii) other religions, in your country?

Chapter 9
Two Chinese Religions
From material contributed by
Tongshik Ryu

INTRODUCTION

The Chinese view of the world is expressed in the principle of *Yin* and *Yang*. This principle is present in all three of China's religious traditions: Confucianism, Buddhism, and Taoism.

The principle of *Yin* and *Yang* is based on the idea that opposites belong to each other. Two things which appear to be against each other actually belong to each other and make one complete whole. The Chinese find examples of this in opposites such as good-evil, light-dark, hot-cold, dry-moist, male-female, Heaven-Earth. All that exists is an expression of the underlying *yin* and *yang*. *Yin* and *yang* complement and balance one another: together they made a perfect whole. This principle is often expressed visually by the symbol:

This principle explains why, before the People's Republic was established in 1949, many Chinese followed two religions, Confucianism and Taoism. Confucianism stressed the responsibility which people have towards each other, while Taoism looked beyond people to the way of nature. Both, however, balance each other within the life of the Chinese people as a whole.

This principle also explains why both these religions, Confucianism and Taoism, appear to teach mainly social behaviour. Their teaching about behaviour in this world must be balanced by prayer and religion.

CONFUCIANISM

A. CONFUCIUS, THE GREAT TEACHER

Confucius, the founder of Confucianism, was born in 551 BC in the province of Lu. He came from a poor family. His father died when he was three years of age, and Confucius had to make his own way in the world. The hardship and poverty of those early years helped him to understand the common people.

From childhood he showed a great love for learning. By the time he was twenty he had opened a school and become a teacher. His method was not to discover new ideas, but only to transmit the wisdom of the ancients. His only aim in teaching was to give a faithful interpretation of the past to others. The reputation of his personality and wisdom spread rapidly, and he attracted many followers.

After service as a government officer in Lu for a short time, he left his own country and travelled from state to state for fourteen years, seeking for a ruler who would accept his counsel. In time he was able to return to his own country, Lu, but by that time he was too old to be an officer. Therefore he spent his last five years teaching, and in editing the great Chinese books. He died in 479 BC, at the age of seventy-two.

Confucius became more famous after his death. He never intended to found a new religion, but the prince of Lu erected a temple in his honour, and sacrifices were offered to him. This was the beginning of Confucianism as a religion of China. The custom of building temples in honour of Confucius has continued into the present century. Until 1912 the emperor offered sacrifices in his honour twice a year, in the spring and the autumn.

B. THE SCRIPTURES OF CONFUCIANISM

Confucius and his disciples collected, edited, and interpreted the writings of earlier Chinese philosophers and teachers. His disciples also collected the sayings of Confucius himself. There are two collections which constitute the Scriptures of Confucianism. They are the Five Classics and the Four Books.

THE FIVE CLASSICS

1. The *Book of Changes*, or *Yi Ching*, is a manual of divination, to assist in seeing future events. It consists of a series of ancient diagrams, together with later commentaries upon them.

2. The *Book of History*, or *Shu Ching*, is a collection of documents ascribed to Emperors from Yao down to the early Chou dynasty. It is

a moral and religious narrative which teaches the lesson that Heaven blesses only virtuous rulers with peace and prosperity.

3. The *Book of Songs*, or *Shih Ching*, is a collection of three hundred short poems, most of which belong to the Chou period in which Confucius lived.

4. The *Book of Rites*, or *Li Ki*, is a code of rules about worship, and about social and family relationships. It remains to this day the authoritative guide for Chinese morality and ethics.

5. The *Annals of Spring and Autumn* records events in the state of Lu over three hundred years.

THE FOUR BOOKS

These were put together in the eleventh century AD, the time of the Sung dynasty. These works formed the basis of the education of the ruling class, and the text of the examinations by which government officers were recruited.

1. The *Analects*, the sayings of Confucius, which were compiled by his disciples.

2. The *Mencius*, the sayings of the most prominent of his successors, Mencius (371–298 BC). He made philosophical comments on Confucius's teaching.

3. The *Doctrine of the Mean*, and

4. The *Great Learning* are parts of the treatises of the *Book of Rites*.

C. THE TEACHINGS OF CONFUCIUS ABOUT LIFE

THE MEANING OF BENEVOLENCE

The central idea of the Confucian ethic is expressed in a sentence from the *Great Learning*. This describes the goal of life to be the discovery of 'the way of cultivating the self, managing one's household, governing the nation, and establishing world peace'. Thus the way to bring happiness to one's home, nation, and the entire world, is by taking care of one's own personal character and conduct.

Confucianism teaches that there are five virtues: Benevolence, Righteousness, Propriety, Wisdom, and Trustworthiness. Among these Benevolence, or *Jen* in Chinese, is the greatest. Confucius did not give any theoretical definition of these virtues. His definitions are descriptions of virtue in action. For instance, Confucius gave different answers to the questions raised by disciples about the nature of *Jen*.

Chung-Kung asked, 'What is Benevolence?'
The Master said: '. . . to treat people as though we were attending a high sacrifice; not to do unto others what we would not that they

should do unto us; to breed no wrongs in the state and breed no wrongs in the home.' (*Analects* XII, 2)

Fan Chih asked: 'What is Benevolence?'

The Master said: 'To love mankind.' (*Analects* XII, 22)

Confucius said: 'He who can practise five things in dealing with the Empire may be accounted to have benevolence.' The five things are 'Politeness, liberality, good faith, diligence, and generosity. Being polite, you will not be slighted; being liberal you will win the people; having good faith, you will be trusted by others; having diligence, you will be successful; being generous, you will be worthy to employ others.' (*Analects*, XVII, 6)

FILIAL PIETY (The respect of a son for his father)

In Confucianism, particular regard is given to the family as the basic unit of society. It is recognized as the foundation of the whole political and social structure of any human community.

Confucianism teaches that there are five basic human relationships. These are: ruler and subject, father and son, husband and wife, elder and younger, and friend and friend. Out of these five, three have to do with the family. In the family the father-son relationship is the foundation of all others, and depends upon the son's proper respect for his father. This sort of respect, therefore, is the keystone of the Confucian teaching about behaviour. In China even loyalty to the ruler is understood in the same way.

The duties of sonship have two forms, the physical and the spiritual. To fulfil his physical duties, a son should pay due attention to the bodily needs of his parents; he should care for his own body as a legacy received from his ancestors; and he should rear children to provide for the family continuity. To fulfil his spiritual obligations, a son should obey his parents, remember them after death by annual sacrifices, and win success and honour to bring glory to the family name.

The duties of sonship includes not only obedience to living parents, but also service to the dead. People pay homage to the departed by holding appropriate ceremonies. At this point the duties of sonship are a bridge between practical duties in this world, and the concerns of religion for a life beyond this one.

OPTIMISM (for a definition of 'optimism' see p. 56)

Mencius taught that human nature is good, because man is the embodiment of the Tao which is good (see p. 98). According to his teaching, evil is due either to environment or to education. This was the basis of Confucian optimism in ethics.

Chu-Hsi (AD 1130–1200), the founder of Neo-Confucianism, re-affirmed Confucian optimism. Chu-Hsi believed that the whole universe is based on *Li*, or principle. According to him, a man's nature or character is his *Li*, which is part of the *Li* of the Universe, and is the same in all men. But each man's *Chi*, or substance, is different, and individual differences depend on the differences of *Chi*.

According to this teaching people's appearances differ, but the basic nature of all people is the same, for all possess the same *Li*, which is good. This basic *Li* shows itself in the Five Virtues: Benevolence, Righteousness, Propriety, Wisdom, and Trustworthiness. Man's basic nature is good.

According to Chu-Hsi, unenlightened people are those who fail to allow their basic nature to be revealed, because of their craving for things. This is due to the impurity of their *Chi*. Therefore it is necessary for people to rid themselves of wrong appearances, and return to their basic nature, or *Li*. This is why the *Great Learning* is important: it helps people to do this. Thus Confucian teaching is optimistic: it teaches that people are basically good.

D. CONFUCIANISM AS A RELIGION

There are opposing views as to whether Confucianism is actually a religion. Some people say that it is not, because it is chiefly concerned with behaviour in this world. Whenever Confucius was questioned about other-worldly matters, he drew the questioner's attention to the affairs of this world. When he was asked about serving the spirits of the dead, he answered, 'While you are not able to serve men, how can you serve their spirits?' Asked about death itself, he answered again, 'While you do not know life, how can you know about death?' (*Analects*, XI, 11). Confucius shifted the emphasis from heaven to earth, from other-worldliness to this-worldliness.

Confucius, however, never denied the existence of 'Heaven', or *Shang Ti*, the Supreme Ruler. For him Heaven was the power on which everything depends. Life and death, wealth and honour, are all in Heaven's hand. The following story illustrates Confucius's attitude:

> When the Master was affrighted in Kwang, he said, 'Since the death of King Wen, has not this been the home of good order? If Heaven had condemned good order, later mortals would have missed their share in it. If Heaven upholds good order, what can the men of Kwang do to me?' (*Analects*, IX, 5)

Confucius put strong emphasis on the importance of human relationships, but he based his teaching on the ancient belief in Heaven.

Although it has no creed or ecclesiastical organization, Confucianism is still a religion to the Chinese. This is not only because it is based on the belief in Heaven, but also because it points towards important principles which give meaning and direction to their lives.

There are, however, religious practices which are related to the teachings of Confucianism. They are these: the worship of Heaven or *Shang Ti*, the ceremony in praise of Confucius, and ancestor worship.

THE WORSHIP OF HEAVEN

Confucius's name has been associated with the cult which was established as the state religion of China in the second century BC, and held this position until 1912, when dynastic rule in China came to an end. The centre of this state religion was Heaven or *Shang Ti*. Chinese people thought of *Shang Ti* as the personal god who has a righteous purpose in governing the world. The emperor made the annual offering to *Shang Ti*.

The worship of *Shang Ti* expresses the belief that the state is built upon the pattern of the family. The emperor was regarded as the son of Heaven. He was appointed by Heaven to rule the world, and so Heaven was his father whom he had to serve as a son. Therefore the emperor had to make an annual offering to Heaven.

CULT OF CONFUCIUS

Confucius never considered himself the founder of a new religion. The Chinese never made him a god, but respected him as their great teacher or sage. In due time, however, people gave such reverence and devotion to the memory of Confucius that it gradually became like a religion. In the fifth century AD, for example, a temple was erected at the site of Confucius's tomb. In 630 the emperor of the Tang dynasty made a decree that all districts in the empire should build temples to Confucius. This spread the cult of Confucius in China. At the same time, in the capital, they established imperial colleges in which the Confucian classics were taught. From then on the people gave Confucius the title of Supreme Saint, and worshipped him at annual ceremonies.

ANCESTOR WORSHIP

Ancestor worship is at the centre of Chinese religion. There are two reasons for ancestor worship: one is the son's respect for his father which is the central virtue in Chinese teaching, and the other is the belief that people continue to live with their ancestors. The Chinese believe that the world of living people and the world of those who have died are not two worlds but one. (See reference to *Yin* and *Yang*, p. 89.)

During China's long history ancestor worship has passed through many changes, but the basic structure of it remains the same.

'Ancestor worship is at the centre of Chinese religion' (p. 94).

A Chinese woman whose family have settled in Sarawak lights incense sticks at an altar dedicated to their ancestors.

'In Shinto the only difference between the living and the dead is the place where they are' (p. 57).

A Japanese widow pours water over her dead husband's tombstone in order to 'refresh his spirit'.

What good do you see in these customs? In what ways do you and your family commemorate your ancestors?

Ancestor worship centres about the tablet, the funeral, and the grave. Among these the tablet occupies the most important place. The tablet, upon which the names of ancestors are written, is kept in the main hall of the house for four generations. Offerings which consist of food, incense, flowers, and candles, are placed before the tablet. The manner and time of offering vary, but a basic pattern can be observed. The head of the house lights three sticks of incense and places them in the incense burner; he then bows three times and asks for a blessing.

Formal offerings are made on the anniversary of the birth and death of the departed. The most important offerings are on the last day and the first day of the year, when the whole family gathers together. This is a time of reunion of the living and the dead.

CONFUCIANISM IN THE PRESENT DAY

Unlike Taoism, the Communists in China have severely criticized Confucianism. Mao Tse-Tung, the leader of the Communist party, once wrote that emphasis on the honouring of Confucius and the reading of the Classics are parts of that feudal culture which must be overthrown.

Throughout its history, China has seen many changes in its government, but has not itself been changed to any great extent. For more than two thousand years, Confucianism has been the ruling religion in China. It is a difficult task, therefore, to remove Confucianism from Chinese culture, and the Chinese way of life.

STUDY SUGGESTIONS

WORD STUDY

1. What is the difference in meaning between 'Annals' and 'Analects'?
2. One collection of Confucian Scriptures is known as the 'Five Classics'. Which of the following dictionary meanings of the word 'classic' is applicable in this case?
   (a) Ancient Greek or Roman literature; (b) a traditional event; (c) a book of enduring importance; (d) a typical or standard example.

REVIEW OF CONTENT

3. (a) In what year was Confucius born and into what sort of family, and in what year did he die?
   (b) What was his profession?
4. (a) Did Confucius himself write down the Chinese Scriptures?
   (b) What books are included in the 'Five Classics'?
   (c) What is the name of the second collection of Confucian Scriptures, and what books does it contain?

5. Two of the important teachings of Confucianism are about (a) filial piety, and (b) optimism. Summarize these teachings and compare them with Christian teaching on the same subject.

6. (a) 'The cult (of heaven) was established as the state religion in the second century BC' (p. 94). When did it cease to be the state religion and why?

(b) What is *Shang Ti*, and what was the connection between *Shang Ti* and the Imperial family of China?

7. Compare Confucian ancestor worship as described on p. 96 with the practices of (a) the Ga, and (b) the Maori.

8. What is or was 'Neo-Confucianism'?

BIBLE STUDY

9. Read Exodus 20.1–20. 'Confucianism teaches that there are five virtues' (p. 91).
What are they, and which, if any, of the Ten Commandments does the exercise of these virtues seem to fulfil?

10. Read 1 Corinthians 13.1–7. Contrast St Paul's teaching about 'Love' with Confucius's teaching about 'Benevolence'.

DISCUSSION AND RESEARCH

11. Name six other pairs of opposites which illustrate the principle of *Yin* and *Yang*.

12. What teaching in Hinduism can be compared to the Confucian teaching about *Li* and *Chi*, and why?

13. Give three or four reasons why you think the Communist party has tried to stop Confucian teaching in China.

14. 'Some people say that Confucianism is not a religion' (p. 93). Why do they say this? What is your opinion?

TAOISM

A. LAO TZU AND TAO TE CHING

According to tradition, the founder of Taoism was the Old Master, Lao Tzu. We know very little about him except that he was born in 604 BC, was a keeper of the imperial archives at the capital of Chou, and retired and disappeared in middle life.

All that we know about Lao Tzu is contained in the book, *Historical Records*, by Szu-Ma-Chien (146–85 BC). One particular episode in this record shows what sort of man Lao Tzu was:

> Confucius once visited Lao Tzu to consult him about a certain ceremony. Lao Tzu's answer baffled the great sage:
> 'A good merchant conceals his treasures as though his warehouses were empty. The sage of highest worth assumes a countenance and outward appearance which suggest that he is stupid. Put aside your haughty aims, your many needs, your affected robes, and exaggerated importance. These add no real value to your person.'
> Confucius departed and later described to his disciples what sort of man Lao Tzu was:
> 'Of birds, I know that they have wings to fly with; of fish, that they have fins to swim with; of wild beasts, that they have feet to run with. For feet, there are traps; for fish, nets; for wings, arrows. But for the dragon, I cannot know how he ascends on the winds and clouds to heaven. I have seen Lao Tzu. Today I have seen a dragon.'

When Lao Tzu departed from the capital city of Chou, the officer stationed at the frontier asked him to write a book. Lao Tzu wrote a book of poems in two parts, of about five thousand words. The subject of this book, which came to be known as the Book of *Tao-Te-Ching*, was an explanation of the Creative Principle (*Tao*) and of Human Virtue (*Te*). It remains to this day as the basic text for all Taoist thought.

B. THE TEACHINGS OF TAOISM

THE CREATIVE PRINCIPLE, TAO

Lao Tzu taught that there is a creative principle, *Tao*, which existed before the world. *Tao* is invisible, inaudible, and intangible. But it is not 'nothing': it is the ground of all being, and it is the way in which nature and the universe exist. It is behind and beneath all. It produces and nourishes all. Therefore *Tao* is sometimes called 'Mother' because all things come from, and are nourished by it. 'Out of Tao, One is born; out of One, Two: Yin and Yang (see p. 89); out of Two,

Three: Yin, Yang, and breath; out of Three, the created universe.'
Tao is the origin of heaven and earth, the creative principle; it is also
the Way in which heaven and earth now live.

Although *Tao* is the creative principle, it is not the creator. Lao
Tzu apparently did not think of Tao as a personal being, as Christians
and Muslims think of God. The 'great virtue' of Tao is that it does
everything but desires nothing; it is 'emptiness', which does not compete
with other forces but is content with itself. When human beings express
this same virtue of contentment, they live good lives. This teaching
was the foundation of Lao Tzu's teaching about behaviour, and it
showed itself in the three teachings about human life which follow.

HUMAN VIRTUE, TE

1. *Inaction in Nature:* In Chinese thought, nature is something which
happens by itself. Man's part in nature is to be quiet and passive, so
that *Tao*, the creative principle of the universe (see p. 98), may act
through him without hindrance. Man must let Tao be Tao in him;
he must do nothing on his own but must simply follow the *Tao*—or
Way—of nature.

Lao Tzu renounced culture and civilization because they were the
products of human activity. Accordingly, he insisted upon inaction in
ruling the people:

> Let the people be innocent of knowledge and desire . . . by action
> without deeds all may live in peace.
> Banish wisdom, discard knowledge, and then the people shall
> profit a hundredfold.

2. *Non-Competition in Emptiness:* 'Non-Competition in Emptiness'
is the other side of the principle of 'inaction in nature'. 'Inaction'
refers to a person's outward actions: 'emptiness' is the corresponding
inner state. It means the absence of desire. 'Attain the utmost in
emptiness, hold firm to the basis of tranquillity.' When a person becomes
tranquil, he obtains power to overcome all things without having to
compete with others.

Lao Tzu emphasized the superiority of humility and of avoiding
competition with others:

> The wise man chooses to be last, and so becomes the first of all;
> Denying self, he is saved.
> The highest goodness is like water; water benefits all things and
> does not compete with them. It dwells in the lowly places that
> people despise, but in doing so it is close in nature to the Tao.

3. *Contentment with What Is:* This is another expression of inaction

in nature and of non-competition in emptiness. When a person is free from desire and has emptiness of spirit, and acts by simply following the way of nature, he can know and attain contentment. The blessedness of the Taoist is the blessedness of the man who expects nothing: 'There is no greater sin than the desire for possession, no greater curse than the lack of contentment.' Where there is no contentment, there is no happiness. In these ways, Lao Tzu taught the way of happiness.

C. TAOISM AS A RELIGION

It is said that Chin Shin Huang Ti, who became Emperor of China in 221 BC, adopted Tao as a religion which would bring him eternal life. During the years Taoism has become mixed with Buddhist beliefs, and also with the beliefs and practices of various local religious groups. One belief was that the 'Queen of the West' had a peach tree in her garden which bore fruit once in a thousand years. Those who ate this fruit attained immortal life.

During the twelfth century AD there was a movement of reformation within Taoism. The most influential people in this movement were the 'Perfecting the True' sect, which survived until the time when the Communist Republic was established in China.

Wong Chung Yang (1112–1170) founded this sect in 1163. His teaching followed that of Lao Tzu very closely. He emphasized the need for human beings to be in harmony with nature in order to achieve calmness and simplicity. This sect advocates strong self-discipline. All priests leave their homes and go to live in monasteries where they adopt a vegetarian diet. The central headquarters of this sect is the White Cloud Temple near Peking.

The distinctive characteristic of 'Perfecting the True' Taoism is its *syncretism*, or combination of beliefs. It is influenced very much by Buddhism, but it tries to combine Taoism, Buddhism, and Confucianism into a single religion.

D. PRESENT-DAY TAOISM

Two major Taoist sects have existed during the period from the end of the nineteenth century up to the time of the Communist revolution in China. These are called the 'Pervading Unity of Tao' and the 'Hall of the Tao'. Their beliefs and practices have been carried on chiefly by secret societies. These modern forms of Taoism teach about Tao (see p. 98), but they say that Tao is a universal energy, of which man is a part. By submitting to this energy man can obtain health, wealth, many children, and a peaceful life. Members of these modern Taoist

'Taoism has been mixed with Buddhist beliefs and practices. Members of modern Taoist sects worship images from all religions' (pp. 100, 102).

This calm-looking image of a Taoist deity dates from the Sung dynasty (AD 960–1279), when reform movements were emphasizing self-discipline as the way to calm and simplicity.

How far do any pictures or statues of Jesus with which you are familiar express the character of Christian teaching?

sects use charms, magical phrases, and incantations in order to bring themselves into a right relationship with the Tao.

One of the peculiar features of these sects is that they worship images from all religions, including Christianity, and they also use rituals from a number of different religions.

When the People's Republic of China came into existence in 1949, the Government dissolved most Taoist organizations. But Taoism is not extinct in China, and the new Communist regime has latterly encouraged it. In 1957 the China Taoist Association was formed in Peking, and the first head of the association was a member of the central committee of the Communist party. The aims of the Association are to unite Taoists throughout the country, to promote the traditions of ancient Taoism, and to support the socialist reconstruction of the country.

STUDY SUGGESTIONS

WORD STUDY

1. Which of the following words would you *not* use to describe to someone the nature of Tao?
   emptiness   inaction   nothingness   struggle   quietness   simplicity   creativity   contentment   competition

REVIEW OF CONTENT

2. (a) Who was the founder of Taoism and when did he live?
   (b) What two books are the sources from which we learn of the beginnings of Taoism and its teaching?
3. 'Many Chinese follow two religions: Confucianism and Taoism . . . balance each other within the life of the Chinese people as a whole' (p. 89).
   Explain this statement.
4. For what reason is Tao sometimes called 'Mother'?
5. What are or were the chief characteristics of the 'Perfecting the True' sect on the one hand, and the 'Pervading Unity of Tao' and 'Hall of the Tao' sects on the other?

BIBLE STUDY

6. Compare the teaching of Lao Tzu with the teaching of Jesus about humility in Luke 14.7–11; Matthew 20.24–28; and Matthew 23.8–12. Compare also Lao Tzu's teaching with the Beatitudes in Matthew 5.1–10. What does the Lord Jesus ask for *more* than 'non-competition in emptiness'?

DISCUSSION AND RESEARCH

7. (a) What are the three principles for human behaviour which Taoism teaches?
   (b) Do you agree with them? Give your reasons.
   (c) In what ways are these three principles like the Christian way of love as described in 1 Corinthians 13? What more is there in the way of love than there is in the three principles of Taoism?
8. In what ways do you think that Taoism, as encouraged by the new communist regime in China, may 'support the socialist reconstruction of the country' (p. 102)?

Chapter 10
Judaism

Note: In agreement with other books in this series, the name 'Israelites' is used until the end of the Exile in Babylon, and the name 'Jews' after that time.

A. THE JEWISH PEOPLE

1. THE CONQUEST OF PALESTINE

The story of the Jewish people is a long one. Their ancestors were groups of Semites called Hebrews, who came out of the desert country of Arabia. They tried to settle in the rich and fertile lands on the borders of Arabia which scholars call the Fertile Crescent. Semitic peoples have been doing this all through the centuries even until today.

At first the ancestors of the Israelites were content to live as visitors in Palestine, without any permanent settlements. Then they moved into Eastern Egypt at a time when Semitic kings, the Hyksos, ruled the country. After a time Egyptian kings regained control of Egypt. They used the Israelites as labourers and treated them cruelly.

Moses led the Israelites out of Egypt back into the desert, and there he united the different tribes into one group. They began to be one people, dedicated to the worship of the one living God. This departure from a life of slavery in Egypt is known in Israelite history as the 'Exodus'.

During the next two or three hundred years, the Israelite tribes succeeded in taking possession of most of Palestine. They were not the only people to live in Palestine. Other peoples had been there from long before. They had many names but the general name for them was *Canaanites*. Other tribes from the desert also tried to gain possession of Palestine at this time, and so did the Philistines who came from across the Mediterranean Sea.

2. THE JERUSALEM KINGDOM

At first the Israelite tribes acted independently of each other, though sometimes two or three of the tribes joined together to defend themselves against invaders. About 1040 BC they were all joined together under the rule of a single king. David and Solomon were the greatest kings, and built the royal city of Jerusalem. They extended their rule over neighbouring kingdoms, and conquered the Philistines. There was great prosperity because of foreign trade. Priests were able to organize the worship of the Temple in new and beautiful ways; writers, poets, and thinkers began to write books.

3. THE TWO KINGDOMS

After the death of Solomon, the Israelites split into two kingdoms. The smaller kingdom in the south was Judah, and its capital was Jerusalem. The larger kingdom, in the north, was Israel, and its capital was Samaria.

Palestine was a small country, lying between Egypt and Syria. On the east was desert. The roads between Africa and Asia ran through it. The great Empires of Babylon and Assyria in Iraq sent their armies westwards into Syria, but the kings of Egypt tried to stop them; Egypt wanted to control Syria. Foreign armies marched through Palestine, and often attacked her cities. Sometimes the two Israelite kings fought against each other.

The two kingdoms continued for some centuries after the death of Solomon. Sometimes they had periods of prosperity: sometimes they passed through periods of weakness and poverty. In 721 BC the Assyrians destroyed the northern kingdom of Israel and burnt Samaria. They nearly captured Jerusalem. Later, in 587 BC, the Babylonians did capture Jerusalem, and killed the king.

4. THE EXILE

After the fall of Jerusalem the leaders of the Jewish people were taken as labourers to Babylon and other countries. In exile, they learnt to worship God without the help of their Temple in Jerusalem. They learnt many new things about God and about prayer.

In 538 BC a Persian king, named Cyrus, extended the Persian Empire westwards and conquered Babylon. The Persian kings permitted the Jews to return to Palestine. Several groups returned at different times, and slowly they rebuilt the Temple, and restored the walls round Jerusalem. Jewish governors ruled in the city, but they were under the authority of the Persian kings, and, later, of the Greek kings.

5. THE MACCABEES AND THE HERODS

In 166 BC the Greek king, Antiochus Epiphanes, tried to make the Jews turn away from their religion. A few did so, but most Jews rebelled against him. The Maccabees, a family of priests, became their leaders, and under them the Jews made themselves independent. For about a hundred years, the Jewish high-priest ruled a small kingdom in Jerusalem. Then the Romans conquered the Greeks, and ruled Syria and Palestine from 63 BC onwards. For a few years they allowed the high-priests, and then the half-Jewish family of the Herods, to rule different parts of Palestine in their name; but Roman officials later ruled in Judea and Jerusalem. In AD 66 the Jews attempted to become independent again, but they failed. After a bitter struggle the Romans captured Jerusalem and destroyed the Temple (AD 70). Jews all over the Empire were forced to pay contributions for the upkeep of the Temple of Jupiter in Rome.

6. THE DISPERSION

From the time of the first exile onwards some Jews lived outside Palestine, and in time many of them moved even further away. By 100 BC, there were groups of Jews living in most of the important cities of the Roman Empire, as well as in Syria, Egypt, and Arabia. These Jews spoke Greek, but they kept their own religion and their own customs. Some were attracted by Greek philosophy.

After the Romans destroyed Jerusalem, the Jews outside Palestine kept their religion alive. Through the centuries, they spread all over Europe, and then into America. The members of most Jewish groups kept close to each other. They were often good at business and sometimes became very wealthy. Other people did not understand them and often ill-treated them. Sometimes kings and other rulers seized their wealth, sometimes they made them dress in a distinctive way, sometimes they killed large numbers of them. The Jews often experienced hard times, but most of them kept true to their religion and customs. Some groups tried to fit themselves more closely to the people around them, but many believed that God would one day bring their nation back to Palestine.

7. THE RETURN

In the twentieth century, many Jews have returned to Palestine. The British Government, who had control of Palestine after the Great War of AD 1914–18, allowed a large number to do so. During Hitler's persecution of the Jews in Germany, and especially after the Great War of 1939–45, the numbers returning to Palestine increased rapidly. In AD 1948, the Jews in Palestine set up an independent Jewish state, and called it Israel. It is now a strong modern state. Not all Jews, however, believe that this is the true solution to the problem of their religion's future. Instead, many Liberal Jews believe that their duty is to contribute the teachings of Judaism to the nations of which they are members and citizens. They do not accept the separate existence of the State of Israel.

B. THE GOD OF ISRAEL

During the course of their long history the Jews learnt many things about God. They learnt them first, in a very simple form, during their years in the desert, before their tribes conquered Palestine. After the conquest of Palestine, many of the people forsook the desert ways

'In the twentieth century many Jews have returned to Palestine. They still face many difficulties' (p. 106).

These demonstrators in Jerusalem were protesting in 1970 against the refusal of the USSR to allow Russian Jews to leave for Israel.

What 'difficulties' do people face when religious and national loyalties conflict?

and mixed their religion with the religion of the Canaanites. But, through the work of the prophets and others, the Israelites learned other ways, and their beliefs slowly became clear and definite.

The following sections describe the Israelites' main beliefs about God as they were at the period when their Scriptures were finally gathered into one book, the Old Testament. They have continued to be the beliefs of most Orthodox Jews down to the present time.

(a) *God is a living person.* The Jews know God to be a living person. At first they called Him 'Yahweh'. This name may be translated as 'The Living One'. They know that God is always present, wherever they go, at all times. Jews do not use the actual name 'Yahweh', because they honour the name so highly. In some of the quotations from the Old Testament which follow in this chapter we have used the name *Yahweh* instead of the more usual translation, 'the LORD'.

(b) *Human beings cannot make a picture of God.* The Jews know that God is greater than anything which men can think of. (See p. 2.) They believe that it is foolish and wrong to try to make an image of Him. Even so, in early times, some of the Israelites imitated other tribes and tried to do so. In early times, the Israelites used plain upright stones to represent God's presence; later they believed that even this was wrong.

(c) *God has chosen Israel to belong to Him in a special way.* The Jews believe that God has chosen their nation to be His people in a special way. He is their God: they are His people. 'If only you will now listen to me and keep my covenant, then out of all peoples you shall become my special possession; for the whole earth is mine. You shall be my kingdom of priests, my holy nation' (Exod. 19.5–6). They believe that God has chosen them, and that He has given them the Land of Palestine. They say that God has made a special agreement, or covenant, with them.

They also believe that God intends to bless the whole of mankind through His chosen people Israel. 'Many nations shall come and say, "Come, let us climb up on to the mountain of the Lord, to the house of the God of Jacob, that He may teach us His ways and we may walk in His paths." For instruction issues from Zion, and out of Jerusalem comes the word of the Lord' (Mic. 4.2).

(d) *God is King of the whole world.* The Jews believe that the one living God rules the whole world. He brought the world into being. He gave life to the first man and woman. He controls the nations. He controls the powers of nature and uses them to help or to punish men.

At first the Israelites may have believed that there were other gods besides Yahweh. But they came to believe that Yahweh was the only living God. And so, from an early period in their history, they did not believe that any gods existed except the one living God, whom they called Yahweh.

I know that Yahweh is great, that our Lord is above all gods.
Whatever Yahweh pleases, that He does, in heaven and earth,
in the sea, in the depths of ocean.
The gods of the nations are idols of silver and gold, made by the hands of men.
They have mouths that cannot speak, and eyes that cannot see;
they have ears that do not hear, and there is no breath in their nostrils.
Their makers grow like them, and so do all who trust in them.
Blessed from Zion be Yahweh, who dwells in Jerusalem.
O praise Yahweh. (Ps. 135.5–6, 15–18, 21)

(e) *God asks men to behave justly and with compassion.* Before the Temple was destroyed, the Jews worshipped Yahweh as other peoples worshipped their own local or national deities. They offered sacrifices and gifts to Him. But the Jews knew that Yahweh required more than that from them. God asks men for right behaviour. Because God had chosen them to be His people, they were bound even more than others to keep the Laws which He gave them. To do this is the most important thing in life.

God has told you what is good; and what is it that Yahweh asks of you?
Only to act justly, to love loyalty, to walk wisely before your God. (Mic. 6.8)
Do what is right and just; that is more pleasing to Yahweh than sacrifice. (Prov. 21.3)

All through their history, from the earliest times, the Jews have believed that God, 'the Judge of all the earth', Himself always acts in justice. (See Gen. 18.25.)

C. THE GOD WHO SPEAKS

The Israelites believed that God made His will known to men.

1. THE LEADERS

They believed that in the first centuries of their history God had spoken to the leaders of their nation. He had made His commands known to them. Their history began when He spoke to Abraham: 'Yahweh said to Abram, "Leave your own country, your kinsmen, and your father's house, and go to a country that I will show you"' (Gen. 12.1). He spoke to Moses all through the long journey from Egypt, and especially at Sinai when He made the Covenant between Himself and Israel. He spoke to Joshua, who began the conquest of Palestine, to Samuel who anointed the first kings, to David, and to many others.

2. THE PROPHETS

Many of the kings failed to keep the covenant with Yahweh. Some of them worshipped the deities of other nations for political reasons. Many of them ruled unjustly. Many of the ordinary people also joined with the kings in the worship of Ba'al and Astarte, who were deities worshipped by the Canaanites and other peoples of the Near East. The older inhabitants of Palestine, the Canaanites, associated Ba'al and Astarte with rain and storm, and believed that they gave fertility to the crops and flocks. In many towns and villages the Israelites joined with the Canaanites when they went to worship and to feast in the 'high places' which they set aside for Ba'al and Astarte. Sometimes they lay with the temple prostitutes.

God spoke to His people through the preaching of the prophets. The prophets were among those who stood firm in the old religion of Yahweh which the Israelites had brought with them from the desert. The main beliefs of this religion were those described in section B. The prophets preached to the people and tried to bring them back to the true way of Yahweh. They warned the people that Yahweh would punish them in order to bring them to repentance. At other times the prophets encouraged the people to trust in Yahweh and to do what pleased Him. They preached in words which they believed God had given them to preach in His name.

Sometimes a number of prophets lived and worked together in groups. Many, however, acted on their own. Some lived hard and lonely lives. Some kings listened to their preaching, but others, together with many of the people, rejected their words. A few prophets only pretended to be speaking in God's name, and there were others who worshipped Ba'al.

3. THE SCRIPTURES

The last of the Jewish prophets died in the second century BC, but the messages of the prophets were treasured in the Scriptures, together with the Law which had first been given to Moses on Sinai. The Jews therefore treasured their Scriptures and read them to discover what God's will was for their nation.

These Scriptures were written during the course of nearly a thousand years. They are divided into three groups.

(a) *The Torah.* These five books record the Laws which the Jews believe God gave to Moses. They also narrate the story of the first entry into Palestine and the story of Moses.

(b) *The Prophets.* These books record the messages which different prophets preached to the people. They also narrate the story of the conquest of Palestine and the history of the Kingdoms until the Exile.

(c) *The Writings*. These books include: the book of hymns (psalms) which were used in the Temple, a collection of proverbs, certain other poems by 'wise men', and books narrating the later history of the Jews.

A Council of Jewish scholars met at Jamnia in about AD 100. They issued a list of the books which they believed God had given to reveal His will. They are all written in Hebrew, and these are the books which Christians call the Old Testament. There are a few others, written in Greek, which are similar to the third section, the Writings. They were written between 300 BC and AD 100.

Since the time of the Exile, the Jews have read from the Scriptures at their services of worship. They believe that God reveals His will to them through these books. The most important of them in Jewish eyes are the books of the *Torah*, the Law.

STUDY SUGGESTIONS

WORD STUDY

1. (a) What is the difference in meaning between 'exile' and 'exodus'?
   (b) Describe the two events in the history of the Israelites known as the Exodus and the Exile.
2. What is the actual meaning of each of the following Hebrew words? *Torah Yahweh*

REVIEW OF CONTENT

3. Who or what were the following?
   Canaanites   Philistines   Maccabees   Ba'al   Assyrians   Herods   Jamnia   Hyksos
4. Why was each of the following important in the history of the Jews?
   Antiochus Epiphanes   Solomon   Cyrus   David
   Adolf Hitler   Joshua   Moses
5. Summarize the Jews' five main beliefs about God as expressed in the Old Testament and still held by Jews today.
6. In what chief ways do Jews believe that God has made His will known to them?
7. What is the connection between the Jewish Scriptures and the Christian Scriptures?

BIBLE STUDY

8. Read Genesis 22.15–18; Deuteronomy 28.1–14; and Isaiah 2.1–4 and 61.1–9. What do these passages show us about the Jews' beliefs about:

111

(a) Their relationship with God?
(b) Their relationships with other nations?
Do you think that the words of God as expressed in these passages have come true? Do you think they will come true? How do you think these passages should be interpreted?

9. Are there many Jews living in your country today? If so, what is their position in society? What attitude do people of other religions show towards them?

10. 'The prophets preached to the people and tried to bring them back to the true way of Yahweh. They warned the people and at other times encouraged them' (p. 110).
Are there any 'prophets' in your country today who preach as the Jewish prophets did? If so, to what religion do they belong, and how seriously do people listen to them?

11. Do you think God does 'choose' nations (other than the Jews) for special purposes? Do you think of your own nation in this way?

D. THE DAY OF THE LORD

The first kings, David and Solomon, made Jerusalem an important city. In their time, it was the capital of a rich kingdom. No other Jewish kings ruled so great a kingdom. Ever since then, Jews have looked back to David's time as the greatest period in the history of their people.

1. THE DAY OF THE LORD

The prophets preached during a time of great disappointment, when the Hebrew kingdoms were small and weak. Foreign armies marched across their territories and besieged their cities. The Israelites were in danger of capture and of exile into foreign lands. The prophets preached that God would judge and punish His people because they had worshipped other gods and broken His laws. But they did not believe that God would completely destroy them. They believed that God would do a great thing in order to restore the prosperity of His people, after He had brought them to repentance.

So the prophets preached that God would restore Israel to her own land. He would bring back His people from exile. He would establish justice and righteous dealing in their society. He would restore prosperity to the land and make trees and flowers to grow in the desert.

A time is coming, says Yahweh,
when the ploughman shall follow hard on the reaper,

and he who treads the grapes after him who sows the seed.
The mountains shall run with fresh wine,
and every hill shall wave with corn.
I will restore the fortunes of my people Israel;
they shall rebuild deserted cities and live in them,
they shall plant vineyards and drink their wine,
make gardens and eat the fruit. (Amos 9.13–14)

The prophets often called this time of promise, 'the Day of Yahweh':
it was the time when God Himself would put things right.

Although the prophets preached that the Kingdom of God would
centre upon Jerusalem, some of them also promised that His peace
and righteousness would come to all the nations. Micah, for example,
prophesied that God would bless the whole of mankind through the
people of Israel (see p. 108). A later Jewish hymn expresses this great
hope in these words:

With the coming of thy Kingdom
    The hills shall break into song,
And the islands laugh exultant
    That they to God belong.
And all their congregations
    So loud thy praise shall sing,
That the uttermost peoples, hearing,
    Shall hail Thee crowned King.

The Jewish hope was that those who had died would also share in the
coming Kingdom: 'Many of those who sleep in the dust of the earth
will wake, some to everlasting life and some to the reproach of eternal
disgrace' (Dan. 12.2). The Yigdal hymn composed about AD 1300 in
Rome finishes with these words:

Our secret things are spread before His face;
In all beginnings He beholds the end.
He measures the saint's reward to his desert;
The sinner reaps the harvest of his ways.
Messiah He will send at end of days,
And all the faithful to salvation lead.
God will the dead again to life restore
In His abundance of almighty love.

2. THE 'ANOINTED SAVIOUR'

Sometimes the prophets spoke as if God Himself would bring about
the deliverance which they promised. At other times they promised
that God would send a chosen leader who would act as His agent.

Some of the prophets promised that the coming Saviour would be a descendant of the family of David. He would restore the ancient kingdom of David in Jerusalem. God would give him gifts of wisdom and strength and God's Spirit would inspire him.

A shoot shall grow from the stock of Jesse (the father of David),
and a branch shall spring from his roots.
The spirit of Yahweh shall rest upon him,
a spirit of wisdom and understanding,
a spirit of counsel and power,
a spirit of knowledge and the fear of Yahweh . . .
He shall judge the poor with justice
and defend the humble in the land with equity . . .
They shall not hurt or destroy in all my holy mountain;
for as the waters fill the sea, so shall the land be filled with the knowledge of Yahweh. (From Isa. 11.1–9)

Because the kings had been anointed to act as God's servants, the coming King was often referred to as 'the anointed one', the *Messiah*.

During the centuries, the hope for God's coming Kingdom has been expressed in different ways. On the one hand, the Jewish prophets emphasized that God often worked through weakness. His servants were often humble persons who knew suffering and pain, and who brought deliverance to others by carrying the burden of their sins and sorrows. The prophet who preached among the Jews during the Exile in Babylon and whose messages are recorded in Isaiah 40—55, expressed this insight. He suggested that God asked for a humble and loving ministry of this kind both from the nation of Israel and from the prophets. In the last two centuries before the destruction of Jerusalem in AD 70, some groups of Jews tried to live out these ideals of service and of dedication to God. They set up communities in the desert country near the Jordan river and elsewhere, and lived lives of discipline and of prayer.

On the other hand, some Jews in the second century BC began to suggest that the coming Saviour would be a supernatural person who would suddenly appear with God's authority. They called him the 'Son of Man', after Daniel 7.13–14, even though in Daniel 'the Son of Man' is said to be 'the people of the saints of the Most High' (7.27), i.e. the people of Israel.

From the time of Jesus onwards, when the nation as a whole rejected His claim to be the Messiah, the Son of God (p. 161), the Jews did not speak much about a coming Saviour. They placed greater emphasis on their belief that God Himself would restore His people. They believed that He would do this when Israel kept the Law in truth. (See section F, p. 117.)

The Jews have always kept alive their belief that God would restore His people of Israel to Palestine, and establish a great kingdom of peace and righteousness. Because of this hope, they have remained brave during many centuries of hardship. Many Jews have kept their religion pure and many believe that their hopes will soon be fulfilled, because the State of Israel has been established in Palestine again.

E. WORSHIP

1. THE PLACE OF SACRIFICE

At first the Israelite tribes offered gifts and sacrifices to Yahweh wherever they were. On their journeys through the desert they carried with them a small tent, and they placed this in the centre of their camps as a sign of God's presence among them.

After their settlement in Palestine, the Israelites set aside special places for the worship of Yahweh, but they often also used the Canaanite sanctuaries. Sometimes people prayed to Yahweh and also to Ba'al and Astarte in the same place. It was a time of confusion. People could not truly combine the pure worship of Yahweh with that of Ba'al.

Solomon built a great Temple in the new royal city of Jerusalem, and the Israelites then looked towards this as the centre of their religion. They believed that Yahweh had marked this Temple with His name, and that He was present in a special way in the dark, secret room which was deep inside the Temple. In time it became the rule that a true worshipper of Yahweh could only offer a sacrifice to Him in the Temple at Jerusalem. Since the destruction of the Temple in AD 70 no Jew has been able to do this.

2. PRAYER AND PRAISE

The Jews sang praises to God when they offered sacrifice. They sang hymns of thanksgiving when they won a victory in war, or when they crowned a new king. They offered special prayers when they faced great danger, or when they suffered a great sickness or disaster. The priests and Temple servants (called Levites) at Jerusalem collected these hymns and prayers together, and thus made the book of Psalms.

During the Exile, when the Temple was in ruins, the Jews continued to worship God and to pray to Him. They used to meet together to do this wherever they were, especially on their holy days, the Sabbaths. They could not offer sacrifice because they were not in Jerusalem, and so they found other ways to worship God. In particular they offered prayers and read the Scriptures.

Ever since that time the Jews have built special buildings, called synagogues, in which to praise God and to pray to Him. Wherever a community of Jews is living, they gather regularly in their synagogue for worship, and especially on the Sabbath days. Their prayers and hymns are often very beautiful: here are two prayers from the modern Authorized Daily Prayer Book used in Britain, and a modern hymn which is sung at Pentecost.

The Lord reigns;
The Lord has reigned;
The Lord shall reign for ever and ever.
Blessed be his name,
Whose glorious Kingdom is for ever and ever.
The Lord he is God.
Hear, O Israel: the Lord our God, the Lord is one.

We give thanks unto thee,
For thou art the Lord our God and the God of our fathers.
The God of all flesh,
Our Creator
And the Creator of all things in the beginning.
Blessings and thanksgivings be to thy great and holy name,
Because thou hast kept us in life and hast preserved us;
So mayest thou continue to keep us in life and to preserve us.
O gather our exiles to thy holy courts,
To observe thy statutes,
To do thy will,
And to serve thee with a perfect heart;
Seeing that we give thanks unto thee.
Blessed be the God to whom thanksgivings are due.

Could we with ink the ocean fill,
Were every blade of grass a quill (i.e. a pen),
Were the world of paper made,
And every man a scribe by trade—
   To write the love
   of God above
Would drain that ocean dry;
   Nor would the scroll
   Contain the whole,
Though stretched from sky to sky.

3. THE FEASTS

The Jews keep special religious feasts in the course of the year. In the springtime they keep the Feast of Passover. In the desert, their forefathers had offered to God newly born animals from their flocks and herds. After the Exodus with Moses, they kept the same feast in

116

memory of their miraculous rescue from slavery in Egypt and of the time when many Egyptians died of a sudden illness, but the Israelites were 'passed over'. They continue to keep this festival until present times. At the same time they clear away all the leaven (yeast) which remains from the past year, and they start the new year afresh with new leaven after seven days without using it. Every Jewish family still keeps the Passover each year. It is their most important feast.

Later in the year they keep the Feast of Pentecost. They offer to God the first harvest of their fields and lands, and emphasize also the mission of Israel in making God's will and purpose known to mankind. Later again, at the Feast of Tabernacles, they celebrate the harvest and keep a religious festival. Where possible, the Jews celebrate this festival by taking their meals or sleeping in temporary structures decorated with fruit and foliage of all kinds.

Jews celebrate these last two feasts with joy and feasting, and they give a share to the poor and needy. There are two other feasts when the Jews remember great victories of the past, called *Purim* and *Chanukah*.

Rosh Hashanah is the name given to the solemn New Year Festival, when special prayers are said and special hymns are sung. This is followed by ten days of penitence, when individual Jews seek to put right any wrong which they have done to others. Then comes the Solemn Day of Atonement, which is spent in fasting, penitence, and prayer; the day concludes with the congregations in the synagogues making a solemn declaration of faith.

F. THE LAW

1. THE LAWS

The Jews believe that God has chosen them to be His special people. Their first duty, therefore, is to obey His Law, and it is the duty of the priests to teach the Law to the people. They believe that Moses received the most important of its rules from God on the holy mountain of Sinai.

The Ten Commandments are the basis of the Law. They state basic human duties:

I am Yahweh your God who brought you out of Egypt, out of the land of slavery.
1. You shall have no other god to set against me.
2. You shall not make a carved image for yourself. . . . You shall not bow down to them or worship them.
3. You shall not make wrong use of the name of Yahweh your God.

'Wherever a community of Jews is living they gather regularly in the synagogue for worship, especially on the Sabbath days; and every Jewish family keeps the Passover each year' (pp. 115, 116).

Saturday prayers still continue, even in the synagogue in Moscow. In Tunisia Jewish children prepare dough for the unleavened bread of the Passover, and an old man supervises the baking of it.

What do you notice in the pictures which shows that the people are Jews?

4. Remember to keep the Sabbath day holy. . . . The seventh day is a Sabbath of Yahweh your God.
5. Honour your father and your mother.
6. You shall not commit murder.
7. You shall not commit adultery.
8. You shall not steal.
9. You shall not give false evidence against your neighbour.
10. You shall not covet your neighbour's house; you shall not covet your neighbour's wife, his slave, his slave-girl, his ox, his ass, or anything that belongs to him. (From Exod. 20.1–17.)

The Law itself covered the whole of people's lives. For example, there are rules in it for:

the offering of sacrifice,
the keeping of the feasts,
matters of marriage and inheritance,
the administration of justice,
the rule of the king,
the conduct of war,
the treatment of slaves, prisoners, and foreigners,
personal and social hygiene.

2. THE ORAL LAW

The written Law did not, however, answer every question about right conduct or the correct way to worship. So the priests and others continued to give rulings about the Law after the books were written. The Jews called these rulings the 'oral law'.

The people who taught the oral law were called *Rabbis* and *Scribes*, and those who kept the rules strictly were called *Pharisees*. We read about them in the Gospels. After the time of Jesus, the work of the Rabbis continued. Their teaching is collected in the great Jewish book called the *Talmud*. The spirit of their teaching is expressed in a little Jewish book called *Pirqe Aboth*, which was compiled about one hundred years after the time of Jesus from sayings of famous Jewish teachers. It is included in the Talmud. Although it was written a long time ago, it is used and loved by Jews, and a special edition was prepared for Jewish soldiers who fought in the British Army in the war of 1939–45. Here are a few extracts from it.

Simon the Just used to say—The world stands upon three things: the Law, Worship, and the showing of kindness.

Hillel said: Be of the disciples of Aaron, one that loves peace, one that loves mankind, one that brings them near to the Law.

Gamaliel said: Study of the Law together with ordinary work is good: labour in them both makes sin forgotten.

Study of the Law without ordinary work ends in failure and causes sin.

Hillel said: Do not separate yourself from the congregation; do not be sure of yourself till the day of your death; do not judge your neighbour until you stand in his place.

Akadja said: Keep in view three things and you will not come into the power of sin. Know where you come from, and where you are going to, and before whom you must give strict account. You came from a drop (of semen): you go to the place of dust, worms, and maggots: you must give strict account before the King of the Kings of Kings, the Holy One, blessed be He.

3. THE KEEPING OF THE LAW

The Rabbis have done much to keep alive the spiritual life of the Jewish people. They taught that the true Jew accepts the Law because of his love for God, and tries to keep every single commandment in it, even those about food, clothing, and work. These have made it difficult for Jews to become full members of the communities amongst whom they live, because their way of life is different from that of others. But their ideal is a great and noble one; it is that men should live pure and humble lives, and that they should love and trust God.

Every day, when they leave or enter their homes, Jews solemnly repeat the declaration which is the heart of their religion:

Hear, O Israel, the Lord is our God, one Lord, and you must love the Lord your God with all your heart and soul and strength. These commandments which I give you this day are to be kept in your hearts; you shall repeat them to your sons, and speak of them indoors and out of doors, when you lie down and when you rise (Deut. 6.4–7).

STUDY SUGGESTIONS

WORD STUDY

1. What is the origin of the word 'Passover'?

2. (a) What does the word *Messiah* mean, and to whom do the Jews give this name?
   (b) What is the difference between the Jewish and Christian use of the word?

REVIEW OF CONTENT

3. What do the Jews mean when they speak of the 'day of the Lord', and what do they believe will happen on that 'day'?

4. What did the phrase the 'Son of Man' suggest to some Jews in the time of Jesus? What do you yourself understand by this phrase?
5. (a) What is the special importance of Jerusalem in Jewish worship?
   (b) Where and when do Jews hold worship services today?
   (c) Name one form of worship which Jews offered to God in Old Testament times, but which they can no longer offer? What do they do instead, and why?
6. In what way are the Hindu festivals of Onam and Pongal like the Jewish feasts of Pentecost and Tabernacles?
7. Who or what were the following?
   Rosh Hashanah   the Talmud   Pharisees   the Sabbath
8. 'The Jews believe that their first duty is to obey God's Law' (p. 117).
   (a) Why do they believe this?
   (b) How do they find out what God's Law is?
   (c) What do they believe will happen if they fail to keep God's Law?

BIBLE STUDY

9. 'Their first duty is to obey the Law' (p. 117). Read Matthew 5.17–48; 22.37–40; Mark 7.1–23. What did Jesus teach His disciples about obedience to the Law?

DISCUSSION AND RESEARCH

10. 'Micah prophesied that God would bless the whole of mankind through the Jews' (p. 113). Read Micah 4.1–4; Zechariah 9.9–10; Isaiah 61.1–11.
    What is the Christian interpretation of these verses?
11. If there is a synagogue within reach of your home or college, arrange to attend a worship service there. Afterwards describe those parts of the worship which you as a Christian felt able to share in. Was there any part in which you felt it would be wrong to take an active share?
12. Why do Christians sometimes call their holy day, Sunday, the 'Sabbath'? What are the chief differences between the Jewish Sabbath and a Christian Sabbath?
13. The Rabbis made many hard rules which have made it difficult for Jews to become full members of the communities amongst whom they live (p. 120). What other people, if any, do you know who have rules which separate them from their neighbours? What is the neighbours' attitude to such people likely to be?

PART 4

THREE INTERNATIONAL RELIGIONS

Introduction

In this Part we discuss the three religions, Buddhism, Christianity, and Islam. They are like each other in several ways:

1. Each one looks back to a particular person as the founder of the religion.

2. Each one has followers in many different countries.

3. Each one has sacred Scriptures to be the guide to belief and conduct.

4. Each one promises to bring its followers to the Heaven (of God) beyond death.

Thus in each chapter the different sections are arranged in the same general order:

1. We study the life and teaching of the Founder.

2. We study how the religion spread over the world and the different groups which practise it.

3. We study the beliefs of the religion, how its members act in daily life, and how they worship and pray.

But although these religions are like each other in some ways there are also great differences between them, e.g.:

1. Each religion refers to its founder in a different way.

2. Each religion teaches that salvation comes to human people in a different way, and that people must do different things to receive salvation.

3. Each religion describes God's relationship with the world in a different way.

The most important thing in Buddhism is to escape from the pain of suffering by purification of the self.

The most important thing in Christianity is to be delivered from the power of evil and to live joyfully and purely as God's children by His love and power made known through Christ.

The most important thing in Islam is to fulfil the duties which a person owes to God, the Ruler of All.

Chapter 11
Buddhism

From material contributed by
Lynn de Silva

Buddhism is the religion of hundreds of millions of people—perhaps as many as 500 million—who live in lands stretching from the island of Sri Lanka to the islands of Japan, and throughout large areas of the Asian mainland. Like Christianity and Islam it is a missionary religion, and has today spread to countries in the West.

Buddhism claims to be one of the most reasonable of the world's great religions. Its teaching about belief and conduct is designed to meet human need, and to solve man's spiritual problems without reliance on the supernatural. In this Buddhism differs from other religions: it has no place for God, nor for a Saviour; it puts salvation completely within man's control. It is sometimes called a 'Do-it-yourself' religion.

Buddhism has been in existence for more than 2,500 years. It has been a great civilizing force, and has inspired art, literature, and other cultural activities. Today it is the state religion of Burma, Thailand, Tibet, Cambodia and Laos; the religion of the majority in Sri Lanka; and the faith of a very great number of Chinese, Japanese, and Koreans.

Buddhism has two main divisions, and many sects. The two main divisions are: *Theravada* (or Hinayana) *Buddhism*, which is followed by people in southern Asia, particularly in Burma, Thailand, and Sri Lanka; and *Mahayana Buddhism*, which is followed by people in China, Japan, Tibet, and Mongolia. Both these schools of thought owe their basic teaching to a man named Siddhartha Gautama, whose life and example has become a source of profound inspiration to millions of his followers.

A. THE FOUNDER OF BUDDHISM

Many legends are told about the life of the Buddha, the founder of Buddhism, and it is now difficult to distinguish historical facts from popular stories. It seems clear that he was born in the sixth century BC, and was brought up in what is now Bihar in Eastern India. This was probably at Kapilavathu, capital city of the Sakya state to which his family belonged. The following account of his life is based on the stories about him which most people accept.

The Buddha's family name was Gautama (or Gotama), and his personal name Siddhartha, though this is not often used. His father was Suddhodhana, an aristocratic Hindu chieftain, and his mother Mahamaya. The young prince was brought up in princely luxury.

'Like Christianity and Islam, Buddhism is a missionary religion, and has spread to countries in the West' (p. 123).

Dr Góza Rács, Secretary of the Buddhist Mission in Budapest, Hungary, teaches a convert about the Noble Eightfold Path.

How does your Church prepare people who wish to become Christians?

It is said that he had three palaces, one for the cold season, one for the hot, and one for the season of rains. During the four rainy months female minstrels entertained him, and he did not come down from the palace. He had all the comforts and pleasures of life. Because he was the one and only son, his father took great pains to provide all he needed, and to educate him so that he could succeed him as the chieftain of the clan.

Gautama's education consisted not only of the various branches of learning taught by the great men of his time, but also of skill in all the manly arts, especially archery, in which he excelled. At the age of sixteen he married a beautiful wife, Yasodhara, having won her favour in an archery contest. From this time on for about thirteen years he led a life of luxury and domestic happiness. His father took all precautions to guard his son from anything that would cause him pain or displeasure, but he could not do this for ever. The time came when the young prince saw the cruel realities of life.

The prince once drove through the streets of the city, in a gaily decorated chariot, when suddenly an old man with grey hair tottered out of a hut, dressed in nothing but rags. His eyes were dim and his teeth had fallen out. When the prince saw him, he was greatly distressed, and returned home, in horror and disgust, abandoning his trip to the Royal Garden for sports.

On another day as the prince drove in his chariot he heard a cry calling for help. He looked round and saw a sick man twisting his body about in the dust, groaning and moaning and gasping for breath. Again he was filled with dismay and returned home.

On another occasion the prince saw a corpse being carried by a crowd of people who were weeping and wailing. The prince was struck dumb and returned home in silence. He went into his room and began to think about the mystery of life. He realized the sorrow which is present in the life of all men. He felt in himself despair, pain, and sorrow. Later he used the term *dukkha*, loosely translated as 'suffering', to express this fact of human life. He thought to himself: 'There is a getting born and a growing old, a dying and a being reborn. But, alas, no escape is known from this suffering, not even from old age and death. When shall such escape be revealed?'

He found the answer to this question on another occasion when he saw a serene and dignified hermit clothed in flowing orange-coloured robes. (A hermit is a person who lives in a simple way, by himself, often in isolated places, in order to be free to pray.) He lived a life of peace in the midst of unrest, of security in the midst of insecurity. So the prince made up his mind to renounce the world, like the hermit, and to go in search of peace and security from the suffering of this mortal life.

One day, when he was twenty-nine, in the very day when a much-longed-for son, Rahula, was born to him, Gautama left his family and home, resolving not to return until he found the solution to the riddles of life. He went deep into a forest, shaved his head, clothed himself in the yellow robes of a hermit, and for six years he sought for a solution. He sought for knowledge from famous philosophers of his day, and practised extreme forms of asceticism ('asceticism' means living a hard life without comfort or luxury, in order to discipline one's body or to pray). Eventually, through starvation, he became dreadfully thin and weak. Five ascetics admired him and joined him as companions. But it was not for long. He realized that extreme asceticism was not the way, and he began to take his normal food again. The ascetic friends then deserted him.

Finally Gautama sat under a peepul-tree, and vowed that he would not move until he had found the answer to his quest. Mara, the tempter, attacked him, and tried to frighten him with storms, torrential rains, and blazing weapons, and to seduce him by offering him the wealth of the world. But Gautama was unmoved. Then, after forty-nine days of meditation, on a full-moon night in the month of May, at the spot now known as Buddhagaya in Bihar, he made his final struggle and achieved enlightenment. He had found the solution to the riddle of life. Thereafter he became known as the Buddha, which means 'Enlightened One'. The word for enlightenment is 'bodhi', and the tree under which he won enlightenment came to be known as the Bodhi-tree or Bo-tree.

The Buddha was thirty-five years old when he attained enlightenment. For forty-five years after that he travelled up and down northern India, teaching and preaching the message of hope and happiness, and making many converts. He lived a life of unceasing activity. It is said that he slept for only two hours at night. He passed away at the age of eighty at Kusinara on a full-moon day.

B. THE TEACHINGS OF BUDDHISM

1. THE FOUR NOBLE TRUTHS

The first sermon of the Buddha, which he preached soon after his enlightenment to the five ascetics who had been his companions, contains the kernel of his teaching. In this sermon he discussed the problem of suffering, and pointed to a path of action by which a solution can be achieved. This is an outline of his sermon:

> Revered monks, the man who has withdrawn from the world should not approach either of the two extremes. He should not approach the one which is connected with lust through sensuous pleasures,

because it is low, foolish, vulgar, ignoble, and profitless. He should not approach the other which is connected with asceticism because it is painful, ignoble, and profitless. Avoiding both these extremes, revered monks, take the middle road . . . which brings insight and knowledge, and leads to tranquillity, to enlightenment, to peace.

And, revered monks, what is this Middle Road that leads to Peace? It is the Noble Eightfold Path, namely, Right Speech, Right Action, Right Livelihood, Right Effort, Right Mindfulness, Right Concentration, Right Views, Right Thought (see pp. 128, 129). The Middle Road, revered monks, leads to Peace.

Now, revered monks, *this is the Noble Truth as to sorrow.* Earthly existence indeed is sorrowful, decay is sorrowful, disease, death, union with the unpleasing, separation from the pleasing, is sorrowful. The wish which cannot be fulfilled is sorrowful; in brief, to walk the path of desire is sorrowful.

Again, revered monks, *this is the Noble Truth as to the origin of sorrow;* the recurring desire which is associated with enjoyment and seeks pleasure everywhere, is the cause of this sorrow. In other words, it is the desire for sense-pleasures, the desire for individual existence, and the desire for self-annihilation.

Again, revered monks, *this is the Noble Truth as to the cessation of sorrow,* and to the acquiring of happiness. It is the cessation of this desiring so that no remnant or trace of it remains. It must be abandoned, renounced, and escaped from.

And once more, revered monks, *this is the Noble Truth as to the road which leads to the cessation of sorrow.* It is indeed the Noble Eightfold Path.

As soon, revered monks, as my knowledge and insight concerning these Four Noble Truths became complete, I knew that I had attained supreme and full enlightenment. I became aware and fully convinced that my mind was liberated; that existence in its unhappy form had ended; that there would no more be any unhappy survival.

Thus spoke the Blessed One. The five monks, rejoicing, welcomed the word of the Blessed One.

Let us now carefully examine this sermon.

1. *The first Noble Truth is that suffering is a universal fact.* The Buddha preached in the Pali language, and the Pali word he used for suffering is *dukkha.* This is a word that has a deep philosophical meaning and is very difficult to define. It includes the ordinary meaning of suffering such as misery, distress, despair, agony, suffering of body and mind. It also means change, emptiness, imperfection, conflict.

Thus the Buddha started off with the truth of common human experience. He dealt with a realistic situation. He was concerned with the human predicament, the suffering which is always present in the life of men and women. By declaring that all existence is *dukkha*, the Buddha did not mean that all life is suffering and nothing else. While he was extremely sensitive to the universal fact of human suffering, he discovered a way out of it which brings true and lasting happiness. That is why the Buddha is said to have had a radiant and cheerful disposition. He often compared himself to a physician. The physician's first concern is to diagnose the disease, however unpleasant and terrifying it may be. This is what the Buddha did in the Second Noble Truth.

2. *The second Noble Truth states the cause of suffering.* The cause of suffering is desire. It is hungering, desiring, and craving for self-satisfaction. It is the ceaseless striving for pleasures and sensations which, though they give some satisfaction for the moment, only arouse more desire. People seek for self-satisfaction through things which they believe they can experience because they do not know the true nature of all things, that they are impermanent. Attachment to things is therefore due to ignorance; ignorance leads to desire, and desire to suffering.

3. *The third Noble Truth declares that there is a state in which there is complete freedom from suffering and bondage.* It is a state of unspeakable joy, happiness, and peace. This state is called *nirvana* (*nibhana*).

4. *The fourth Noble Truth declares the way that leads to nirvana.* It is known as the *Noble Eightfold Path*. It is also referred to as the Middle Way between the extremes of self-indulgence and self-torture, both of which are profitless. The Middle Way consists of eight duties or principles of conduct which are as follows:

Morality:
(1) Right *Speech*—abstaining from untruthfulness, tale-bearing, harsh language, and vain talk.
(2) Right *Action*—abstaining from killing, stealing, and sexual misconduct.
(3) Right *Livelihood*—earning a living in a way not harmful to any living thing.

Concentration:
(4) Right *Effort*—avoiding evil thoughts and overcoming them, arousing good thoughts and maintaining them.
(5) Right *Mindfulness*—paying vigilant attention to every state of the body, feeling, and mind.
(6) Right *Concentration*—concentrating on a single object so as to induce certain special states of consciousness in deep meditation.

Wisdom:

(7) Right *Views*—understanding the Four Truths.
(8) Right *Thought*—freedom from ill-will, lust, cruelty, and untruthfulness.

This Eightfold Path leads to insight and wisdom which dispel ignorance. Its fruit is serenity, knowledge, and enlightenment which is *nirvana*— the state of perfect peace and bliss.

Thus the Buddha did not claim to be a saviour who can take upon himself the sin and suffering of mankind. He claimed only to be a guide, a teacher of the Way. Having gained deliverance from suffering, he pointed the way for others to follow. To follow is to gain spiritual emancipation, not as a gift of divine grace but as a conquest won by man's intellect and will on his own responsibility. Man must work out his own salvation by his own efforts; no one can do for him what he must do for himself. This emphasis on self-effort, self-conquest, self-emancipation, is fundamental in the Buddha's teaching.

By oneself evil is done, by oneself one is defiled. By oneself evil is left undone, by oneself alone one is purified. Purity and impurity depend on oneself. No one purifies another.

Thus Buddhism teaches a man to trust himself and summon his powers within him to achieve his goals in life. The clarion-call of Buddhism is sounded in the following words: 'Be ye refuges unto yourselves; be your own salvation. With earnestness and high resolve, work out your salvation with diligence.'

It is important, however, to notice that although Buddhism teaches that each person must work out his own salvation without the help of a Saviour, yet both branches of Buddhism also teach faith in the Buddha. In Mahayana Buddhism the Buddhas assume the role of saviours. In Theravada Buddhism, the worshipper in the daily chant says, 'I take refuge in the Buddha.'

2. THE DOCTRINE OF ANATTA

Buddhism does not teach that man has an eternal, indestructible soul. Instead Buddhism says that there is 'no-soul' (*an-atta*). This doctrine of 'no-soul' is implicit in the Buddha's teaching about suffering. Since all things are subject to *dukkha*, to pain, decay, and death, there can be nothing permanent; all things change and are impermanent. Hence there cannot be anything which is not subject to the law of change.

It was by thinking about life that the Buddha arrived at the conclusion that there is no soul or self. The so-called 'I', said the Buddha, is only a combination of ever-changing forces which together make up a being.

These forces include the sensations of sight, hearing, and touch, the activities of the mind, and the qualities of things as they are, such as solidity, heat, and movement. Where these forces act together there is a 'being' which takes a certain form and is given a name.

Because the forces which combine to make this 'being' are changing from moment to moment, this 'being' is also continually changing. A thing or person, of any sort, is never the same for two consecutive moments. It is like a cinema picture, which is made up of thousands of individual drawings, each separate and distinct, but which follow one another on the screen with such rapidity that it appears to be continuous. Thus the combination of physical and mental forces creates an illusion that there is a 'person', when in fact there is no permanent self. It is this illusion that begets the notion of 'I', 'me', 'mine', and this in turn produces desire or craving. This produces selfishness, egotism, ill-will, hatred, conceit, pride, attachment, and all other evils we can think of. All this is what suffering means.

The cure for all the evils in this world, therefore, lies in getting rid of this false idea of the self. A person must realize that the so-called self is only a combination of ever-changing mental and material elements which make up a succession of changes and nothing more. A human person is a no-soul, *anatta*.

3. KARMA AND REBIRTH

If at death a person has not realized the true nature of being by completely destroying the desire for life, then this desire gathers fresh life and forms a new mind-body complex, a new 'being'. Life will continue as long as there is desire, and it is the law of *karma* that keeps the process going.

The law of *karma* may be described as the law of cause and effect. Everything is the result of some prior cause, and is itself the cause of something else which will follow. What a man sows he shall reap. As an Indian proverb has it:

Who plants mangoes, mangoes shall he eat.
Who plants thorn-bushes, thorns shall wound his feet.

Good actions produce good results and bad actions produce evil results.

The law of *karma* operates by itself. No God can interfere with this law. Prayers, ceremonies, rites, and offerings cannot alter this law. It is a law that holds good in every department of the universe.

As long as there is *karma*, a being will be born and reborn in various states in accordance with his good or bad deeds. This continued existence, birth after birth, is called *samsara*, reincarnation. *Samsara* embraces the whole cycle of existence: past, present, and future.

Behind us there stretches a vast vista of past lives, and before us lies the possibility of innumerable lives as long as *karma* persists. In reincarnation a person may be born as an animal, a ghost, or a god, and may undergo suffering or enjoy pleasure in proportion to his bad or good deeds. (The doctrines of *karma* and *samsara* are also Hindu doctrines: see p. 68.)

A question that inevitably arises is: If there is no soul or person, who is it that is reborn? Is it the same person that is reborn or is it another? The traditional Buddhist answer is that one who is reborn is neither the same nor is he another. There is nothing that passes from one life to another, but it is one's own *karma* in a previous life that brings about the new life. The new life is not the same as the previous life, but the new life is not an altogether different one, because of the law of *karma*, or cause and effect.

This is difficult to explain. Buddhist lore is full of parables to help explain this paradox, that the one born is neither the previous one nor yet a different one. When a man lights a light from another light, one light does not pass over to another light. The properties of the new light are the same as the previous one, but the two are not identical. The birth process of a butterfly is another illustration. It was first an egg and then it became a caterpillar. Later it developed into a chrysalis, and finally evolved into a butterfly. The butterfly is neither the same as, nor totally different from, the caterpillar. The chain of existence will continue as long as there is desire for existence.

4. NIRVANA THE GOAL

Must the weary round of existence, life after life, continue for ever? 'No', said the Buddha. His primary concern was to point out a way of putting an end to reincarnation. This is the Middle Way, consisting of the eight steps whose goal is *nirvana*.

The literal meaning of the word *nirvana* is 'dying out' or 'extinction', as of a fire. Using this simile, the Buddha said that the world is in flames, kindled by the fire of desire. The process of rebirth is a rekindling of this fire from one flame to another flame, and this keeps the fires of birth, old age, decay, death, pain, despair, anxiety, etc., constantly burning. *Nirvana* is the extinguishing of this flame, the flame of desire. With that the life process as we know it comes to an end. In a sense this is annihilation, but it is not the annihilation of the self, because, according to the doctrine of *anatta*, there is no self to annihilate. It is rather the annihilation of the illusion of the self. And with this, all that clusters round or supports this illusion—the thirst for life, lust, greed, selfishness, desires, appetites, and all forms of suffering —are annihilated. The fire has gone out because there is no longer any fuel to feed it.

Nirvana is not just nothing. It is called 'the harbour of refuge', 'the cool cave', 'the island midst the floods', 'the place of bliss', 'liberation', 'safety', 'the home of ease', 'the end of suffering', 'the supreme joy'.

Nirvana is an experience of bliss which can be attained in this life in this world, and not a state that can be attained only in the distant future. Nor is it a state that only few can attain. Everyone is capable of this attainment, although very few or hardly any achieve it in full measure in this life. In the sacred books of the Buddhists there are numerous stories of saints who experienced the unbounded peace and joy of *nirvana*.

Buddhism also teaches about the bliss of the saints (or perfect ones) after death. This is called *parinirvana*. Because the saint has no more desire there is no more rebirth for him. What exactly happens to the saint we cannot say for certain. The human mind is incapable of describing that state. However, a well-known passage describes it as a state 'where there is neither solid nor liquid, neither heat nor air, neither this world nor any other, neither sun nor moon, neither arising nor passing away nor standing still, neither being born nor dying, neither substance nor development nor any basis for substance'. *Nirvana* is not a personal state, but an unconditional state of bliss and ultimate happiness. Such is the goal of the Buddhist to which the Noble Eightfold Path leads.

5. THE PATH OF HOLINESS

The person who perseveres in the Noble Eightfold Path will pass through 'Four Stages of Holiness' wherein he will, step by step, gain freedom from the 'Ten Fetters' which bind people to the existence of suffering.

1. The *First Stage* is that in which a person becomes entirely free from the first three of these 'fetters':

(a) The false belief that he has a real unchanging soul.

(b) Doubt about the Buddha.

(c) Addiction to rituals as a means of deliverance from suffering, together with all charms, rites, ceremonies, worship, or other forms of dependence on superhuman agencies.

A person who has attained to this 'First Stage' of the 'Path' can never be reborn except as a god or man—he is forever freed from rebirth in the lower forms of life. He is called 'Stream-Winner'.

2. The *Second Stage* is that in which a person is almost, but not quite, freed from the power of the next two 'fetters'. Such a person may return once to the existence of man—after an existence as a god in one of the heavens. He is called 'Once-Returner'.

3. The *Third Stage* is that in which a person becomes absolutely freed from the fourth and fifth 'fetters':

(d) Sense-Pleasures. This includes every conceivable form of desire for pleasure—lust, natural affection, legitimate gratification of the physical senses, even many mental and social delights which are normally considered to be good and helpful.
(e) 'Anger'. This includes all ill-will or hatred that would lead to a desire to see another injured.

The person who has attained to this 'Third Stage' can never be reborn on earth, but passes to the highest heaven, whence he reaches *nirvana*. He is called 'Non-Returner'.

4. The *Fourth Stage* is that in which a person becomes perfectly free, after having cast off the remaining five 'fetters':

(f) The desire for existence in a bodily, material form, in one of the lower Heavens.
(g) The desire for existence without a bodily, material form, as a god in one of the higher Heavens.
(h) Pride.
(i) Restlessness.
(j) Ignorance.

The person who has attained this 'Fourth Stage' is free from any rebirth—he has attained *nirvana*. He is called 'Holy One'.

STUDY SUGGESTIONS

WORD STUDY

1. 'Buddha' means 'Enlightened One' (p. 126). Which of the following words would you use to explain the meaning of 'enlightenment'? knowledge lightning insight illumination brightness liberation luminosity levity serenity severity
2. The following are important words in Buddhist thought. How would you translate them into English?
   dukkha nirvana karma anatta
3. Explain the meaning of the word 'Noble', with examples from life, in not more than 100 words.

REVIEW OF CONTENT

4. Draw a sketch map to show the countries where Buddhism is chiefly practised today.
5. (a) Who was the founder of Buddhism, when did he live, and to which country did he belong?

(b) Can you name any Christian saints who were converted to a religious life for the same reasons as the Buddha?

6. What are the two main divisions of Buddhism, and in which countries is each chiefly followed?

7. (a) What was the important question to which the Buddha wanted to find the answer?
   (b) How and where did he find it?

8. (a) What did the Buddha mean when he preached about the 'Middle Road that leads to peace'?
   (b) What were the 'Four Noble Truths' which expressed the answer to the Buddha's question?

9. What Buddhist teachings are the same as those of Hinduism?

10. What are the 'ten fetters' which hold a man back from reaching *nirvana*?

BIBLE STUDY

11. Read Ephesians 4.21—5.21. What do you find in the Middle Way of Buddhism which is like the Way of the Christians?

12. Read Revelation 4, 5, 21, and 22. What is the chief difference between *nirvana* and the 'heaven' for which Christians hope?

13. Read 2 Corinthians 3.18—4.7 and 1 Peter 2.9–11. Contrast the salvation which Christians believe they have in this present world with the Buddhist hope of attaining ultimate happiness one day.

DISCUSSION AND RESEARCH

14. (a) How would you explain the law of *karma* to someone who asked you whether or not Buddhists believe in life after death?
    (b) 'Who plants mangoes, mangoes shall he eat.
       Who plants thorn-bushes, thorns shall wound his feet.'
    What proverbs do you know, in your own or any other language, which express the idea that 'What a man sows he shall reap'?

15. 'The Buddha arrived at the conclusion that there is no soul or self. . . . The cure for all the evils in this world lies in getting rid of this false idea of the self' (pp. 129, 130). What 'evils' are caused by the idea of the self? Do you agree that they can all be cured by getting rid of that idea? Do you think that human beings *can* wholly get rid of that idea?

16. Buddhism teaches that to attain *nirvana*, people must pass through four stages, in each of which they overcome certain 'fetters'. Compare these 'fetters' with the 'sins' which Christians try to overcome. Do you agree that we should try to overcome our sins in a certain order?

C. MONASTIC BUDDHISM

The goal that Buddhism has set is far beyond the reach of the common man, and the principles of the Eightfold Path are far too difficult for ordinary people to practise. To do so demands detachment from the turmoil of daily life, renunciation of all attachment to things of the world, and the cutting of all ties that bind people to passing phenomena, including family ties. This kind of life is possible only for a few. Therefore, there grew up from very early times a monastic system.

Although the vast majority of Buddhists are laymen, there are also the monks, who are considered to be the followers of the ideal. A Buddhist monk can be easily recognized in the Theravada countries. He shaves his head and he wears a yellow robe. He lives alone or in one of the many monasteries which are scattered throughout the Buddhist world. He is expected to live a life of utmost simplicity, owning no personal property, or money, and he is supposed to get his food only by begging. Hence he is called a *bhikku*—a beggar.

A *bhikku* must lead a very simple life. His possessions must be the bare minimum. Strictly speaking he is allowed to possess only eight articles: the three separate pieces of his robes, a girdle, a begging bowl, a water-strainer (to avoid swallowing living creatures), a razor to shave his head, and a needle to repair his robes.

Monks are permitted to take meals only between sunrise and noon. Their diet is usually vegetarian, made up of the food which they have been given. They must not pick and choose from what is in the bowl, but eat whatever is served, even animal flesh. They must not desire tasty food, but eat only for the purpose of sustaining life.

In Theravada countries, monks do not marry, but certain Buddhist sects in Korea and Japan permit their monks to do so.

In Thailand and Burma almost all males spend at least a few weeks of their lives as monks in a monastery. This period is regarded as part of their education, for which the State makes adequate provision. Almost all of them go back to lay life, although some may continue to be monks for the rest of their life.

Monks live in communities. Twice a month, the monks within a particular area gather together for a ceremony of confession at which the 227 monastic rules are recited. Those who have broken any of these rules must make confession, and receive pardon from their community.

A Buddhist monk is expected to spend his time in study and meditation, in recitation of the sacred texts, and listening to such recitation by other monks. His duties are to preach (particularly on the 'Sabbath' days and special occasions), to officiate at funerals, to perform certain ceremonies, and to provide for the religious education of the young. He may also participate in chanting before weddings. But his main function, so far as the layman is concerned, is to serve as an example of the Buddhist way of life and point the path toward *nirvana*.

The monks do not claim any priestly rights. Their communities are simply bands or brotherhoods of the more earnest followers of the Buddha, with two chief aims: whole-hearted devotion to travelling the Eightfold Path, and energetic efforts to propagate the Buddha's teaching for the welfare of all beings.

D. THE EXPANSION OF BUDDHISM

During the life-time of Gautama Buddha, and after his death, Buddhism spread throughout India. From the very beginning Buddhism had a missionary character, and the Buddha sent out his disciples to preach, saying:

> 'Go ye, O Bhikkus, and wander for the gain of many, out of compassion for the world, for the welfare of gods and men. Let not two of you go the same way. Preach, O Bhikkus, the doctrine which is glorious in the beginning, glorious in the middle, glorious in the end, in the spirit and in the letter. Proclaim a perfect and pure life of holiness.'

Through the untiring efforts of zealous missionaries the faith spread far and wide. Many, high and low, were converted to Buddhism. The most spectacular conversion was that of the great Indian emperor, Ashoka, who reigned from 269 to 237 BC. After a career of bloody conquest, by which he extended his domains, he was filled with disgust and dismay, and found peace in Buddhism. He became a lay disciple at first, but later adopted the life of a monk. He based the religion of the State on the peaceful tenets of Buddhism.

During his time, Ashoka sent Buddhist missionaries to various countries, not only to those near India, but, it is claimed, even as far as Egypt, North Africa, Syria, and Macedonia. These missionaries preached what is today known as Hinayana or Theravada Buddhism, and it is well established in Sri Lanka, Burma, and Thailand.

In the course of time, however, Buddhism developed a more liberal form, which later came to be known as Mahayana. Its beginnings can be traced back to about 200 years after the death of the Buddha, but it flowered and flourished in the first century AD. It is this form of Buddhism which spread to the northern countries—China, Korea, and Japan—where it took firm root.

According to a legend, a Chinese Emperor who lived about AD 65 dreamed that a golden image of the Buddha appeared from out of the West. So he sent messengers beyond the Himalayas to find out the truth about this dream. These messengers, it is said, came back bringing with them the teaching of the Buddha. It is possible that in those early days Buddhist missionary monks made their way northwards across the mountain passes, while Chinese pilgrims travelled in the opposite direction in search of the teaching of the Buddha. We have records of two such pilgrims. One of them, Fa-Hsien, left China in AD 399, and, after undergoing immense hardships in central Asia, spent fifteen years in India. He compiled an eye-witness account of India and its people which is still studied by historians. The other pilgrim, Hsuan-Tsang, left China in AD 629, crossed the Gobi desert, and arrived in India, where he spent sixteen years making a deep study of Buddhism. He returned to China, taking with him many books and manuscripts. Subsequently he translated Buddhist literature into Chinese, with the assistance of his pupils. It is said that more than a thousand volumes were translated. The court of the Tang dynasty, during whose time he lived, became filled with converts to Buddhism.

From China, Buddhism spread to Korea and Japan. Japan is today the stronghold of Mahayana Buddhism. In the seventh century AD, the important Japanese Prince Shotoku embraced Buddhism, and the Japanese accepted this doctrine, along with Chinese culture. Buddhism came to Japan as a highly developed religion associated with the great civilizations of India and China. Possibly because of this fact, Buddhism made a great impact on the life of the people and held a larger place in Japanese than Chinese life. Today Buddhism is a vital force in Japan (see p. 54).

Buddhism also penetrated into Tibet and existed in scattered monasteries. But about AD 750 an Indian Buddhist monk named Padma Sambhava crossed the mountains into Tibet and preached a different and peculiar form of Buddhism, which is known as Tantrism. This is a mixture of Mahayana Buddhism, certain magical and mystical doctrines derived from Hinduism, and ancient religious practices used in Tibet. Tantrism includes prayers, ritual dances, exorcism of devils, and magic spells.

E. THE BUDDHIST SCRIPTURES

The Scriptures of Buddhism were written in much the same way as the New Testament. Gautama's followers wanted first of all to record the exact words of their master and the rules he had laid down for the monastic life, and secondly to collect the interpretations of his teaching given by leading scholars. These form the *Theravada* Scriptures, known as the 'Canon of the School of Elders', and are regarded as embodying the more authoritative and conservative traditions in Buddhism.

Then, later on, Buddhist sects in different countries made their own collections of holy books, to add to the earlier texts. These reflect rather more liberal traditions and include stories, epics, and poems, as well as doctrinal teaching. They became known as the *Mahayana* Scriptures, or 'Greater Vehicle'. Scholars of the Mahayana countries have referred to the Theravada Scriptures as *Hinayana* or 'Lesser Vehicle', because they are less broad in scope, though probably they are closer to the original teaching of Gautama Buddha himself.

1. THE THERAVADA SCRIPTURES

The earliest complete collections of Buddhist texts have come down to us in the Theravada Canon, which forms the accepted Scriptures of Burma, Cambodia, Laos, Sri Lanka, and Thailand.

These Scriptures, written in the Pali language, are believed to have been put together in Sri Lanka in the first century BC. Though based on oral traditions brought there by Buddhist missionaries about two centuries earlier, they were not actually written down till some 600 years after Gautama's death.

The Canon is known as the *Tripitaka* (Three Baskets) because it consists of three separate collections of texts. These are:

(a) *Vinaya-Pitaka* (the Discipline Basket), containing five books of detailed regulations for the lives of monks and nuns.

(b) *Sutta-Pitaka* (the Discourse Basket), containing collected discourses of the Buddha, together with shorter sayings, and covering all of his teaching.

(c) *Abhidhamma-Pitaka* (the Metaphysical Basket), containing the writings of later scholars on doctrine and ethics.

Each of the three Pitakas is further divided into a number of separate books. The *Abhidhamma-Pitaka* is chiefly used by the monks. The *Sutta-Pitaka* contains the most popular and widely-read texts of the Theravada Tradition. It includes the *Dhammapadda*, or 'Way of Virtue (or Truth)', a collection of poetry which is probably the best known of all the Buddhist sacred texts.

2. MAHAYANA SCRIPTURES

The earliest Scriptures of the Mahayana countries come from North India. They were written in Sanskrit, between AD 100 and 800. There is no one Mahayana canon. Each country came to have its own collection, written in its own language, e.g. Chinese, Tibetan, Nepali, Korean, Japanese. Like the Theravada Scriptures, however, they are divided into three chief categories:

(a) *Vinaya:* rules for religious orders.

(b) *Sutras:* discourses—corresponding roughly to those in the Theravada *Sutta-Pitaka*.

(c) *Shastras:* philosophical discussions.

But these Mahayana books quickly developed into a much more varied collection, including works of a more legendary and popular nature. Most widely read among them are the *Lalita Vistara*, a vivid and detailed account of the future coming of the Bodhisattva (see below), and the *Saddharmapundarika*, or 'Lotus of Wonderful Law', which represents the Bodhisattva almost as an omnipotent God who controls the entire universe.

F. MAIN BUDDHIST GROUPS

1. BUDDHISM IN THERAVADA COUNTRIES

The doctrine of Gautama Buddha has remained the ideal in the southern countries of Sri Lanka, Burma, and Thailand. It is known as *Theravada* (or Hinayana) Buddhism and its doctrine and ideals have been described in section B of this chapter. The worship offered to the Buddha is described in section G.

In these countries, however, as well as elsewhere, Buddhist teaching among the ordinary people has been mixed with other religious beliefs and practices. These are mentioned in section H of this chapter.

2. MAHAYANA BUDDHISM

About 200 years after the death of the Buddha, a group of his disciples disagreed with the others over the interpretation of the Buddha's teachings. They preached a doctrine which was less severe and more suited to the needs of ordinary people. This liberal movement was probably the beginning of a new form of Buddhism which flowered and matured in the first century AD. As we have seen, this form of Buddhism became known as *Mahayana*, or 'the Greater Vehicle'. It is the religion of the northern countries of Asia, China, Korea, and Japan.

The Mahayanists taught that faith and devotion were sufficient to enable a person to be a true Buddhist and achieve the highest spiritual goals. Rigorous practices and intellectual attainments were not absolutely essential. Thus, in the northern countries, salvation by faith became one of the main teachings of Mahayana Buddhism.

The aim in Theravada Buddhism was that a person should achieve *nirvana* (see p. 131). In Mahayana Buddhism, however, another aim was put before the believer: to become a *Bodhisattva*. A Bodhisattva is a compassionate person who has made a vow to reach supreme and perfect illumination in order to help all other human beings gain the same illumination or salvation. He postpones entering nirvana in order to transfer his merit to those who call upon him in prayer. A Bodhisattva puts himself at the service of others and is prepared to undergo any suffering for the sake of others. Through enormous toils and sufferings he is able to attain Perfection, which qualifies him to be a Buddha, and by attaining this he is able to confer marvellous blessings on others. Mahayanists believe that everyone can become a Bodhisattva and attain Buddha-hood.

The Buddhists in Mahayana countries also believe in a number of especially great Bodhisattvas and Buddhas who are able to save others by transferring to them the merit which they themselves have acquired. These Buddhas are not people who actually lived, and they are, in some ways, simply manifestations of the one Buddha reality, of which Gautama Buddha was one manifestation. These great Buddhas are believed to be enthroned in different heavens in the midst of assemblies of gods and saints. In Japan, Vairocana is the great Buddha (see p. 54), but in China Amitabha Buddha is prominent. Amitabha Buddha means 'the Buddha of Infinite Light'. It is said by some that he was once a Buddhist monk who refused to accept Buddha-hood for himself until he was permitted to transfer to others some of the merit which he had acquired. Although Amitabha was not an actual historical person as Gautama was, he is believed to be a glorious redeemer. His chief virtue is compassion or love, and he is believed to inhabit a heaven known as the 'Great Western Paradise', or the 'Pure Land'. All good Buddhists, monks or laymen, can hope to go to this paradise. In one of the ancient books this paradise is described as a place:

> surrounded by radiant beams of light and brilliant jewels of untold price. In every direction the air resounds with harmonious tunes, the sky is full of radiance, large heavenly birds of paradise are flying to and fro. Some of the beings in paradise are singing in adoration of the Buddha while others are posed in serene meditation. Amitabha Buddha sits on a lotus seat like a gold mountain in the midst of all glories, surrounded by his saints.

All that one needs in order to enter this paradise is faith in Amitabha Buddha or even the repetition of his name. Faith means trust in the all-sufficiency of Amitabha's grace, and the renunciation of self-dependence or trust in one's own self-sufficiency. A Mahayana creed expresses this faith in these words:

> 'I believe in him as the highest being. Because of the sinfulness of men and because of their suffering, Amitabha Buddha was incarnate and came upon earth to save men; and only in his suffering love is there hope for me and for the world. He became human to become its saviour, and no one but he alone can help. He watches constantly over all who trust in him and helps them.'

Mahayana Buddhism offers hope for all, and it has a very great influence over the people of northern Asia. Prayer, adoration, and worship became the most powerful factor in Mahayana devotion. The Mahayanists reverence Gautama as a great teacher, but they worship Amitabha and other great Buddhas as merciful saviours.

A goddess known as Kuan Yin gives personal form to the ideas of mercy and love. She is the goddess of compassion who guides the faithful to the promised land. She is sometimes compared to the Catholic Madonna. The Mahayanists have come to give her worship and honour equal to that which they give to Amitabha. Statues of this goddess are placed in Mahayana monasteries and homes.

3. ZEN BUDDHISM

As Buddhism spread to the northern countries, it divided into numerous sects with variations in doctrine. One of these sects is *Zen* Buddhism, which originated in China and then spread to Japan. Zen Buddhism has had an impact in many countries outside Japan, and this form of Buddhism is better known in the West than any other.

According to a legend, a disciple of Gautama Buddha once approached him with a gift of a golden flower, and asked him to preach the secret of his teaching. Gautama took the flower, held it aloft, and with fixed attention gazed at it in silence for some time. By this act he indicated that the secret of his doctrine lay not in words, but in the act of meditation on the flower itself. Zen doctrine is supposed to have descended from this mystical act, and the word *Zen* in Japanese means 'contemplation'. Zen has as its goal insight or enlightenment, like that which Gautama achieved under the Bo-tree (see p. 126). Zen teaches that people can attain enlightenment by contemplation.

This doctrine matured in China at the end of the fifth century AD. Its founder was an Indian mystic missionary named Bodhidharma about whom there is an interesting legend. When Bodhidharma came to North China, the Emperor Wu Ti of the Liang dynasty, who was a convert to Buddhism, sent for this missionary who had come from India. In the course of conversation, the Emperor asked him how much merit was due to him because of the donations he had made to the Buddhist order, and in continuing the translations of the sacred Buddhist books. The monk replied gruffly, 'No merit at all.' The Emperor was shocked. Bodhidharma went on to explain that knowledge gained from books is worthless; no one gains merit by doing good works; only meditation gives a person direct insight into reality. To demonstrate what this meant, Bodhidharma is said to have retired to Mount Su where he spent nine years continuously meditating with his face to a wall, saying nothing to anyone.

The main tenet of Zen Buddhism is that enlightenment does not come from the study of scriptures, or from philosophical speculation; rather it comes from a sudden flash of insight into things which a person is given during disciplined meditation. A person may need to take ten years learning to meditate before this happens. Books, preaching, discussion, theories, or austerities are of little importance. The experience of enlightenment happens suddenly, like a flash of lightning. It is like a laugh which spontaneously occurs when one suddenly sees the point of a joke.

Zen disciples are trained with acts, not with words. A Zen teacher might strike a student with a stick, shout at him, set him a riddle or a puzzling story to think about. All these are designed to train the mind to see the truth. Zen monks lead lives of extreme simplicity, begging for their food, working in the fields, and meditating. In recent times European thinkers have been attracted to Zen Buddhism because of its ideas of simplicity and intuitive inspiration.

4. MODERN MOVEMENTS IN THAILAND

The headquarters of the World Fellowship of Buddhists have been in Thailand for many years. Modern developments in that country are, therefore, of great interest, and provide an example of what is happening in many Buddhist countries today.

(a) *A revival of the practice of meditation:* In the late 1940s a movement began to revive meditation in Thailand, and by 1970 there were many hundreds of meditation centres throughout the kingdom. There are two main types of meditation: the first, *Meditation for Concentration*, has tranquillity as its goal, and the second, *Meditation for Insight*, has *nirvana* as its goal. Both monks and laymen take advantage of the meditation centres, which are mostly in temple compounds. Meditation masters, some of them quite famous, give instruction in meditation at these centres. Some people receive their instruction in the evenings after work is done, while others go to live for short or long periods at a centre. Some practise meditation on their own under the guidance of radio broadcasts by experts. By these means many attain calmness and the ability to face life's tasks in a more creative way. Many consider that meditation is the real heart of Buddhist practice.

(b) *Education:* For the past sixty years the twelve-year curriculum of studies for monks has remained largely unchanged. It consists mostly of studies in the life of the Buddha and his disciples, the monastic discipline, ethics, Buddhist proverbs, the Scriptures and commentaries, and the Pali language in which the Scriptures and commentaries were written. Many chants are memorized. These courses are now often held for laymen as well.

Because of the growth of modern education and the influx of new ideas from abroad, secular subjects are beginning to be added to the monks' former curriculum, both at the high school level and at the two universities for monks.

'The headquarters of the World Fellowship of Buddhists is in Thailand; developments there provide an example of what happens in many countries' (p. 142).

Stupas (see p. 151) at the Wat Pho temple in Bangkok attract many pilgrims, while monks celebrate a festival at the temple's chief altar.

Buddhists show their affection and respect for the Buddha in relaxed and informal worship. A senior monk, Phra Ratanavedi, looks after the Wat Pho temple's administration and charity projects.

What likenesses, if any, do you see between this temple and Christian places of worship? What *un*likenesses do you see?

STUDY SUGGESTIONS

WORD STUDY

1. What do *Mahayana* and *Hinayana* mean, and why were these names given to the two separate groups of Buddhist Scriptures?
2. What is the meaning of the Japanese word *Zen*?

REVIEW OF CONTENT

3. (a) Describe the life of a Buddhist monk.
   (b) Why are Buddhist monks known as *bhikkus*, or 'beggars'?
   (c) What are their two chief aims?
4. At about what dates were (a) the Theravada and (b) the Mahayana Scriptures first put together, and in what language was each first written?
5. Name the three parts of the Theravada Scriptures, and say what sort of writings each contains. Which is the best known book among them?
6. What are the chief differences between the Mahayana and the Theravada Scriptures?
7. Give three examples of countries or regions to which Buddhism was carried by the activities of the monks.
8. What are the following, and how do they vary from the more ordinary forms of Buddhism?
   Tantrism Zen Dhammapadda
9. 'Buddhism teaches "salvation by one's own efforts"' (p. 145).
   But this did not satisfy the religious hopes of ordinary Buddhists. How did Mahayana Buddhism provide saviours to whom people could pray?
10. Compare your answer to Q. 9 above with the ways in which the followers of Confucius began to pray to him.
11. Who were the following?
    (a) Amitabha Buddha
    (b) Kuan Yin
    (c) Bodhidharma

BIBLE STUDY

12. Read Matthew 10.5–16 and 40–42.
    In what ways are the rules for Buddhist monks like the directions which the Lord Jesus gave to His disciples?
13. Read John 1.1–4 and 14; 2 Corinthians 8.9; Philippians 2.6–8.
    What differences are there between Jesus Christ and the great Buddhas of Mahayana Buddhism?

DISCUSSION AND RESEARCH

14. Jesus has been called 'the man for others'.
    What teaching in Buddhism reminds us of this principle of self-giving?
15. Find out what Buddhist groups, if any, there are in your country. To which tradition or sect do they belong? Are their numbers increasing or decreasing? How and when did Buddhism come to your country?
16. In Thailand and Burma almost all males spend a few weeks of their lives as monks (p. 135). Find out what effect, if any, this custom has on the daily life of the people in these countries. What effect might it have in your own country if everyone had to spend part of their life as a monk or nun?
17. Some of the modern movements in Buddhism are aimed at improving social conditions. In what ways, if any, are developments of this sort related to Buddhist teaching about the Four Noble Truths?
18. In what ways is Mahayana Buddhism more like the Christian faith than Theravada Buddhism? What is the great difference between Mahayana Buddhism and Christianity? (See Q. 13 above.)
19. Zen Buddhism is attractive to some people living in European countries. Discuss what you think it is which attracts them in this way.

G. WAYS OF WORSHIP

The Buddhist ideal is to attain salvation by one's own efforts, without the help of a supernatural saviour (see pp. 127–133). Meditation and attention to behaviour and right thinking, therefore, take first place in the lives of Buddhists. This is clearly seen in the description of Buddhist monasteries which we have given in section C, and in Zen Buddhism. (See section F. 3: also F. 4.)

But in both Mahayana and Theravada countries people rely on the help of the Buddhas, and pay honour to them in the temples. This section describes how Buddhists do this. Especially important are the gifts which are made to the Buddha and his monks.

The attitude of people to the Buddhas in Mahayana countries has been described in section F. 2. In Theravada countries the average Buddhist thinks of Gautama Buddha as more than a man. He believes that the Buddha is *Devatideva*—the God above God—who lives, knows, and loves, and is worthy of all adoration. In this way Buddhists make their teaching a religion like other religions. In worshipping the Buddha they express their wonder at the mystery of life, and they find in him the person with supreme authority in whom they may trust.

The strictly orthodox Buddhist, however, although he may regard the Buddha as the greatest man who ever lived, and the most enlightened teacher of gods and men, still thinks of him as a man who once lived and is now no more.

1. THE REFUGES AND THE PRECEPTS

Every act of Buddhist worship begins with the recital of the formula of homage to the Buddha:

'Homage to Him, the Blessed One, the Exalted One, the fully Enlightened One.'

This is followed by the *Three Refuges*:

'I go to the Buddha as my Refuge; I go to the Doctrine as my Refuge; I go to the brotherhood of monks as my Refuge.'

Immediately after this the *Five Precepts* are taken. The observance of these precepts is the least that is expected of every Buddhist. They are not commandments, but resolutions made by each individual. The worshipper can 'take' these precepts by himself or he may have the assistance of a monk. In the latter case the worshipper repeats the precepts after the monk recites them. The following are the precepts:

1. I undertake to observe the precept to abstain from destroying life.
2. I undertake to observe the precept to abstain from taking things not given.
3. I undertake to observe the precept to abstain from sexual misconduct.
4. I undertake to observe the precept to abstain from false speech.
5. I undertake to observe the precept to abstain from taking distilled and fermented liquors that cause intoxication and heedlessness.

2. OFFERINGS

Worshippers offer offerings at all places of worship. They are of various kinds—flowers, oil-lamps, or candles, incense, food, drinks, and requisites for the monks.

When a worshipper offers flowers he may recite the following, meditating on the impermanence of life:

'I offer this mass of flowers, fresh-hued, odorous, and choice, at the sacred lotus-like feet of the Noble Sage. I adore the Buddha with flowers and through this merit may there be release or may I attain *nirvana*. As these flowers must fade, so does my body march to the state of destruction.'

When the worshipper offers oil-lamps or candles, he may say:

'I offer these bright lights that dispel darkness to the Omniscient
One, the Light of the three worlds who has destroyed the darkness of
ignorance.'

The offering of lights is believed to bring rich stores of merit that last
for endless ages.

When the worshipper offers food, he may say:

'O Lord, receive with favour this noble food which we have prepared
for Thee; accept it in compassion for us. I offer this delicious food
to the Lord in deep reverence. May this food-offering of mine
destroy all my sins and enable me to attain *nirvana*.'

Similar prayers accompany other offerings. Every offering is considered
to bring some merit.

3. PRAYERS AND INVOCATIONS

Worshippers offer prayers and invocations for human needs and
material blessings. The following is a well-known prayer in Sri Lanka:

'May there be rain in due season and the crops be plentiful.
May the kings be righteous and the country become prosperous.'

There is a similar prayer in Thailand which begins with a number of
verses extolling the virtues of the Buddha, and ends with a prayer
asking for his blessings. The following are the first and last stanzas
of this long prayer:

'I worship with bowed head the Supreme Lord Buddha of the ten
strengths who has boundless wisdom, who is the highest of creatures,
who gives help with mercy, who receives worship, who is without lust
or desire. . . . The merit of my worship has been stored up safely by
the world's Refuge, who has inestimable wisdom. May all disease and
misfortune perish. May clouds giving rain in abundance cause it to
rain.'

The prayer for pardon is very important. In Sri Lanka a worshipper
asks pardon from the Triple Gem (The Buddha, the Doctrine, and the
Brotherhood of Monks) for any sins committed by thought, word, or
deed:

'Forgive me O Lord, for any sins I have committed against Thee in
thought, word, and deed. I resolve not to do any wrong deed against
Thee hereafter.'

In the same way forgiveness is prayed for from the Doctrine and the
Brotherhood of Monks.

The Burmese use a similar but more detailed prayer. It has become so popular that it is known as the Buddhist Common Prayer. It runs as follows:

'I beg leave! I beg leave! I beg leave! In order that any offence which I may have committed either by deed or by mouth or by thought may be nullified, I raise my joined hands in reverence to the forehead and worship, honour, look at, and humbly pay homage to the Three Gems: the Buddha, the Law, and the Brotherhood once, twice, three times, Lord.

And because of this meritorious act of prostration may I be freed at all times from the Four States of Woe, the Three Scourges, the Eight Wrong Circumstances, the Five Enemies, the Four Deficiencies, the Five Misfortunes and quickly attain the Path, the Fruition, and the Noble Law of *Nirvana*, Lord.'

4. TRANSFERENCE OF MERIT

Very frequently worshippers make offerings in the name of deceased relatives, especially gifts of robes, utensils, medicines and food for the monks. The merit gained by making these offerings is transferred to the dead, and to gods, and other beings. After doing such a meritorious act, a worshipper says:

'By this meritorious act may our beloved dead be benefited. May they attain happiness. . . . Just as the rivers filled with water by rain flow into the sea and fill it, so may the merit of this offering be transferred to our dead relations.'

One of the formulas used in Thailand is as follows:

'May these gifts of mine be credited to my relatives, to my mother and father especially. May all my relatives, especially my mother and father, share in this giving according to my wishes.'

In Burma the formula is:

'I share the merit of this deed with my parents, friends, and relatives, and the spirits and all living beings. May the earth bear witness.'

5. PILGRIMAGES

A pilgrimage to a sacred place is considered to be a meritorious deed, and the more pilgrimages a person makes the greater is his merit. It is therefore the ambition of every Buddhist to visit as many sacred places as many times as possible during his life-time. The Buddha himself declared that there are four places that one should look upon with emotion, namely, the birthplace of the Buddha, the place of his Enlightenment, the place where he preached his first sermon, setting in motion the wheel of the Dharma, and the place where he passed away into nirvana. One should go on pilgrimage to these places because 'whoever dies with peaceful heart, while wandering in pilgrimage to such shrines, upon the breaking up of the body shall be reborn beyond death in the blissful heaven-world'. These words have over the centuries inspired millions of pilgrims, monks, nuns, and lay devotees, to make long journeys braving all dangers, from remote parts of the Buddhist world, to worship at these sacred places in the land where the Buddha was born. It was considered to be particularly meritorious to walk all the way on foot, undergoing some amount of hardship.

There are also sacred places in the Theravada countries to which thousands go on pilgrimage. One of the most popular places in Sri Lanka is a mountain 7,500 feet high, on which the Buddha left an imprint of his foot. This mountain is named Sri Pada, meaning 'Sacred Footprint'. It is also known as Adam's Peak. It is a place to which Buddhists, Hindus, Christians, and Muslims go on pilgrimage. During the pilgrim season, thousands wend their way to the summit of this holy mountain, bringing various offerings, and carry out their devotions.

According to a legend, the Buddha is believed to have left the print of his left foot on Adam's Peak and then, in one stride, crossed to Thailand where he left the impression of his right foot on a rocky hillside in Phrabad. This is a place that attracts thousands of pilgrims.

6. CEREMONIES AND FESTIVALS

Buddhist ceremonies and festivals are numerous. One of the most important is the ceremony known as *Pirit*. This is supposed to have been approved by the Buddha, as a way of warding off the malice of demons or evil spirits, and to give blessing.

In the Pirit ceremony Buddhist monks hold one end of a long thread and the congregation holds the other end while squatting on the floor. The middle of the thread is twisted round the neck of a new clay pot filled with water. The monks chant selected texts from the Buddhist Scriptures, called *Parittas*. When the chanting is concluded, the thread is broken into pieces and tied round the wrist and neck of those assembled, and at the same time the sanctified water is sprinkled on all.

'To ward off all calamities, to bring to fulfilment all rich blessings, for the destruction of all suffering, for the destruction of all fear and for the destruction of all disease and sickness recite the Parittas.'

Monks chant the Pirit ceremony in temples or homes, or in temporary recitation-halls or pavilions specially constructed for that purpose. The period of chanting extends from one hour, to one day, a week, or even longer periods, according to the occasion. Apart from its use as a protection against evil and disease, the ceremony is held on other occasions such as the inauguration of a new house, the starting of a journey, or the beginning of a new business.

Buddhists all over the world celebrate the festival known as *Vesak*. *Vesak* is the name of the lunar month that falls in May, and the full-moon day in that month is called Vesak day. It is the most holy day for Buddhists. This sacred day has a threefold significance. It is said that the Buddha was born, attained enlightenment, and died on a full-moon day in the month of May.

Buddhists celebrate Vesak on a large scale, with great festivity. They decorate and illuminate temples, houses, and streets, and hold special services for instruction and edification. On this sacred day white-clad devotees, men, women, and children, crowd the temples and halls; they perform their religious rites at the *stupa*, the Bodhi-tree, and the Buddha image, and squat on the ground to observe the Precepts, meditate, and listen to the teaching.

On this most holy day, especially, the Buddhist devotee sends out thoughts of loving kindness to all living creatures, and to the dead, recalling to mind the words of the Buddha's Discourse on Loving Kindness: 'Cherish in your hearts boundless goodwill to all that lives.' Buddhists send out thoughts of love not only to those near and dear to them, but to enemies, all living creatures, animals and insects, and those living in other realms. For this each devotee must first cherish loving kindness in his own heart, and then transmit it to those of his own family, then friends, and relations, and so on in widening circles until he permeates the whole world with radiant thoughts of love. Thus by possessing a happy and peaceful mind, a boundless heart full of compassion and understanding, pity and goodwill towards all beings, a follower of the Blessed One will find strength to tread the Noble Eightfold Path that leads to the end of suffering and the realization of nirvana—joy unspeakable.

H. POPULAR BUDDHISM

The religion of the ordinary people in Buddhist countries is a mixture of Buddhist teaching and other religious beliefs and practices. We have already seen how Buddhism was mixed with Shinto in Japan (chapter 7) and with Taoism in China (chapter 9 C), and Buddhists in Korea often worship the gods of the Shamans (chapter 6). Buddhist temples may contain the images worshipped in other religions.

There are, however, three objects in Buddhist temples which are particularly associated with the Buddha.

1. *Relic Worship:* After the death of Gautama Buddha, his mortal remains, such as his teeth, hairs from his head, and his collar-bone, were carefully preserved. They are kept safely in the many tower-like shrines which exist throughout the Buddhist world. These are called

stupas (meaning 'mound'), or pagodas. Since there are millions of these *stupas* scattered throughout Asia, not all contain relics of the Buddha. Some contain relics of the Buddha's disciples or of those worthy of being honoured, and others, reminders of the Buddha, such as images, sacred writings, and prayers.

When a devotee enters a temple he first worships the *stupa*, going round it three times in a meditative mood, keeping the object of worship, namely, the *stupa*, to his right. Then he worships, either prostrating, kneeling, squatting, or standing with hands cupped together. Worship of the *stupa* is believed to bring great merit. The relics of the Buddha are planted like quickening seeds at the centre of the *stupas*. The worshippers believe that they exert a living influence on the building, and keep alive for all time and all men the spiritual power of the Buddha.

Every temple has a *stupa*, and some of them are of enormous size. One of the biggest in Sri Lanka, the Abhayagiri Dagaba, when originally built, had a diameter of 327 feet and was 405 feet high, being only fifty feet less than the highest of the Pyramids in Egypt, or the dome of St Peter's in Rome, and fifteen feet higher than St Paul's Cathedral in London. One of the best known *stupas* is the Shwe Dagon Pagoda. This pagoda on a hilltop in Rangoon has a central tower surrounded by spired shrines, and is covered with gold leaf. It is a common sight to see laymen sweeping the pavement of the Shwe Dagon Pagoda, or putting on gold leaf which they have bought, over the outside of the pagoda's central tower. The latter is an act of great merit and can be done only by men. Women, however, can buy gold leaf and hire men to put it on the tower.

Building a *stupa* or contributing to building one is an act which brings great merit, and some of the ancient kings in Theravada countries spent enormous amounts of money to build *stupas* and acquire merit.

2. *The Cult of the Bodhi Tree:* There is a Bodhi tree within the precincts of every monastery. Worshippers pay respect to this sacred tree because the Buddha attained Enlightenment under one, and after that paid his own respect to the tree. It is said that he spent one whole week standing in front of the tree, gazing with unblinking eyes full of gratitude and love. Later on he himself commended the worship of the Bodhi tree. There is a strong belief that a god resides in every Bodhi tree. Some people believe that the tree itself is a god. The homage and reverence paid to the Bodhi tree is considered to be homage and reverence paid to the Buddha himself.

3. *Worship of the Buddha Image:* Strictly speaking image worship is quite out of place in Buddhism. Gautama Buddha never wanted to be worshipped in any way. In the early days there were no Buddha images. He was represented by symbols such as the wheel, the foot-print,

'Today image-worship occupies a central place in the devotional life of Buddhists' (p. 153).

In Fiji a woman prays in a corner of her home set aside as a shrine for relics and images.

This huge stone Buddha (right) is at Swayambhuna, one of the most sacred places in Nepal. According to legend it was visited by Gautama himself.

What effect does worship of an image have on one's belief about the divinity associated with the image?

the seat on which he sat, or by the shape of his shadow which was supposed to be impressed on rocks. It was not until four or five centuries later that he was represented by images. Today image-worship occupies a central place in the devotional life of Buddhists.

Images of Gautama Buddha show him in one of the three postures: (1) standing, (2) seated, and (3) reclining. Making an image for public worship is a great event attended by rituals and ceremonies. Many Buddhist homes have small images of the Buddha. His shrine in a home is an object of worship, and it is also believed to be a source of blessing and magical protection.

I. THE BUDDHIST

'Suffering and the enduring of Suffering'—this sums up the whole philosophy and religion of Buddhism, and the aim of every Buddhist is to be free from suffering. He believes that suffering is self-made, i.e. the result of past *karma*. Thus every man depends on himself alone for his salvation, not on God.

Though every Buddhist regards *nirvana* as his ultimate goal, the highest and holiest he can aim at, for ordinary people it seems very far away, and not everyone wants to get there too quickly. Ordinary lay Buddhists, as well as the monks, spend much of their time and money in performing acts of merit in order to be reborn in happy conditions, and to enjoy material blessings along the way to higher states of consciousness. And while meritorious deeds are done to make sure of rebirth in a happier condition, magical practices are regularly used to gain material blessings.

Emphasis on the inner quality of life, however, is a characteristic of Buddhists. They take the Three Refuges and follow the Precepts regularly, especially on *poya* days, and spend time in meditation to develop spiritual qualities.

General belief in *karma* and rebirth does not mean that all Buddhists strictly follow the orthodox teaching about who or what actually continues to live through the process of *samsara*. Most believe that the same person goes on living after his earthly life ends. This is clearly shown by funeral prayers which express the hope that the mourners may meet the departed again in some future birth.

Note: The Buddhist described here belongs to the Theravada tradition. The Buddhist of the Mahayana tradition is described in section F. 2 above.

STUDY SUGGESTIONS

WORD STUDY

1. The Buddha is sometimes addressed in worship as *Devatideva*. What does this word mean?

2. What are: (a) the Three Refuges? (b) the Five Precepts?
3. What do Buddhists believe about prayers and offerings on behalf of people who have died?
4. (a) Describe the ceremony of *Pirit*. What is the purpose of this ceremony?
   (b) What is *Vesak* day, and why is it specially important to Buddhists? Describe some of the ways in which they observe this day.
5. 'Every temple has a *stupa*.' What are the stupas chiefly used for?
6. The stupa, the Bodhi tree, the Buddha image are the three main objects of worship in Buddhist temples. What is the importance of each?

BIBLE STUDY

7. 'Self-effort, self-conquest, self-emancipation are fundamental to the Buddha's teaching' (p. 129). Read Luke 10.21–22; 11.1–4; John 14.5–14. Jesus sought to put His disciples into a living relationship with God so that they might receive grace and help from Him. Do you think that this difference between the two teachings is important? Give your reasons.

DISCUSSION AND RESEARCH

8. 'The Buddhist ideal is to attain salvation without the help of a supernatural saviour' (p. 145).
   Why, then, do you think that so many ordinary Buddhists pray to the Buddha and Bodhisattvas for help?
9. Compare the 'Five Precepts' with the 'Noble Eightfold Path' (p. 128). Which steps in the 'Path' are *not* included among the precepts? Why do you think they are omitted?
10. Compare some of the prayers quoted on p. 147 with the prayers of the Dinka (pp. 21–23), and those which Jews use (p. 116). Can you find any in which the ideas and feelings are similar in all three religions?
11. With which Christian festival can *Vesak* day be compared?
12. (a) Buddhists are often said to be among the most gentle, unselfish, and peaceful people, because this is what their religion demands. But some people ask if they can really be called unselfish, since all their actions are aimed at gaining merit. What is your opinion?
    (b) Read the description of the 'ordinary Buddhist' on p. 153. Does he sound the sort of person you would like to have for a neighbour?

Chapter 12
Christianity

A. JESUS CHRIST

At the centre of Christianity is Jesus Christ. Christians believe that He was both human and divine. They accept His teaching and try to follow it. They believe that by His death He reconciled mankind to God. They believe that by His resurrection He overcame death and evil, and that He gives new life to those who trust in Him. We begin our study of Christianity by looking carefully at His life and teaching.

1. HIS FAMILY AND HOME
Jesus was born in the year which according to present-day calendars is counted as 4 BC. He was the son of a Jewish mother, named Mary, who was then a virgin. Her future husband, Joseph, was a carpenter in the village of Nazareth in Galilee. Both Mary and Joseph belonged to the Jewish royal house, but their families were village craftsmen. The ruler of Galilee was King Herod, who belonged to a family which was only half-Jewish. Herod held his authority by permission of the Roman Emperor. The Romans had conquered Palestine and Syria a few years before, and a Roman governor ruled Judaea to the south of Galilee. Judaea was the homeland of the Jews, and contained the ancient capital city of Jerusalem.

Galilee was Jewish territory, but people of other races lived there as well. A trade-route ran through it between Syria and Egypt. Nazareth was one among many other small villages and towns in the hills round the Lake of Galilee. It was close to the open countryside, with its vineyards and olive-orchards, its little fields and open pasture land. Jesus grew up in this farming country. In His teaching He told many stories about the farmers and fishermen, the householders and merchants among whom He lived.

Jesus grew up in Nazareth. He learnt to read at the local village school, in the synagogue. Like Joseph He did the work of a carpenter, and lived at home with His mother and Joseph's children. He spoke the Aramaic dialect which was common in Galilee.

Like other Jews, He worshipped in the synagogue on the Sabbath days. He also visited the Temple at Jerusalem on some of the great feast days. He accepted the Jewish faith and the Jewish Scriptures (see chapter 10).

2. HIS TEACHING AND MINISTRY
When Jesus was about thirty years old, He began to proclaim 'the kingly rule of God'. In the open-air, and sometimes in the synagogues,

He preached to those who would listen. He gathered together a group of disciples.

Jesus taught people to recognize God's authority as King, and to accept God's claims upon them. He showed God's royal power in action by healing those who were sick, and by setting free those who were in the grip of evil.

There were four main themes to His teaching:

(a) *God's rule is more important than anything else in life.* Because God's rule is so important, Jesus called upon people to repent and to turn away from evil. God's rule is not something in the distant future; God is already present as King. People must be prepared at any time to give account of their lives to God. They must be ready to give up everything else in order to win a share in His Kingdom. Only those who keep God's laws in their inmost thoughts truly love Him. Those who do this, and search for God's kingdom in all things, are the people who are truly happy. To find out God's will and to do it is the most important thing in life. Jesus made God's rule the one aim of His whole life. 'My food,' He said, 'is to do the will of him who sent me and to accomplish His work' (John 4.34). He Himself spent long hours in quiet prayer to God.

(b) *God cares for all.* Jesus made friends of all, even of those who did not keep the strict laws of the Jewish religion (see p. 120). He told three stories in which He taught how God cares for people:

1. God, He said, is like a *shepherd* who searches for a sheep which has strayed. The shepherd sometimes suffers in doing this, and risks his life on the wild hills.

2. God is like a careful *housewife*. She will turn the whole house upside down in order to find a coin which she has lost.

3. God is like a *father*, who waits patiently for his foolish son to return home, and welcomes him unconditionally when he comes.

God has no favourites. God gives His love to all alike. Jesus saw in every shower of rain and in every sunrise signs of God's loving care for all men, good and bad alike. (See Luke 15; Matt. 5.43–48.)

Jesus brought the love and power of God to all who were in need. He healed the lame and the crippled, the blind and the deaf, the lepers and the sick. Others who were mentally ill He healed in their minds. On three occasions Jesus restored to life people who had died. In storms on the Lake of Galilee, His words calmed tempests of wind and waves.

Jesus made friends of people who had allowed themselves to be mastered by evil. By His friendship He brought them back into the community of God, and helped them to overcome evil. Jesus said: 'Those who are well have no need of a physician, but those who are sick; I came not to call the righteous, but sinners' (Mark 2.17).

Jesus taught His disciples to rely on God's loving care:

Therefore I tell you, do not be anxious about your life; what you shall eat or what you shall drink, nor about your body, what you shall put on. Is not life more than food, and the body more than clothing? Look at the birds of the air: they neither sow nor reap nor gather into barns, and yet your heavenly Father feeds them. Are you not of more value than they? . . . And why are you anxious about clothing? Consider the lilies of the field . . . Therefore do not be anxious, saying, 'What shall we eat?' or 'What shall we drink?' or 'What shall we wear?' . . . Your heavenly Father knows that you need them all. But seek first his kingdom and his righteousness, and all these things shall be yours as well . . . Are not five sparrows sold for two pennies? And not one of them is forgotten before God. Why, even the hairs of your head are all numbered. Fear not; you are of more value than many sparrows. (Matt. 6.25–34; Luke 12.6, 7)

(c) *God's true children are those who love as He loves.* Jesus taught His disciples to reflect in their own behaviour the love which God showed to them.

What I tell you is this: Love your enemies and pray for your persecutors; only so can you be children of your heavenly Father, who makes his sun rise on good and bad alike, and sends the rain on the honest and the dishonest. If you love only those who love you, what reward can you expect? Surely the tax-gatherers do as much as that. And if you greet only your brothers, what is there extraordinary about that? Even the heathen do as much. There must be no limit to your goodness, as your heavenly Father's goodness knows no bounds.

You must love your enemies and do good; and lend without expecting any return; and you will have a rich reward: you will be sons of the Most High, because he himself is kind to the ungrateful and wicked. Be compassionate as your Father is compassionate. (Matt. 5.44–48; Luke 6.35–36 NEB)

On the day of judgement, Jesus taught, the heavenly Judge will judge people according to the way in which they were neighbours to those who were in need.

Then the King will say to those at his right hand, 'Come, O blessed of my Father, inherit the kingdom prepared for you from the foundation of the world;

'God's true children are those who love as He loves . . . people like Mother Teresa of Calcutta, who spend their lives in caring for others' (pp. 157, 174).

List some of the ways in which Christians of your church are able to care for others, and some of the ways in which they are failing to do so.

for I was hungry and you gave me food,
I was thirsty and you gave me drink,
I was naked and you clothed me,
I was sick and you visited me,
I was in prison and you came to me . . .
Truly, I say to you, as you did it to one of the least of these my brethren, you did it to me.'

The opposite will also be true: those who refuse to help others will find that they have refused to help the heavenly Judge himself. (See Matt. 25.31–46.)

Jesus knew, however, that people were often tempted to do evil. He knew that evil was present in their hearts. He called His disciples to repent and to change the direction of their lives, and He promised them that God would give them His Spirit and make them new people. He taught them also to pray to God, their Father, for the coming of His Kingdom and deliverance from evil.

(d) *God's love is present, in a special way, in the person of Jesus.* Jesus knew that He was able to reveal God's will and nature in a way that no one else was able to do. Thus He said:

'I thank Thee, Father, Lord of heaven and earth, for hiding these things from the learned and wise, and revealing them to the simple. . . .' Then turning to his disciples he said, 'Everything is entrusted to me by my Father; and no one knows who the Son is but the Father, or who the Father is but the Son, and those to whom the Son may choose to reveal him.' Turning to his disciples in private he said, 'Happy the eyes that see what you are seeing! I tell you, many prophets and kings wished to see what you see, yet never saw it; to hear what you hear, yet never heard it.' (Luke 10.21–24 NEB)

Jesus expressed His close relationship to God by using the Aramaic word *Abba* in His prayers. The word 'Abba' was used by little children in the home, and meant 'Father dear'. He knew that, in a very special way, He was the Son of God. Thus He said: 'I am the way, and the truth, and the life; no one comes to the Father, but by me. If you had known me, you would have known my Father also' (John 14.6–7).

Jesus invited people to become true members of God's Kingdom by becoming His disciples. 'Come to me,' He said, 'all who labour and are heavy laden, and I will give you rest. Take my yoke upon you, and learn from me; for I am gentle and lowly in heart, and you will find rest for your souls. For my yoke is easy, and my burden is light' (Matt. 11.28–30). If a person rejected Jesus's invitation, he rejected God who had sent Him. Those who built their lives on His teaching built securely. Those who neglected it would find their lives collapsing in ruins (Matt. 7.24–27).

Jesus described His task as that of breaking into the house of Satan, the 'prince' of evil spirits, to set his prisoners free. He did this when He healed the sick and welcomed the outcasts. He did it when He taught His disciples about the caring love of God and showed them how to respond to it. 'If you continue in my word,' He said, 'you are truly my disciples, and you will know the truth, and the truth will make you free' (John 8.31–32). By His actions, He was breaking Satan's power over men.

3. HIS SUFFERING AND DEATH

At the time of Jesus, the Jews were looking for the coming of a deliverer. They believed that God would send him, as the Scriptures had promised (see pp. 113, 114).

1. Most Jews expected that the coming deliverer would be a warrior king, like the great David who had founded Jerusalem nearly one thousand years before (see p. 104). This king, they thought, would expel the Romans and other foreign rulers from the land of Israel. He would restore a Jewish kingdom which would dominate the world. They spoke about him as 'the Christ', the 'Anointed' of God.

2. Other Jews expected that a miraculous deliverer would come from heaven. He would carry out God's will in the world with God-given authority and power. They referred to him as 'the Son of Man'.

Jesus himself used this title, 'Son of Man', especially when talking about the end of the world. He also accepted the title 'Messiah'.

But He did not do as many Jews expected. He chose instead to act as the Servant of God in the way which some of the prophets had followed. This was a way of suffering and of humble service. The Servant of God would save God's people by sharing their difficulties and their sufferings. He would overcome evil by carrying its burden of shame and failure himself (see p. 162).

Because Jesus chose this way of bringing deliverance, there was conflict between Himself and many other Jews about God's will for their nation. When He began to preach publicly, He first prepared himself by spending forty days alone in the desert. He rejected the temptation to establish God's kingdom by political means or by demonstrations of supernatural power. He made up His mind to obey God in all things. The temptation to seek God's kingdom in wrong ways, however, pressed on him all through His ministry. His disciples, as well as the people, expected Him to be a king like David. (See Luke 4.1–13; John 6.15; Mark 8.27–38.)

The conflict reached a crisis when Jesus rode into Jerusalem as king. His first action was to purify the Temple, in order to make it a place of prayer for men of all races. To do this was more important to Jesus than attacks on the Roman soldiers whose fortress overlooked the Temple. But His action disappointed the people, and turned them against Him (Mark 11.1–19).

The Jewish religious authorities were already hostile towards Jesus for a number of reasons:

(a) They resented the teaching which Jesus gave to the people. He was not an authorized teacher. He was only a village carpenter from the northern province of Galilee, but He gave His own interpretation of the Law.

(b) Jesus appeared to be careless about religious customs like ceremonial washing, and He made friends with irreligious people. He also differed from the religious authorities in what He taught about the observance of the Jewish holy day, the Sabbath.

(c) Jesus criticized the religious teachers because of the great importance which they gave to the oral traditions. These were detailed regulations which Jewish teachers added to the written Law of the Scriptures, in order to ensure that it was strictly kept. (See p. 119; Luke 11.42, 46.)

The final conflict took place in Jerusalem when one of Jesus's disciples betrayed Him to the Jewish authorities. After a night trial, they handed Him over to the Roman governor on a charge of blasphemy, and when that failed, of treason. The Romans executed Him as a criminal on a cross outside Jerusalem, with two others.

Jesus accepted the torture and insults which His enemies heaped upon Him, and prayed for their forgiveness. 'When they came to the place which is called the Skull, there they crucified Him, and the criminals, one on the right and one on the left. And Jesus said, "Father, forgive them; for they know not what they do" ' (Luke 23.32–34).

4. THE LIVING LORD

On the second day after Jesus's death, He came to His disciples and they knew that He was alive. They realized that He now possessed authority and power which were quite different from those of ordinary human people. They knew that God had raised Jesus from the dead.

Jesus came to His disciples in a visible form on several occasions during a period of forty days. Then He commissioned them to take His message to the whole world. After that, they never saw Him in the same way again. They believed that He had 'ascended into heaven'.

Shortly after this, when they met together in prayer, they experienced something which changed their whole lives. They felt themselves inspired and strengthened in a completely new way by the Spirit of God. With His power to help them, they began to tell others what they had seen and heard.

In speaking to others about their Lord, the first Christians had to explain who Jesus was. One of the ways in which their leaders, the Apostles, did this was by referring to Him in special ways. They said things like the following:

Jesus is *the Christ*. He is the chosen agent of God. His task is to establish God's rule in the world.

Jesus is *God's chosen Servant*. He brought healing and forgiveness to men by suffering for them.

Jesus is *the divine Lord*. He has authority over the universe.

Jesus is *the Son of God*. He came from heaven to reveal God's character and His will. (The title 'Son of God' is closely linked with the title 'the Christ'.)

Jesus is *the Word of God*. He is God's thought and will expressed in a human life. He is God's Agent at work in the world.

These titles expressed the apostles' belief that Jesus was alive, and that He had come into the world in order to reveal God's nature and will to men.

The apostles had also to explain why their Lord had endured such suffering and death upon a cross. This was not an accident, because Jesus had been prepared for it. He had even referred to it beforehand, on a number of occasions, as something which He had to face because it was God's will.

The Old Testament passages, from which the title, 'the Servant', was taken, provided one answer to the question 'Why did Jesus die?' They described the task of the Servant as that of suffering on behalf of others. This kind of suffering is called 'vicarious suffering'. It is a kind of suffering which is well known by people of all kinds, especially those like nurses and teachers who care for others, or who have the task of leadership. Every nurse knows what it costs her to nurse a sick patient properly. Every true leader knows that being responsible for others can often be a heavy burden. They suffer vicariously for others.

The title of 'the Servant' was an important one for the apostles. It reminded them of what Jesus had said about His death. The purpose of the Servant's work, according to the Old Testament Scriptures, was to re-establish the covenant, or solemn agreement, between God and His people (Isa. 42.6; 49.5. See p. 108). Jesus knew that this was the purpose of His death. At His Last Supper with His disciples, He spoke about the new covenant, and brought His disciples within it. By means of the loaf and cup of wine which He shared with them, He gave them a share in the new covenant which He was establishing between God and men. 'This cup (of wine),' He said, 'represents my blood, the blood which seals the covenant, shed for many' (Mark 14.24).

The apostles used other ideas also in order to answer the question,

'Why did Jesus die?' Often they used ideas which were associated with sacrifice. Both Jews and Gentiles understood these ideas. The apostles used them to express their belief that Jesus had died in order to create a new relationship of love and trust between God and men.

1. The death of Jesus was the perfect sacrifice. By means of it, those who worship God may come to Him without fear (1 John 1.7–9).

2. His death was the costly ransom paid to set people free from slavery to evil (1 Pet. 1.18–19).

3. His death was the act of suffering by which He Himself carried the consequences of human sin and took them away (1 Pet. 2.24; 2 Cor. 5.21).

4. His death was the act of love by which God has reconciled people to Himself (2 Cor. 5.19–20).

5. By His death, He defeated the powers of evil and broke their hold over human beings (Col. 2.15).

6. His death fully revealed the nature of God's love (1 John 4.7–10; 2 Cor. 5.19).

As time went on, the apostles' understanding grew and deepened. They began to see that Christ's victory over evil affected the whole universe. They also believed that the Son of God had been God's agent in the act of creation, even before He had become man in Jesus of Nazareth. One of them expressed it in this way:

He is the image of the invisible God, the first-born of all creation; for in him all things were created, in heaven and on earth, visible and invisible, whether thrones or dominions or principalities or authorities—all things were created through him and for him. He is before all things, and in him all things hold together. . . .

For in him all the fullness of God was pleased to dwell, and through him to reconcile to himself all things, whether on earth or in heaven, making peace by the blood of his cross. (Col. 1.13–20)

The early Christians, therefore, worshipped the Lord Jesus with awe and love. They thought of Him as the heavenly Lord. When John saw Him in a vision, he saw Him like this.

He was clothed with a long robe and with a golden girdle round his breast. His head and his hair were white as white wool, white as snow. His eyes were like a flame of fire. . . . His face was like the sun shining in full strength. When I saw him, I fell at his feet as though dead. But he laid his right hand upon me, saying, 'Fear not, I am the first and the last, and the living one. I died, and behold I am alive for evermore.' (Rev. 1.13–18)

STUDY SUGGESTIONS

WORD STUDY

1. Jesus used the word *Abba* in speaking to God in His prayers. What does this word mean, and what does it tell us about the relationship between Jesus and God?

2. (a) The suffering and death of Jesus on the cross is called 'vicarious' suffering. What does this mean? Give some examples of 'vicarious suffering' in everyday life.

   (b) The Pope is sometimes called the 'Vicar' of Christ, and in some churches a minister is known as 'Vicar'. These titles come from the same root-word as 'vicarious'. What do you think they mean? (Use a dictionary to check your answers.)

3. Which four of the following words and phrases would you find most useful in explaining the work of an Apostle?

   teacher   scholar   finder   founder   witness   messenger   marshal   watcher

REVIEW OF CONTENT

4. Write a short summary, in not more than 200 words, to describe the life and death of Jesus.

5. What were the four main themes of Jesus's teaching?

6. (a) 'There was conflict between Jesus and many of the Jews about God's will for their nation.' What were the reasons for this conflict?

   (b) For what other reasons were the Jewish religious authorities hostile to Jesus?

7. The Apostles used various titles for Jesus, to express their beliefs about Him. What did they mean to express by each of the following?

   (a) The Christ   (b) God's Chosen Servant   (c) The Divine Lord
   (d) The Son of God   (e) The Word of God

BIBLE STUDY

8. Read Matthew 5.43–48; Matthew 6.25–34; Luke 6.35–36. What do we learn from these passages about God's love for human beings?

9. Read Mark 8.27–38; Luke 4.1–21; John 6.15. What do we learn from these passages about Jesus's way of bringing deliverance to the world?

10. 'Jesus had died in order to create a new relationship of love and trust between God and men . . . His victory over evil affected the whole universe' (p. 163).

    Read the following passages and then describe in your own words some of the ways in which Jesus, by His death, overcame evil and renewed men's relationship with God.

2 Corinthians 5.19–21; Colossians 2.15; 1 John 1.7–9; 1 John 4.7–10; 1 Peter 1.18, 19; 1 Peter 2.24.

(In this chapter Bible references have been put in some places, though not in all cases where they would be helpful. The student would find it a good exercise to work through the chapter adding references where he thought they would be helpful.)

DISCUSSION AND RESEARCH

11. 'The Jews were looking for the coming of a deliverer ... who would expel the foreign rulers. ... But Jesus did not do as many Jews expected' (p. 160). Many countries today look for the coming of new leaders to deliver them from political oppression or from foreign rulers. How do you think people would react if revolutionary leaders were to behave as Jesus did, instead of fighting political battles or carrying on guerilla warfare?

12. After Jesus's death His disciples believed that He had ascended into heaven.
    (a) What do you think they meant by this?
    (b) What do you yourself believe about it?

13. Can you think of any *important* element in the teaching of Jesus which has been omitted in Section A. 2?

14. 'The Jewish religious authorities resented the teaching which Jesus gave, for a number of reasons. He appeared to be careless about religious customs and He made friends with irreligious people' (p. 161).
    (a) How much importance do the religious authorities (i.e. Church leaders) in your country attach to the observance of religious customs? Do they encourage or discourage friendliness between Church members and irreligious people, or between Christians and people of other religions? Are they right to do so?
    (b) A Christian student in India said: 'If I make friends with people who are not Christians I find it difficult to obey all the rules of the Church.' His college room-mate said: 'If I only make friends with Christians, how can I obey the commandment to love my neighbours, and faithfully witness to God's love for *all* people?' Which student do you think was right?

15. 'I died, and behold I am alive for evermore' (Rev. 1.18).
    (a) Many people today try to live in accordance with Jesus's teaching, but do not claim to believe in His resurrection. Do you think they have the right to call themselves Christians?
    (b) What difference would it make in your own life if you did not believe that Jesus is 'alive for evermore'?

16. Read again chapter 10, section B. Discuss what are the links between the Old Testament and the teaching of Jesus.

B. THE GROWTH OF THE CHURCH

Note: The word 'Church' has two meanings in English. It can mean the building in which Christians worship; and it may also be used to mean a group of Christians who worship and meet together. In this book we use the word mostly in the sense of 'a group of Christian believers'. Such a group may be a small number of people who live in one village or town, or a very large number of Christians from many places who belong to one denomination. The word may also mean all Christians, of all times and all places, who belong to the one Church of Jesus Christ. When it means a building we use a small 'c'.

1. THE MISSION OF THE CHURCH

The apostles believed that people must receive the gifts of Jesus Christ by faith. People must respond to the living Jesus themselves, with love and with trust, in order to enjoy the gifts which He offers them. Paul, who was an apostle, expressed it like this: 'If on your lips is the confession (i.e. public declaration), "Jesus is Lord", and in your heart the faith that God raised him from the dead, then you will find salvation. Faith is awakened by the message, and the message that awakens it comes through the word of Christ' (Rom. 10.9 and 17 NEB).

From the earliest times Christians have made it their chief task to tell the story of Christ to others. They call this story 'the Gospel', which means 'the good news'. It is news about God's forgiveness and about the new power which the Spirit of God can give to Christian believers. During the centuries, many Christians have devoted themselves to this task in many different parts of the world. As a result of their labours the Church has grown so that today there are Christian communities in most parts of the world.

2. THE GROWTH OF THE CHURCH

(a) *From Jewish Palestine into the Roman Empire* (*about AD 30–100*). The first Christian Churches were groups of believers living in Palestine. They spoke Aramaic, and the centre of the movement was in Jerusalem. Despite opposition from the high-priests and some of the Pharisees, Christians continued to be closely linked with the Temple, and used the Jewish Scriptures.

When persecution followed the martyrdom of Stephen, a Christian leader in Jerusalem, Christians took the message about Christ into what is now Lebanon and Syria. At the great Roman city of Antioch, the Church welcomed Gentiles, i.e. non-Jews, into the Christian community for the first time. Then the Church there sent out missionaries to Cyprus and elsewhere. Through their work, and through the witness of ordinary Christians, Christian communities were established in many of the cities of the Roman Empire. As a result, Greek replaced Aramaic as the language used in the Church. Christians used new words and new ideas to teach and to spread their message of good news. The Christian Church was no longer a sect within the Jewish religion. It was becoming much more catholic, or world-wide, in its teaching, and its membership. When the Romans destroyed Jerusalem in AD 70, the link between the Christian Church and Jewish Jerusalem was finally broken.

(b) *The Establishment of the Church in Southern Europe (about AD 100–313)*. At first, the authorities of the Roman Empire took very little notice of the Church. Most Christians, then as now, were law-abiding and honest people. Their growing numbers, however, soon forced the government authorities to take action.

In those days, there were ceremonies in which men offered worship to the Roman Emperor as if he was a divine being. These ceremonies were a test of a person's loyalty to the government. Most Christians, however, refused to join in these ceremonies. They claimed that the authority of Christ was supreme, and they refused to join in acts which paid divine honours to the human Emperor. Because of this the Roman authorities became hostile to the Church. During the first three centuries of Christian history, there were times when the Roman government cruelly persecuted the Christians. Many were put to death because of their faith.

Despite persecution, however, Churches were founded in many cities within the provinces of the Roman empire both north and south of the Mediterranean Sea. The Church attracted many converts, including educated and wealthy men and women.

In the Roman Empire there was often fighting between rival generals, each of whom claimed the right to be Emperor. In AD 313, after some years of fighting, Constantine defeated his rivals and became Emperor. His mother was a Christian, and he issued the Edict of Milan, a decree in which he formally recognized Christianity as a lawful religion. It soon became the most important religion of the Empire, and the countries of southern Europe have been Christian from the 4th century onwards. The coastal areas of North Africa were also Christian for a time, until the Muslim invasions of the 7th and 8th centuries AD.

(c) *The Eastern Churches and the Advance into Asia (about AD 100–1400)*. In the first two centuries, missionaries carried the message of Christ eastwards from Syria across Iraq and Iran, into central Asia and India. The Syrian Orthodox Church in south India is linked with the preaching of Thomas, one of Jesus's twelve apostles, who went to India.

Edessa, now 'Urfa in Iraq, became an important centre for the Christian Church in the countries east of Palestine. Other Christian

167

Churches had much influence in the Persian empire of the Sassanids, particularly in the fifth and sixth centuries AD. At the time of Muhammad (c. AD 600, see p. 184), there were Christian Churches on the west coast of the Persian Gulf and in southern Arabia. In the north of this area, the kingdom of Armenia, between the Caspian and Black Seas, became Christian.

The Nestorian Church in Persia sent out many missionaries to the north and east, and particularly to China. As a result of their work, Churches were established throughout central Asia, including China and Tibet. This was so during the whole period between the seventh and fourteenth centuries. There were other small Churches in Punjab and southern India.

The Eastern Churches unfortunately became isolated from the Churches in the West. This isolation was partly caused by disagreements about Christian beliefs, but it was also the result of political struggles between the Byzantine and Persian empires, and, from the seventeenth century AD, between European and Muslim governments. The rise of Islam also weakened the influence of the Churches. Today the Eastern Churches, except in Ethiopia and Egypt, are comparatively small and isolated communities.

(d) *Further Growth.* Through the centuries Christians continued to take the good news about Jesus Christ to other parts of the world. We have only space here to outline the main ways in which the Churches grew: details of the story may be found in Church History books. The Church History Study Guides in this series tell the story in detail.

AD 100–1200. Churches were established in Britain, in north-west Europe (the Netherlands and German Bavaria), and in Scandinavia.

AD 850–1500. Churches were established in Bulgaria, Rumania, and in Russia. Christianity became the official religion of the kingdom of Kiev in Russia in AD 988, but the Mongols invaded Russia and destroyed Kiev in AD 1237.

When the Mongol rule was overthrown in the fifteenth century, Moscow became the new capital of Russia. The Russian Church had done much to keep the Russian nation alive during the Mongol invasions, and its influence in Russian history has been very great.

About AD 1500 onwards. Churches were established in South America, both among the indigenous inhabitants and among the settlers, through the Spanish and Portuguese colonies, and somewhat later in North America, where there were British and French colonies. Later there were many immigrants into the United States from all European countries.

About AD 1550 onwards. In the sixteenth century, Portuguese ships first sailed round Africa to India and other Asian countries. They carried with them missionaries of the Roman Catholic Church. Among the greatest were Francis Xavier, who laboured in India and Japan from AD 1542–52; Matteo Ricci, who died in China in AD 1610; and Roberto de Nobili, who died in India in AD 1656. With their companions, they adopted Chinese and Indian ways of behaviour and of thinking. Unfortunately, those who came after them did not always follow their courageous examples.

In the eighteenth and nineteenth centuries, the Protestant countries of western Europe began to extend their political influence, first in India and the East Indies, and then in Africa. At the same time the Protestant Churches began to send missionaries to carry the Christian message of good news to these countries also.

Through all these efforts, Christian Churches have been established in nearly every part of the world, and among people of every race and nation. Unfortunately all kinds of different Christian Churches have done this in a variety of different ways. As a result the Christian Churches have in the past lacked unity, and there has been no common pattern of worship and practice. But in modern times the Churches are working for a new unity among themselves. In many countries most Churches share in a Council of Christian Churches, and they are helped by the World Council of Churches which was founded in AD 1948.

3. THE CHURCHES

Today there are Christians in almost every country of the world. Most of them belong to one of the following main groups of Churches.

(a) *The Eastern Churches*. These Churches are closely linked by their history to the first Churches in Palestine and Syria. They include the Coptic Church in Egypt ($3\frac{1}{2}$ million), the Armenian Church (3 million), the Church of Ethiopia (14 million), and the Syrian Orthodox Church in India ($1\frac{1}{4}$ million). Until modern times, some of their communities have been isolated from other churches and have developed their own distinctive ways of worship and Christian living.

(b) *The Orthodox Churches*. These Churches are linked with the Greek civilization which enriched the countries at the eastern end of the Mediterranean Sea. They also inherit the traditions of the Byzantine empire which ruled Turkey, Syria, Palestine, and Egypt before the Muslim conquests. The main Orthodox Churches are:

The *Orthodox Churches* of the Near East ($2\frac{1}{2}$ million people).

The *Orthodox Churches* in Russia and eastern Europe, Greece and Cyprus (87 millions).

These Churches (and some of the Eastern Churches) use the name 'Orthodox' (meaning right in opinion), to emphasize their strong and living links with the worship and teaching of the first Christian centuries.

'Churches have been established among people of every race and nation' (p. 169).

In the mountains of Peru a wayside cross reminds travellers that they are never beyond the reach of God's guiding Spirit. In Tanzania the Bible is pledge when President Nyerere swears in the new Minister for Foreign Affairs.

What evidences of Christianity (other than church buildings) might a stranger see in your country?

(c) *The Roman Catholic Church.* This great Church of 580 million people preserves much of the Latin civilization of the Roman empire. It is especially strong in southern Europe, and in South America, as well as in other parts of Europe, in North America, and in parts of Asia and Africa. The Roman Catholic Church emphasizes the importance of discipline, and the authority which the leaders of the Church have in deciding what Christians should believe and how they should behave. The Bishop of Rome, the Pope, has supreme authority in the Church as the representative of Christ.

(d) *The Reformed Churches.* During the sixteenth century, Christians in certain parts of Europe, Scandinavia, and Britain attempted to reform the life of the Church. Among other things, they no longer recognized the authority of the Pope, they used their own languages instead of Latin, and they made the worship and ministry of the Church more simple. In some countries, they retained many of the old customs, but in others the Reformers tried to make a completely fresh start. The main Reformed Churches are the Lutheran (77 million), the Anglican (40 million), the Methodist (40 million), the Presbyterian (55 million), and the Baptists (60 million). These Churches are mostly in north-west Europe, in North America, and in Asia and Africa where missionaries of these Churches have worked. In their teaching, these Churches emphasize the authority of the Bible and the importance of personal trust in Christ by every individual Christian. They also claim that each Church has authority to arrange its own worship and way of life.

(e) *The Pentecostal and Independent Churches.* These Churches are in all parts of the world and are growing in numbers very rapidly. They emphasize the authority of the Spirit of God, and claim that He guides and leads them directly in every new circumstance. They do not think that tradition or established authority are important, but keep looking for fresh evidence of God's power and new, spontaneous leadership.

STUDY SUGGESTIONS

WORD STUDY

1. What are the two chief meanings of the word 'Church'. Describe one actual example to illustrate each of these meanings.
2. What is the meaning of the word 'orthodox', and why do some Churches use this name?

REVIEW OF CONTENT

3. What has chiefly caused the growth of the Church into all parts of the world?

4. (a) What was the attitude of the first Christians towards the Jewish religion?

(b) Which event finally broke the link between the Christian Church and the Jewish religious authorities in Jerusalem?

5. (a) What was the attitude of the early Christians towards the Roman State religion?

(b) What happened as a result of their taking that attitude?

(c) When and how did Christianity become recognized as a lawful religion in the Roman empire?

6. (a) In which Asian countries was Christianity first established?

(b) Why did the Eastern Churches become isolated from those in the West?

7. At about what periods was the Church first established in the following areas?

(a) South America (b) Britain and north-west Europe (c) Eastern Europe and Russia

8. Describe briefly the distinguishing characteristics of each of the five main groups of Churches existing today, i.e:

(a) The Eastern Churches (b) The Orthodox Churches (c) The Roman Catholic Church (d) The Reformed Churches (e) The Pentecostal and Independent Churches

9. For what main reasons have Churches in the past lacked unity?

BIBLE STUDY

10. Read John 17.1–4, 20–23; 1 Corinthians 3.18–23; 1 Corinthians 12.12, 13; Ephesians 4.1–16. If you were a journalist, which of the above passages would you choose as 'text' for an article on the subject of Christian Unity? Using this text, prepare brief notes, or a rough outline of the article you would write.

DISCUSSION AND RESEARCH

11. How is your Church connected with the Apostles? By what way did the Church come to you from Palestine?

12. (a) How many Churches or denominations, i.e. different Christian groups, are there in your country or in your town?

(b) To which of the five main groups listed in Q. 8 above does each belong?

(c) Find out which of them are members of (i) the national or regional Council or Conference of Churches and (ii) the World Council of Churches. If any do not belong to either council, find out why they do not belong.

13. It is clear from the passages listed for Q. 10 above that 'divisions' in the Church are against God's will.

(a) What can individual Christians and local congregations do to bring these divisions to an end?

(b) What, if anything, is your own congregation doing to help Christian unity?

(c) What *good*, if any, do you think can come to the Church as a result of disunity?

C. BASIC ELEMENTS IN CHRISTIANITY

1. THE WAY AND THE SPIRIT

One of the first names which other people gave to the Christian community was the name 'the followers of the Way' (Acts 9.2). This name shows that they thought of Christians as people who followed a particular '*way of life*'. This 'way of life' marked them out as different from their neighbours. Christians learnt this Way from the apostles. The apostles taught them the words of Jesus and the Way in which they should live if they wished to be His disciples.

Jesus summed up His teaching about the Way in His last commandment: 'A new commandment I give to you, that you love one another; even as I have loved you, that you also love one another. By this all men will know that you are my disciples, if you have love for one another' (John 13.34–35). The new emphasis in this commandment was not the command to love. The new emphasis was on the quality of love which Jesus asked for. He Himself showed by His life what that kind of love was. It was selfless and continuing care for other people. Jesus was 'the Man for Others'.

When the Christian message was carried into the Gentile countries of the Roman empire, many new converts entered the Church (see p. 167). The apostles and other leaders gave much attention to teaching them the Christian Way of life. It was a Way which was very different from the ways in which most people lived in the towns of the Roman empire. In these towns there was much immorality, and slaves were often treated very cruelly. The leaders of the Church soon came to a common mind about the Way in which Christians were to live. Summaries of their teaching about the Way may be read in their letters, particularly in Romans 12—13, Ephesians 4—6, Colossians 3—4, and 1 Peter.

At the heart of their teaching was the principle of following the Way in which Christ had lived: 'Be imitators of God, as beloved children. And walk in love, as Christ loved us and gave himself up for us.' 'Christ also suffered for you, leaving you an example, that you should follow in his steps.' 'Beloved, let us love one another; for love is of God, and he who loves is born of God, and knows God. . . . And this commandment we have from him, that he who loves God should love his brother also' (Eph. 5.1–2; 1 Pet. 2.21; I John 4.7 and 21).

The apostles did not believe that Christians could live in this Way by their own efforts. They taught that when a person became a Christian by faith in Christ, that person became a new person. God gave to him or her the Spirit of Christ. The Spirit lived within their personalities and strengthened them so that they could live holy and Christian lives. The Holy Spirit renewed their characters and made them more like Christ Himself (Rom. 6.1–4; 2 Cor. 5.17).

All through the centuries since the apostles taught the Christian Way, Christians have tried to live their lives according to the Way of love. Many have failed to do so, and some have not even tried. They have been content to accept the gifts which they believe Christ gives to them, and to have the name of Christians, without letting the teaching of Christ affect the ways in which they live. But many other Christians believe that the most important thing in life is to follow the teaching of Jesus and to live with love to others. They believe that the most important Christian leaders are people like Mother Teresa of Calcutta, who spend their lives in caring for others. They think that it is very important for their Church to find ways in which its members can serve others.

2. THE SCRIPTURES

All Christians recognize the authority of the Scriptures, i.e. the writings contained in the Bible. They believe that they were given to the Church by the will of God. These writings are divided into two parts, the Old and New Testaments.

The Old Testament contains the Scriptures which the Jews collected together during their long history. (See p. 110.) The Roman Catholic and Orthodox Churches also include other books in the Old Testament. These were written between 300 BC and AD 100, and Jews living outside of Palestine included them in their Greek translation of the Old Testament. The books of the Old Testament are the Scriptures which the Lord Jesus and the apostles honoured and used.

The books of the New Testament were all written between AD 50 and 100. The Gospels record what the apostles taught about the life and teaching of Jesus. The other books contain writings by and about some of the first leaders of the Church, the apostles.

When Christians read the Scriptures carefully and prayerfully they are challenged and encouraged by them. They feel that the Spirit of God is addressing them directly. This is a common experience, whether the Scriptures are read individually in private, or by a group of Christians meeting together. Because of this, Christians sometimes refer to the Bible as 'the Word of God': 'God', they say, 'speaks to us through its pages.' Christians read the Bible at all their services of worship, and they use many phrases and words from the Bible in their prayers and songs. A copy of the Bible is usually placed in a central position in a building which Christians use for worship.

3. THE BATHING AND THE MEAL (The Sacraments)

Jesus instituted two practices which Christians have practised ever since.

1. All over the world, people use water in religious ceremonies as the means and a sign of cleansing. The Jews used water in this way when they received a leper who had been healed back into the community (Lev. 14.1–9).

John the Baptist, who was the forerunner of Jesus, preached that men should prepare themselves by repentance for the coming of God's kingdom. John lived near the Jordan river, and he used its waters to bathe his followers as a public sign of their repentance. This bathing was so important a part of his ministry that people nicknamed him 'the Baptizer'. The English words *'baptize'* and *'baptism'* come from a Greek word meaning 'to dip in water', and so 'to bathe'. Today, these special words are used when the bathing is done as a religious ceremony by the Church.

During the early part of His ministry, Jesus and His disciples also used baptism as an outward sign of repentance. After the resurrection the Apostles used baptism as the ceremony by which a person was admitted to the Christian community. In doing this they were obeying Jesus's command (Matt. 28.16–20). Most Christian Churches use baptism in the same way today. In many Churches the leaders of the Church lay their hands on the heads of the newly baptized to show that they also now receive the Holy Spirit.

2. All over the world, groups of friends meet together for conversation and fellowship, and to share a meal together. Among the Jews, at the time of Jesus, groups of men often did this on the evenings before Sabbath days or religious festivals. In the course of the meeting they would share a loaf of bread and a cup of wine together. Before they did this, the president of the group would say 'grace', thanking God for the bread and the wine.

Jesus shared a meal like this with His disciples on the evening before His arrest. He had probably done this on other occasions also, but two things made them remember His Last Supper with them in a special way.

1. It was associated with the Passover meal which Jewish households ate together on one night each year to commemorate the deliverance of their nation from captivity in Egypt (see pp. 116, 117).

2. At the supper, Jesus linked the bread and the wine with His

'Jesus instituted two practices which Christians have practised ever since', i.e. Baptism and Holy Communion (the Lord's Supper) (p. 175).

In Lagos, Nigeria, Bishop Akinyele celebrates Holy Communion in the Anglican Cathedral; in a Methodist Church in Jamaica mothers bring their babies to be baptized; in Brazil an adult convert is received into the Baptist Church by immersion in the local river.

With what events in the life of Jesus are these practices linked?

death which was soon to come, and with the New Covenant which He was establishing between God and men. 'As they were eating, (Jesus) took bread, and blessed (God for it), and broke it, and gave it to them, and said: "Take; this is my body." And he took a cup, and when he had given thanks (to God) he gave it to them, and they all drank of it. And he said to them, "This is my blood of the covenant, which is poured out for many" ' (Mark 14.22–24). Paul says that Jesus commanded His disciples to repeat the action 'in remembrance of Him'. Thus, from the earliest days in Jerusalem onwards, Christians have made the Lord's Supper one of their main acts of worship.

The theology and actions associated with the Lord's Supper have developed in many ways since the time of the apostles. Each Church follows its own customs and rituals. But in every case the service is based on the solemn taking and sharing together of bread and wine. In this way, Christians commemorate the death and resurrection of Jesus, and renew their trust in Him and in God. They also renew their fellowship with each other.

4. STATEMENTS OF BELIEF (CREEDS)

Before a convert is baptized and admitted to the Christian community he is asked to make a statement of his beliefs. At first, this was probably a very short statement such as the phrase 'Jesus is Lord' (see p. 166). As time went on, however, the official statements of Christian belief became longer. Their purpose was to define what Christians believe about God, and to provide a basis for the instruction of new converts. Christian bishops and theologians authorized these statements at meetings called 'Councils'. They used them as tests to decide whether particular Churches taught the faith correctly or not.

These statements are called *creeds*, from the Latin word *credo*, 'I believe'. The most important of them is the one which is known as the Nicene Creed. The Emperor Constantine convened the Council of Nicaea which authorized it in AD 325 (see p. 167). Additions were made to it in the fifth century AD. Most Christian Churches accept it as an authoritative statement of belief, and it is a good summary of Christian beliefs about God.

Christian teaching about God uses the word 'Trinity'. This is not an easy word to explain. Christian teaching about the Trinity grew out of two complementary beliefs which Christians have about God.

(a) Christians believe that God, who created the world and who sustains the whole universe in being, sent Jesus into the world. Jesus prayed to God during His earthly life, and Christians believe that Jesus is a living person even as God His Father is. Furthermore, Christians experience the strengthening and guiding of the Holy Spirit in ways which show that the Spirit also is a personal being, as Jesus is. Thus

Christians believe that when they pray, they worship three distinct personal beings.

(b) On the other hand, Christians believe that these three personal beings are united in the one being and life of the Godhead. They know that in worshipping one they worship all three. They are baptized into the *one name* of the three persons, and they offer united praise to the Holy Trinity as to the one being of God. 'Glory be to the Father and to the Son and to the Holy Spirit: as it was in the beginning, is now, and ever shall be, world without end: Amen.'

Christians join these two beliefs together in the doctrine of the Trinity. This is the belief that the being of God has from all eternity been composed of three centres of personal consciousness, each in constant and living relationship with the other two, the Father, the Son, and the Spirit.

5. THE MINISTERS OF THE CHURCH

During His earthly ministry, Jesus chose twelve men from among His disciples to act as His chosen representatives. 'He appointed twelve, to be with him, and to be sent out to preach and have authority to cast out demons' (Mark 3.14–15). These men were called 'apostles'. This title implied that they were the representatives of the one who sent them and that they possessed His authority. 'He who receives any one whom I send receives me; and he who receives me receives him who sent me,' said Jesus (John 13.20).

The 'apostles of Jesus' held authority in all the Christian communities because they had been His chosen representatives. In each local Church they appointed local men to supervise its everyday affairs. They called them either 'elders' or 'overseers'. From these two Greek words come the English words 'presbyter' (or 'priest') and 'bishop'. From the beginning, these local leaders presided at the Lord's Supper. After the death of the apostles, some of the elders took their place, and the name 'bishop' was given to them.

Thus in almost all the Churches there are men who are authorized, or 'ordained', to preside at services of the Lord's Supper, and who have the responsibility of leadership. In many cases, they are paid to serve in this way, and in some Churches they are forbidden to marry.

Many other people, however, both men and women, share in the ministry of the Churches, whether as people who care for the community of the Church as pastors, teachers, or nurses, or as engaged in the work of mission towards those who are not Christians. All Christians, however, are called to share in the ministry of their Church in one way or another. As in Hinduism and Buddhism, there are societies of monks and nuns who give their whole lives either to prayer, study, and teaching, or to serving the needy.

6. POPULAR CHRISTIANITY

As in other religions, Christians practise Christianity in ways which have become the custom in their own local Churches. Often these practices are the result of strong emphasis upon one particular aspect of Christian belief and teaching. It is not possible in this book to make a detailed study of these popular practices, but some examples are the following:

In the Roman Catholic Church, Christians hold Mary, the Mother of the Lord Jesus, in high honour, and offer reverence to her. They seek her help in prayer, burn candles before her image in church buildings, and carry her image in processions. They believe that blessing and healing come from things which are associated with her.

In many Churches, particularly the Orthodox and Roman Catholic, Christians honour the memory of great Christians who lived in the past. They call them 'saints', and believe that they support the prayers of their devotees.

In some Protestant Churches, Christians treat the words of the Bible with such great respect that they seem to forget that the Scriptures were written by human people.

In some Churches, Christians adopt customs and practices which belong to the Old Testament and do not fit the New. This is so, for example, in some of the newer Churches of Africa.

D. THE CHRISTIAN

Because there are many different Churches, it is not easy to define exactly what ordinary Christians believe and think about their religion. In general, however, it is possible to say the following about them:

(a) Christians worship God as the great Creator of the world, and pray to Him as 'Our Father in Heaven'. They believe that He has the whole world in His care, and that He will bring the world to a good end.

(b) They worship Jesus Christ and the Holy Spirit as one with God the Father. They declare their faith in this respect in one of the Creeds.

(c) They believe that Jesus is the Son of God, who came into the world to rescue them from the power of evil and to make them God's children. They believe that He died in order to do this, and so they feel love towards Him. They believe that He is alive, and so they honour Him as Lord.

(d) They believe that God has chosen special ways by which to reveal His will to the world, and they believe that they know His will through the Bible.

(e) They join in services of Holy Communion, and believe that through the bread and the wine they come into close touch with Jesus.

(f) They believe that the Spirit of God helps and guides people. Some Christians feel and know His influence very strongly.

(g) They try to follow the teaching of Jesus, and they know that they should love other people because He has taught them to do so. Many try to express this love in practical ways.

(h) They accept the leaders of their Church as people who have authority to teach them, and they rely on their counsel and help in times of difficulty. Some, both men and women, are willing to give their whole lives in the ministry of the Church.

(i) They also follow the popular practices which have become part of the life of their own local Church (see examples in section 6, p. 179).

STUDY SUGGESTIONS

WORD STUDY

1. (a) What is the meaning of the Greek word from which the word 'baptism' comes?

(b) What is the meaning of the Latin word from which the word 'creed' comes?

REVIEW OF CONTENT

2. 'One of the first names which people gave to Christians was "followers of the Way".'

(a) Which other religion we have studied is often known as the 'Way'?

(b) What are two important differences between the 'Way' of that religion and the Christian Way?

3. 'The apostles did not believe that Christians could live in this Way by their own efforts' (p. 174).

What or who does enable Christians to follow the way of love?

4. (a) How do the Scriptures used by the Roman Catholic and Orthodox Churches differ from those used by most other Churches?

(b) At about what period was the New Testament written, and what does it contain?

(c) Why do some Christians refer to the Bible as 'the Word of God'?

5. (a) What two quite ordinary practices form the basis of the two 'Sacraments' which Jesus initiated?

(b) What did Baptism signify for Jesus and His disciples?

(c) How was baptism used by the apostles, and how is it used by the Church today?

6. 'Two things made Jesus's disciples remember His last supper with them in a special way' (p. 175).

Which of those two things makes that Last Supper specially important for the Church?

7. Which is the most important Christian Creed, and when and where was it formulated?

8. 'Christians believe that when they pray they worship three distinct personal beings: on the other hand they believe that these are united in the one being and life of the Godhead' (p. 178).
   What is the formal doctrine called that is based on these two beliefs together? How would you explain it to an enquirer?

9. Give examples of three different sorts of 'ministry' in the Church.

BIBLE STUDY

10. In his first Letter Peter described the sort of life all Christians should lead. From this Letter choose, if you can, one verse to illustrate each of the statements on p. 179 about how to recognize a Christian.

DISCUSSION AND RESEARCH

11. (a) What title is given to the ordained ministers of your Church? What is their chief function?
    (b) In almost all Churches men are specially authorized to preside at services of the Lord's Supper. Do you think this is necessary? Give your reasons.
    (c) In some Churches ordained ministers are forbidden to marry. What do you think are (i) the advantages, and (ii) the disadvantages, of this custom?

12. How are the creeds used in your Church?

13. What did the apostles teach about the Christian Way in relation to family life, employment, and citizenship?

14. Do you think the description of ordinary Christians on p. 179 is a true one? Is it true or not about Christians whom you know? Is there any further characteristic you would want to add to the list?

15. Find out more about the rules for Christian monks and nuns, and compare them with those for monks and nuns in Hindu religious orders.

Chapter 13
Islam

Islam is the religion which Muhammad (sometimes spelt Mahomet) preached in Arabia. Those who practise Islam are called Muslims. *Islam* means 'to surrender or to submit oneself for obedience to God': a *Muslim* (sometimes spelt Moslem) is 'a person who surrenders or submits himself to obey God'.

Muhammad preached this religion in Arabia between the years AD 610 and 632. He taught the Arabs to believe in the one living God, and to live as the servants of God. After Muhammad's death, the Arab Muslims carried this religion into Asia and Africa. Today there are Muslims in very many countries of the world.

All Muslims honour Muhammad, whom they call 'the apostle of God'. They accept his book, the *Qur'an* (sometimes spelt *Koran*), as the Scripture which God has given to them. They look back to his life to find guidance for their own behaviour. Because Muhammad is so important to Muslims we begin our study of Islam by looking carefully at the story of Muhammad's life.

A. MUHAMMAD, THE APOSTLE OF GOD (1)

1. ARABIA

(a) *Arabia:* Arabia is a very large country. It is as big as the whole of India and Pakistan. It is, however, very dry and hot, and its people are few in number. Much of it is sandy desert in which only the Bedouin people can live. These desert Arabs live in tents, and journey long distances to find pasture for their flocks of camels, sheep, and goats.

There are oasis areas in Arabia where cultivation is possible. In the north and centre of Arabia, the oases lie along the courses of a few great river valleys. These are dry for much of the year, but after rain they quickly become flowing streams and they retain the moisture in their sandy beds during periods of drought. A high range of mountains down the western edge of Arabia attracts the rain; this makes the western side the most fertile part of the land.

(b) *The Trade-routes:* Trade has always been important in Arabia. Traders carried goods from South Arabia, or ivory, gold, and slaves from Africa, along the west coast to Syria, Egypt, and Europe; they carried goods from India and China up the Persian Gulf in boats, and then overland across the deserts of north Arabia, or landed them in harbours on the south coast and carried them up the west coast.

(c) *Arabia before Muhammad:* Long before Muhammad, there were small kingdoms in Yemen and other parts of south Arabia. Between AD 400 and 600, however, these kingdoms became very weak, and at the time of Muhammad there was no strong kingdom in Arabia.

No one was able to control the Bedouin tribes who lived in the desert. There was constant fighting and raiding between the tribes, and the traders had to find ways of protecting their trading caravans from them.

The Bedouin, however, depended on the oasis regions for dates and other foodstuffs. They also needed the cloth and other manufactured goods which the traders exchanged at the markets for their butter and skins. To meet these needs and to make trade possible, big markets or fairs were held at different places during the year. The fairs lasted for two or three weeks at a time and some of the tribal groups made very long journeys to be present. At the fairs the Bedouin spent their time in races and sports, dances and storytelling, as well as in buying and selling. They gave up fighting, and it was often forbidden to bring weapons into the area set aside for the fair.

The fairs were held near religious sanctuaries, and, at the time of the fair, the Bedouin made a pilgrimage to the sanctuary. The fair was thought to be under the protection of the divinity which was worshipped at the sanctuary. If a man broke the peace by fighting he sinned against the sanctuary and its divinity. In this way each sanctuary provided security for the caravans of merchants and others on their way to the fair which was held near it.

(d) *Religion:* Before Muhammad, the Arabs worshipped many different deities at their sanctuaries:

1. Some of them worshipped objects in the sky, such as the sun or the moon, or one of the planets.

2. They also associated prominent natural objects with the divine powers. These included great boulders, meteorites, groves of trees, high mountains, caves, and springs. Very rarely they used a shaped idol of stone or perhaps of precious metal.

They offered sacrifice near the object which was associated with the deity. If it was a stone, they smeared the blood of the sacrifice upon it. The Arabs often processed round the sacred objects, dancing and chanting praise-songs to the deities.

In the bigger towns, they often housed their sacred object in a tent or a stone building. More often the sanctuary was simply an area set aside for the deity, and marked with boundary stones.

At the time of Muhammad, Christianity was making its way among the tribes on the borders of Arabia. There were also some Jewish tribes in western Arabia, particularly in the Hijaz and in Yemen. These were either Jewish tribes who had emigrated from Palestine, or Arab tribes who had adopted the Jewish religion.

Although Jews and Christians were few in number, their influence spread along the trade-routes. Many Arabs knew some of the Bible stories, as well as Jewish and Christian legends. There were also many poets. Because the poets all used the same language, a common Arabic language was spreading through the tribes. This helped to spread new ideas.

2. THE CALL OF MUHAMMAD

(a) *Mecca and Quraysh:* Muhammad was born in Mecca, near the west coast of Arabia. The great trade-routes between north and south Arabia passed through it, and lesser trade-routes between west and east also began in the neighbourhood. Mecca was an important town because it gave protection to caravans. The Bedouin in the Hijaz allowed the trading caravans to pass peacefully to and from Mecca. In return, the Meccans gave them special privileges when they visited their sanctuary.

The most important sanctuary at Mecca was called the Ka'ba. The name probably means 'squared tent or building'. It contained an idol known as Hubal, which was made out of red sandstone and shaped in the figure of a man. The worshippers threw their offerings into a pit at the foot of the image of Hubal. There were other sacred objects within the Ka'ba and in the area immediately surrounding it. One of these was a black stone meteorite. Muslim pilgrims still touch this stone when they visit Mecca.

The family which had charge of the Ka'ba was that of Qusayy, and they belonged to the Quraysh tribe. They were also responsible for feeding the pilgrims, and for the council chamber and war-banners.

(b) *Muhammad's early years:* Muhammad was born about AD 570. He belonged to the family of Qusayy. His father died before he was born and his mother Amina died when he was six years old. At first, Muhammad's grandfather, 'Abdu l-Muttalib, took care of him, and when 'Abdu l-Muttalib died, Muhammad's father's brother, Abu Talib. Muhammad spent much of his early childhood with a Bedouin foster-mother, Halima, in the desert country outside of Mecca. Muslim historians tell many stories about events which happened to him during his youth.

At the age of twenty-five Muhammad married Khadija, a wealthy widow, who was several years older than himself. He had acted as her agent on a journey to Syria and had conducted her affairs very well. His marriage gave Muhammad independence and leisure. It was a happy marriage, and Khadija bore Muhammad four daughters and two sons. All six children died in infancy except one daughter, Fatima.

(c) *Muhammad's Call:* Arab tradition says that Muhammad was upright, honest, and trustworthy. He was also a deeply religious person. He used to go away by himself to the lonely hills outside Mecca, and stayed there for many hours, sometimes for days at a time.

A tradition says 'Muhammad made West Arabia a sacred area, which only Muslims were allowed to enter.' 'The most sacred sanctuary was called the Ka'ba. Muslim pilgrims touch the black stone (set in its wall) when they visit Mecca' (pp. 197, 184).

Even today only Muslims are allowed to enter Mecca. The Indonesian pilgrims (above) are on their way to visit the Ka'ba, seen (below) through a window grill.

What is your own belief about the value of pilgrimage and touching 'sacred' objects? Is any Christian teaching based on this sort of custom?

His wife sometimes accompanied him. In this way, they escaped from the burning heat of the town.

During these times of loneliness and quietness, Muhammad thought much about men's dependence upon God. He felt very humble and thankful, and he was grieved because his neighbours did not realize their dependence upon God. He realized that judgement would come upon them because of their ingratitude, and he tried to awaken men to their peril. He expressed his thoughts in short vivid poems.

(I swear) by time that passes:
Men are in danger of loss,
Except those who believe and do good deeds,
Who encourage each other to be faithful and steadfast.   (Qur'an 103)

(I swear) by the snorting chargers (i.e. horses),
That strike fire with their hooves,
That gallop in the dawn,
That leave a trail in the dust behind them,
And pass through the midst (of their enemy) in a troop.
Surely Man is ungrateful to his Lord . . .
He is violent in his love for wealth.
Does he not know that on the day (of judgement) his Lord will be well aware of everything men do.
On that day the contents of the graves will be ransacked and all hidden thoughts and feelings brought to light.   (Qur'an 100)

Some of the poems are included in the Qur'an. They touch men's hearts and minds like a flame.

During this period, Muhammad became convinced that he was called by God to proclaim His message to the people of Mecca. On two separate occasions, he saw the vision of an angel who gave him particular words to recite. Muslims believe that these were words from the Heavenly Book which the angel Gabriel revealed to Muhammad. They were the first words of the Qur'an which were sent down to him. (They are now in the Qur'an: 96.1–8 and 74.1–10.) These visions gave Muhammad the courage to preach to his people. He believed that God had called him to be His spokesman, and he believed that God gave him the actual words of the messages which he had to preach.

We may note certain things about Muhammad's call to preach:

1. At first he was unwilling to preach. It was not a task which he sought for his own pleasure or benefit.

2. He was convinced that the messages which he preached were messages from God. He had not invented them. He was only responsible for passing on these messages to others (Qur'an 24.54).

3. At the beginning of his ministry, Muhammad was given visions of the heavenly messenger. They are described in the Qur'an (53.1-18).

4. When Muhammad received his visions, he felt strange physical sensations. For example, when the angel first appeared to him, he 'squeezed' him strongly until he was exhausted. Sometimes he fell to the ground as if sleep had overcome him. Sometimes he shivered or perspired freely. Sometimes he experienced the brightness of light. Similar sensations occurred all through his life, whenever he received revelations of passages from the Heavenly Book. Such sensations are often associated with 'ecstasy' (see p. 47).

3. MUHAMMAD'S PREACHING IN MECCA

(a) *The Qur'an:* Muhammad preached the messages which he received to the townspeople of Mecca. They were short and easy to remember. The lines of these poems rhymed with each other, and their language was strong and rhythmical. They excited those who heard them and made them think.

Muhammad knew that the Christians and Jews read sacred Scriptures at their services of worship, and that they recited them aloud. Because of this, Muhammad called Christians and Jews 'the people of the Book'. He taught the Muslims to recite his messages in a similar way. The number of messages which the Muslims recited in this way was always growing, because Muhammad kept receiving new messages to preach. The Muslims called them 'the recitation', or, in Arabic, *al-Qur'an*. They learnt them by heart so that they could recite them when they met to pray.

(b) *God:* Muhammad tried hard to make his hearers recognize the authority of the one living God. He tried to show them their obligations to Him. Muhammad called God 'Allah'. Arab scholars say that *Allah* is an abbreviated form of the Arabic word *al-'Ilah*. This means 'the (one and only) God', as distinct from all other gods and deities. Before Muhammad preached, some Arabs may have given this title to some of the more important pagan deities.

Some of the Arab poets had also used the name 'Allah' when they spoke about 'the only God', the great Creator of the universe. They were influenced by the Jewish and Christian teachings which were known in Arabia at that time. Other Arabs also were turning from the pagan practices which recognized many gods and goddesses. They were turning towards a *monotheistic* belief in one supreme Creator-god. ('Monotheism' means belief that Divinity is *one* living person.) These Arab thinkers were called *Hanifs*. Their beliefs and those of the Jews and Christians may have helped and encouraged Muhammad.

Muhammad, however, believed in the one living God because he had been called by Him. His beliefs came from his own heart. He knew that he lived in the presence of God. The following passages from the Qur'an speak about God as the Creator of the universe.

Will men not consider
how the camels have been created,
how the heavens have been lifted high,
how the mountains have been set up,
how the earth has been spread flat?
So warn them (about God): your task is to warn. (88.17–21)

Let man consider his food.
(God says): We poured out the rain abundantly,
Then We split the earth,
Then We made the grain to grow,
And vines and plants,
And olives and palms,
And tangled orchards,
And fruits and pastures,
As provision for you and your flocks. (80.24–32)

Muhammad also pointed towards the ways in which God had protected Mecca from attack by the Ethiopians (Qur'an 105).

(c) *Man:* Muhammad's messages often rebuked people for their failure to fulfil their duties to God.

May Man perish! How ungrateful he is.
From what does God create him?
He creates him from a drop (of semen) and fixes his (way of life).
He makes his way easy.
Then he causes him to die and be buried.
Then when he wishes he raises him to life again.
But all the same, Man has not fulfilled what God commanded. (80.16–23)

Man is insolent.
He thinks he is independent—
But he must return to God for judgement. (96.6–8)

Muhammad felt very deeply the importance of the Judgement Day. He believed that at the end all men must return to God and be judged by Him, 'the justest of judges' (95.8). In the Qur'an, God calls men to worship Him and to believe in the message of his prophets. He also calls them to practise good behaviour, and He rebukes those

who do not honour the orphan, who do not feed the poor, who devour the inheritance (of others), who love wealth to excess.

Such men will suffer punishment on the Day of Judgement: None punishes as God punishes, nor binds as He binds. (Compare 89.17–26)

Men are called to climb the steep path of duty: by freeing a slave, by feeding an orphan, by feeding the poor, by being steadfast and compassionate. (Compare 90.12–17)

God will say on the Judgement Day to those who do this:

Return to your Lord, well-pleased, well-pleasing,
Enter among my servants, enter my Garden. (89.28–30)

According to the Qur'an, good conduct means care for one's parents in old age, generosity to the poor and to travellers, modesty in the use of wealth and in conduct, fulfilment of one's duty to relations, the use of fair weights and measures, keeping one's agreement. Adultery and the killing of baby girls were forbidden. (The Arabs sometimes killed baby daughters to avoid the burden of caring for them.) (See 17.9–38.)

Muhammad taught his disciples to seek God's guidance in the whole of their lives. He taught them to do this by praying daily, and Muslims repeat the following prayer every time they pray. It is the opening chapter of the Qur'an, *al-Fatiha*.

Praise (be given) to God (Allah),
Lord of the Worlds.
The Merciful, the Compassionate,
The Ruler of the Judgement Day.
You we worship:
You we ask for help:
Guide us on the straight highway:
the highway of those to whom You have been gracious;
not the highway of those with whom You are angry,
nor of those who go astray.

(d) *Muhammad, God's Spokesman:* Muhammad preached as God's spokesman or prophet. He believed that God had called him to do this, and that God had given him messages which he was to proclaim in His name. When a person accepted the messages Muhammad preached, he also accepted the authority of Muhammad as God's messenger. In many parts of the Qur'an (e.g. 46.7–9) we read how Muhammad's opponents challenged his authority, and how he answered them.

Muhammad believed that the Scriptures of the Jews and Christians witnessed to the truth of the messages which God had given to him for the Arabs (see, e.g., 26.192–198). He was God's spokesman to the Arabs in the way in which other prophets had been His spokesmen to other peoples. The Qur'an contains stories about these other prophets. Sometimes these stories are like those in the Jewish and Christian Scriptures, sometimes they are different. In addition, the Qur'an records the stories of prophets who were known in the traditions of the Arabs. Examples are the stories of Abraham (21.51–73), and of Salih, who was the Arabian prophet to the people of Thamud (26.141–158).

(e) *Preaching and Persecution:* Muhammad preached at Mecca the messages which had been given to him, and he taught those who accepted his preaching to pray and to recite the Qur'an together. The first believers included Muhammad's wife Khadija, his adopted son Zayd, his cousin 'Ali, and his friend Abu Bakr. Many who followed him were poor people, and some were slaves.

At first, there was little opposition to Muhammad's preaching. But, after two or three years, opposition grew.

1. Muhammad's preaching annoyed the most important people in Mecca. He was not wealthy, and did not belong to the most influential of the families of Quraysh. The leaders of the town rejected his claims, and resented the fact that poor people and slaves were allowed to be equal members of the Islamic community.

2. The rich merchants were angry at his attacks on extravagance and wealth. They did not listen to his call for humility, generosity, and moderation. They were unwilling to recognize their dependence upon God and to submit themselves to the authority of His prophet.

3. Muhammad also preached against the lesser deities which the Meccans worshipped. He may not have done this at first, but it soon became part of his message. He denied the existence of all other deities except Allah, the one living God. (See 17.22–23, 39.)

For these reasons the townspeople of Mecca persecuted the little group of Muslims. Those who suffered most were the slaves and those who belonged to the less important families. Muhammad's neighbours insulted him: sometimes they piled rubbish at his door or threw it at him. Once some young men attacked him in the courtyard of the Ka'ba, but his friend Abu Bakr rescued him.

Muslims treasure the stories of the persecutions, and use them to teach children the virtues of courage and steadfastness. A favourite story is that about Bilal, a negro slave. He was one of the first Muslims, and suffered terrible persecution. On one occasion his tormentors stretched him out on the burning sand, and put a great stone on his chest. He remained true to his faith, and Abu Bakr purchased him and set him free. Bilal served the Muslim community by giving the call to prayer (see p. 213), and he accompanied Muhammad on his campaigns.

The Meccans persecuted the Muslims for some years. On two

occasions, groups of Muslims sought refuge in Ethiopia where the king was a Christian, and he allowed them to practise their religion. At Mecca, the clan of Muhammad's family, the Hashimites, were confined within their own quarter of the town for more than one year. Other people in Mecca refused to buy or sell to them, or to make marriage contracts with them. Not all the Hashimites were Muslims, but they still suffered in this way.

(f) *Events leading to the Hijra:* Khadija, Muhammad's first wife, died at the end of AD 619, and his uncle, Abu Talib, died shortly afterwards. Although Abu Talib never became a Muslim, he had protected Muhammad. After his death, Muhammad was in greater danger from his enemies. The Muslim community continued to grow in numbers, but it seemed obvious that Islam would never triumph in Mecca if things remained as they were. Muhammad, therefore, began to look for support outside the town.

At the beginning of AD 620, Muhammad visited Ta'if to seek help. Ta'if was a town forty miles south of Mecca. The countryside round was very fertile, and Ta'if was an important rival to Mecca in trade. The leaders of the city refused to accept Muhammad's appeal for help. They also refused to recognize him as a prophet. After a stay of ten days, the common people drove him from the town. They hooted and threw stones at him. Muhammad was nearly killed, and only escaped with difficulty.

During these months Muhammad suffered many doubts and temptations, but he was encouraged by visions, and by receiving new messages from God. Two of these visions were especially important:

1. *The vision at Nakhla:* On his way back from Ta'if, Muhammad spent the night at a place called Nakhla. Near this place was the sanctuary of the pagan deity called al-'Uzza, which was marked by a sacred stone and a grove of trees.

The Arabs associated such places with beings whom they called *jinn.* They believed that the *jinn* were spirit-demons who lived in the desert, and that they were responsible for all kinds of things and happenings which could not be explained in any other way.

At Nakhla, Muhammad saw a vision. He saw a company of *jinn* listening to the Qur'an and accepting its authority. The vision encouraged him to believe that Islam would triumph in the end despite its present difficulties (46.29–31 and 72).

2. *The Heavenly Journey:* chapter 17, verse 1, of the Qur'an mentions another vision:

May He be praised who took his servant by night from the Holy Mosque to the Furthest Mosque, whose surroundings We have blessed.

God did this in order to show him some of His signs. God truly is the all-Hearing, the all-Seeing.

Muslims believe that this verse refers to a vision in which Muhammad visited Heaven and, in particular, 'the Furthest Mosque' in which angels meet to worship God. In later years the Umayyad rulers called the mosque in Jerusalem 'the Furthest Mosque', *al-Masjid al-Aqsa.*

These visions encouraged Muhammed to continue his work, but his position in Mecca remained difficult. The Muslims needed greater freedom to practise their religion. The opportunity to do this came when Muhammed was invited to Medina.

STUDY SUGGESTIONS

WORD STUDY

1. 'The Arabs were turning to a monotheistic belief' (p. 187). What is 'monotheism'?
2. What is the meaning of the word 'Muslim'?

REVIEW OF CONTENT

3. (a) Why did Muhammad call both Jews and Christians 'the people of the Book'?
   (b) What is the book called which contains all Muhammad's own teaching?
4. Who or what were the following?
   Oases Bedouin *Hanifs* the Ka'ba
5. (a) When and where was Muhammad born?
   (b) What sort of family did he belong to?
   (c) In what two chief ways was Muhammad's personal life different from that of Jesus?
6. In what ways was the religion of the Arabs before Muhammad like that of the Maori (see chapter 5)?
7. In what ways was the preaching of Muhammad in Mecca (see pp. 187–190) like the teaching of the Jewish rabbis (see pp. 119, 120)? Write down side by side those sayings which are almost the same in both messages.
8. Some of the Arab poets were influenced by Jewish and Christian teachings, which led them to believe in one supreme God. What was special about the way in which Muhammad came to believe in God?
9. 'Muhammad preached as God's spokesman' (p. 189).
   (a) Which of the Jewish religious leaders preached in this way?
   (b) How did the people of Mecca receive Muhammad's preaching?
10. (a) Describe, in your own words, the vision which Muhammed saw at Nakhla.
    (b) What effect did this vision have on him?

11. Compare Muhammad's call, with those of: (a) Moses (see Exod. 3.1—4.20); (b) Amos (see Amos 7.12–15); and (c) Jeremiah (see Jer. 1 and 20.7–11).
12. Compare Muhammad's message to people to care for one another, with God's Law for the Israelites as recorded in Leviticus 19.11–18.

DISCUSSION AND RESEARCH

13. Why is it more difficult for rich and important people to accept the preaching of a prophet like Muhammad (or Amos), than it is for poor and humble people?
14. Do you find the story of Muhammad during his years at Mecca an attractive one? If so, what are the features of his work there which attract you?

A. MUHAMMAD THE APOSTLE OF GOD (2)

4. MUHAMMAD'S RULE IN MEDINA

(a) *The Hijra:* The town of Medina was on the west coast trade-route, about three hundred miles north of Mecca. It contained a number of oases, and covered many miles of territory. Two Arab tribes lived in Medina, the Aws and the Khazraj; they were related to each other. Jewish tribes also lived there, particularly Qurayza, al-Nadir, and Qaynuqa'. The old name of the city was Yathrib, and al-Madina means 'the city (of the Prophet)'.

Muhammad first met Arabs from Medina at one of the annual pilgrimages to Mecca. Perhaps some of them had already heard about his activities. At the pilgrimage in AD 621, a few people from Medina promised that they would support Muhammad. A few months later Muhammad sent Mus'ab to Medina to teach them the Qur'an and how to pray.

At the pilgrimage in AD 622, a larger group of Medinans met Muhammad in secret by night. Among them were twelve headmen representing the sub-tribes of the Aws and Khazraj. The Medinans took Muhammad under their protection, and promised to defend him with their lives. They also promised to worship no other god except Allah. During the next few months, numbers of Muslims made their way from Mecca to Medina. In September, Muhammad himself, accompanied by Abu Bakr, succeeded in escaping from the Meccans who were searching for him, and joined the Muslim community at Medina. This journey is known as the *Hijra* (Arabic for 'migration') and Muslims date their years from it. AD 1974 is the Muslim year 1394.

Some of the Medinans who invited Muhammad to their city did

so because they accepted his message. They became sincere Muslims even before Muhammad came to their town. Perhaps they were influenced by the Jews in Medina, and by Muhammad's claims that he preached to the Arabs the same religion which the Jews followed.

Other Medinans invited Muhammad because they hoped he would settle the quarrel between the Aws and Khazraj. These two tribes were always fighting, and needed the help of a third party to maintain peace between them.

In Arabia, the 'holy families' who took care of the sanctuaries were often responsible for this kind of peace-making. Muhammad belonged to the holy family associated with the Ka'ba at Mecca, but he had acted independently, and was becoming well-known as a preacher and religious teacher. He was also distantly related to the tribes at Medina through his mother. It was natural, therefore, for the Medinans to promise their support to Muhammad, and invite him to come to Medina to act as mediator between them.

Soon after his arrival in Medina, Muhammad negotiated agreements between the different groups of people living in the oases. These included the Muslims from Mecca, the Arab tribesmen of Medina, and the Jews. The agreements clearly stated the obligations of each group towards the others. All the groups accepted Muhammad as the person who should decide in disputes between them. He could do this because they accepted him as God's representative. They also declared that Medina was an area set apart for God, and forbade fighting and bloodshed within it.

By these agreements, Muhammad built a new kind of community among the Arabs. It has remained an ideal for Islamic communities ever since. The worship of God was at the centre of the life of the community, through the recitation of the Qur'an and the practice of prayer, fasting, and almsgiving. The chosen leader was Muhammad, the apostle and spokesman of God.

(b) *Muhammad, Prophet and Chosen Messenger:* Muhammad was both *prophet* and *chosen messenger*.

From the beginning the Qur'an included lists of the 'prophets', and, with one exception, they are all people who are mentioned in the Old or New Testaments. One list is the following: 'We inspired you (Muhammad) as we inspired Noah and the prophets after him. And as We inspired Abraham, and Ishmael, and Isaac, and Jacob, and the Tribes, and Jesus, and Job, and Jonah, and Aaron, and Solomon; and We gave David the Psalms' (4.163). In contrast with these Muhammad is called 'the Gentile prophet' (7.157–158).

Another title used in the Qur'an is 'chosen messenger' or 'apostle'. Nine people are given this title in the Qur'an, and each one was sent to a different community. The 'apostles' were more important than the prophets, and a people 'had no argument against God after their chosen messenger had preached to them' (4.165).

Muhammad himself accepted both titles. 'Say: "O people, I am the apostle of God to you all: the apostle of Him to whom belongs the sovereignty over Heaven and Earth. There is no god except Him. He makes alive, and He makes to die. So believe in God and His apostle, the Gentile prophet, who believes in God and His words. Follow him: perhaps you will be rightly guided" ' (7.158).

The Muslims respected Muhammad very highly. They brought young children to him, for him to bless them. They used his washing water as 'holy water'. They asked for his prayers in times of sickness. They believed that his prayers could bring rain in times of drought.

(c) *The Completion of the Qur'an:* Muslims believe that the whole Qur'an is an Arabic copy of the Heavenly Book which was written in Heaven before the creation of the world. But the whole Qur'an was not given to Muhammad at one time: it was revealed to him bit by bit all through the twenty and more years of his ministry, on many separate occasions.

The passages which were revealed to Muhammad at Medina are different in style and length from those which were revealed to him at Mecca; they refer to a number of different subjects:

1. Some passages refer to the *battles, pilgrimages, and other happenings* in which Muhammad and the Muslims took part. These passages were revealed in order to guide them in these changing and sometimes difficult circumstances, and they encouraged Muhammad to believe that he was acting in the name of God. The reader can only understand these passages easily if he knows the events to which they refer.

2. Some passages narrate the *stories of other prophets and apostles.* They warn the Arabs to pay attention to Muhammad.

3. Some passages explain the *relationship between Islam and other religions*, those of the Jews and Christians. (See also p. 189.)

When Muhammad first went to Medina, he faced towards Jerusalem when he prayed, and he adopted other Jewish customs. The Jews in Medina, however, rejected his claim to be a prophet, and argued with him about his version of Old Testament stories. Passages in the Qur'an refer to these controversies (e.g. 4.44–47).

Christians are also mentioned in the Qur'an. At first, they were said to be 'the nearest in love to the believers' (in contrast to the Jews and the pagans), but later they also were rebuked, and, in particular, for their beliefs about Christ. Towards the end of his life, Muhammad was commanded to fight against the Jews and Christians until they submitted to the authority of the Muslims and paid tribute to them (5.82–86; 9.29).

4. Some passages gave directions to guide the Muslim community in

matters of *behaviour*. Some dealt with religious behaviour, such as prayer and conduct on the pilgrimage to Mecca. Some dealt with social responsibility, and the practice of almsgiving. The payment of interest on loans was forbidden. Some laid down the proper punishment for various types of crime, and prohibited drinking wine and acts of immorality. Other passages gave guidance on questions of marriage, divorce, and the settlement of inheritance after a death. Regulations were made for the conduct of trade and commerce. Many of these problems needed to be dealt with because Islam had replaced the old tribal customs and rules with a new loyalty to the community of Islam.

5. THE CONQUEST OF ARABIA

Muhammad lived in Medina for ten years, from the Hijra in AD 622 till his death in AD 632. During this time, the practice of Islam spread all over Arabia. This did not happen easily, but was the result of constant struggle and determination on the part of Muhammad. He made his efforts in four directions: (1) within Medina, (2) to Mecca, (3) to the Arab tribes, (4) outside Arabia.

(a) *Medina:* When Muhammad first came to Medina, he had few resources with which to support those who had come with him from Mecca. He was entirely dependent on the help of those people in Medina who had become Muslims.

Muhammad had hoped for support from the Jewish tribes. The Muslims in Medina even faced towards Jerusalem when they prayed, and they adopted for a time the Jewish fast in the month of 'Ashura. Muhammad was disappointed, however, when the Jews refused to recognize him as a prophet. They became more and more hostile towards him. As a result, Muhammad changed his attitude towards them, and later expelled them from Medina.

Muhammad also extended his authority over those Arabs in Medina who were unbelievers at the time of the Hijra. As time passed, they accepted Islam, for one reason or another.

(b) *Mecca:* After the Hijra, Muhammad set out to win control of Mecca and the trade-routes. At first, Muhammad's forces and resources were less than those of the Meccans, who had the help of some Bedouin tribes. The two sides kept sending small parties of men to spy on each other, and there were many small fights and raids. There were also three big battles, in which Muhammad took part and fought bravely. Only the first, the battle of Badr, was a complete success for the Muslims.

In AD 630, Muhammad entered Mecca at the head of his army. There was hardly any opposition. The Muslims broke the idols in the

Ka'ba in pieces, and the Meccans became Muslims. In this way Muhammad gained control of west Arabia with its trade-routes. A tradition says that Muhammad made the whole of this area a sacred area into which only Muslims were allowed to enter.

(c) *The Arab Tribes:* After the conquest of Mecca, Muhammad's influence spread rapidly. Tribes sent delegations to him from all over Arabia. Their aim was to enter into good relationships with the one who had control over the trade-routes. Muhammad made terms with them. In each case, he insisted that they should perform the prayers and pay the alms-tax to Medina. On some he imposed other taxes, such as a stated part of the year's crops or other produce. He also commanded the destruction of idols.

Muhammad also sent expeditions against some of the more important tribes which were slow in coming to terms with him. Sometimes the Muslims were successful without fighting. At other times there was fighting, and some tribes fought bravely to prevent the destruction of their images and sanctuaries.

6. FOUNDATION OF A WORLD RELIGION

Towards the end of his life, Muhammad began to reach out towards territories beyond the borders of Arabia. The town of Aylah at the northern end of the Gulf of Aqaba paid tribute, and others in the south of Jordan also did so. Muhammad also sent small expeditions against the Byzantine territories in this area. If the tribes and towns in this area chose to remain Christian or Jewish he compelled them to pay tribute. This was much heavier than the alms-tax which he imposed on those who became Muslims. In doing this, Muhammad was acting in accordance with the command given in the Qur'an in 9.29. Muhammad also tried to spread Islam towards the north-east of Arabia and the Persian empire.

Muhammad died in AD 632, eleven Muslim years after the Hijra. During the years at Medina he had created the foundations of the great religion which we know as Islam. He did this in several ways.

1. He taught a way of prayer and worship which people of all kinds and all communities are able to understand, and, if they wish, to practise.

2. He was the instrument by which the Qur'an, the word of God, was revealed to his followers.

3. He brought peace among many of the tribes in Arabia through his authority as the Apostle of God. His treaties began with the words, 'In the name of God and his chosen messenger.' Thus he made it possible for his successors to lead Arab-Muslim armies into the lands of the Byzantine and Persian empires.

4. He taught a pattern of behaviour which has become the basis of law in Islamic communities. It was truly Arabian in origin and suited the customs of Mecca and Medina. It is not completely adequate for modern society (see pp. 211, 212), but it is moderate and, in some important matters, humane.

STUDY SUGGESTIONS

WORD STUDY

1. (a) What is the meaning of the Arabic word *Hijra*? For what event in the history of Islam is it used?
   (b) What is the origin of the name *Medina*, and why was this name given to the city of Yathrib?
2. (a) What is the meaning of the word *Qur'an*?
   (b) Why was this name given to the Muslim Scriptures?

REVIEW OF CONTENT

3. (a) For what reason and in what year did Muhammad move from Mecca to Medina?
   (b) How long did he live there?
4. What were the agreements which Muhammad negotiated in Medina, and what influence have they had on Muslim communities since that time?
5. (a) Explain the statement (p. 194) that 'Muhammad was both *prophet* and *chosen messenger*'.
   (b) Give some examples of ways in which Muslims showed their respect for Muhammad, during his lifetime.
6. (a) What do Muslims believe about the origin of the Qur'an?
   (b) What four different sorts of subjects do the passages which were revealed to Muhammad at Medina deal with?
7. Describe the relationship between Muhammad and (a) the Jews, and (b) unbelieving Arabs, in Medina.
8. For what chief reasons did Muhammad think it important to win control of Mecca?
9. (a) In what four chief ways did Muhammad 'create the foundations of the great religion which we know as Islam' (p. 197)?
   (b) Which of these ways were like the ways in which Jesus can be said to have 'created the foundations' of Christianity?
   (c) In what chief ways was Muhammad's life unlike that of Jesus?

BIBLE STUDY

10. Read Exodus 20.21—23.12. Compare this passage with numbered para. 4 on pp. 195–196, which lists matters of behaviour on which the Qur'an gave guidance for the Muslim community at Medina.

(a) Which verses in the Exodus passage contain laws giving guidance to the Jews on these same matters?

(b) Can you see any similarity between the circumstances in which this sort of guidance was given to the Muslims and to the Jews?

DISCUSSION AND RESEARCH

11. What difference do you notice between the way in which Muhammad worked in Mecca and the way in which he worked in Medina?

12. 'Muhammad made it possible for his successors to lead Arab-Muslim armies into the lands of the Byzantine and Persian empires' (p. 197).

(a) Compare the ways in which Muhammad and his Successors first spread Islam with the ways in which the apostles first spread Christianity.

(b) What do you know of other religions whose leaders made use of political or military power to spread their influence?

(c) Is it always wrong to use such methods? Are there circumstances in which it is right to do so?

13. Muhammad taught a pattern of behaviour which 'is not completely adequate for modern society' (p. 198).

Do you think that any pattern of behaviour taught more than 1,000 years ago can be 'completely adequate' for modern society? In what ways is it likely to be inadequate? What, if anything, can make it adequate?

B. ISLAM IN THE WORLD

1. THE ARAB EMPIRES

Muhammad died in AD 632. His friend Abu Bakr succeeded him. Abu Bakr was not a *prophet* nor was he an *apostle*. His task was simply to continue leading the Muslim community in the way which had been revealed in the Qur'an and which Muhammad had taught.

Abu Bakr continued the policy which Muhammad had begun, and sent armies into Syria and Iraq. They were victorious almost everywhere. In the years between AD 634 and 643, they defeated large Byzantine and Persian armies and conquered Syria, Iraq, Persia, and Egypt.

The local people in Syria and Egypt welcomed the Arab armies. Although they were Christians, they were hostile to their Byzantine rulers, who had treated them badly.

The Arab commanders appointed Muslim governors in the important cities. These governors ruled their territories with the help of the subordinate officials who had previously served the Byzantines or Persians. They used the taxes to pay the Arab armies.

It is difficult to be certain about the reasons why such large Arab armies came out of Arabia at this time. Some say that they did so because they felt called to spread the faith of Islam in all the world. Others say that they did so because the Arabs needed to find more fertile land on which to settle and to pasture their flocks. In fact, Arab tribes have been forced out of Arabia in search of land and food all through the centuries. The difference between the armies of the first Muslims and the ordinary movements of Arab tribes is that the Arab armies were greater in number and that their efforts were much more warlike and energetic. It was Islam which made them so, and which gave them courage and determination. The Arab conquerors themselves believed that they were fighting for Islam, and they were willing to give up their lives in doing so.

After the conquests in Egypt, Syria, and Persia, the Arab commanders continued to send expeditions both towards the west and the east. By AD 720, one hundred years after the death of Muhammad, the following countries had become parts of the one Arab empire: Spain, Morocco, Algeria, Tunis, Libya, Egypt, Palestine, Lebanon, Syria, Iraq, Iran, Afghanistan, parts of Pakistan, and certain areas in the south of the Soviet Union. (We give their modern names so that the boundaries of this great empire can be followed in an atlas.)

The one supreme ruler of this vast Empire was called the 'Successor' of the Prophet Muhammad. The Arabic word for 'successor' was *khalif*. The *khalifs* all belonged to the Quraysh tribe and were kinsmen of Muhammad. The first four 'righteous khalifs' were elected by the Muslim community. After them the khalifs kept the power in their own families. From AD 661 to 750, the Umayyad family ruled in Damascus. The 'Abbasids then defeated the Umayyads and moved the capital to Baghdad in Iraq. 'Abbasid rule came to an end in 1258. Since that time Muslims have never had a single ruler who could be called the one 'successor' to Muhammad. Individuals, however, have often claimed the title. Some rulers even today claim to be descended from the Prophet: among them are King Husayn of Jordan, and the Aga Khan.

The Arab empire continued as one empire for the first hundred years of the 'Abbasid khalifs, and for much longer in the provinces near to Iraq. This Muslim empire was a wonderful achievement, and shows that Islam provides a good foundation on which many different countries may be united in a strong and civilized society.

2. ISLAMIC KINGDOMS

The 'Abbasids removed the capital of the empire to Baghdad in AD 762. Even before then the unity of the empire had been broken. In AD 755 an Umayyad prince, 'Abdu l-Rahman, fled to Spain and established an Umayyad kingdom independent of the 'Abbasid Khalif. During the next few centuries, the Muslim empire continued to break up into separate states. The last 'Abbasid Khalif was killed in AD 1258. He was only a figurehead and, for centuries before then, other rulers had held the real power.

The empire broke up for several reasons:

1. The rulers of the more distant provinces claimed independence of the Khalif.

2. The non-Arab peoples of the empire resented Arab rule.

3. Disputes occurred about religious beliefs and practice. The different sects often tried to settle these disputes by fighting, or by rebellion.

4. Turkish tribes from Central Asia invaded the eastern parts of the empire from about AD 970 onwards. Mongol tribes followed them from about AD 1220 onwards.

Thus from about AD 850 onwards, the story of Islam is told in the histories of many different kingdoms. It is not one story but the stories of many different peoples and of many great civilizations. Among the most important kingdoms were:

The Kingdom of the *Umayyads in Spain* which lasted in some parts until AD 1492;

The Kingdom of the *Fatimids in Egypt* who founded Cairo in AD 969, and that of their successors the *Mamlukes*;

The Kingdom of the *Moghul emperors in India*, from about AD 1500–1700;

The Empire of the *Ottoman Turks*, who ruled almost the *whole Arabic-speaking world* from their capital Constantinople, from about AD 1500 until 1918.

3. THE SPREAD OF ISLAM

Islam has, from the beginning, been closely linked with the Arabs. But it has also spread far beyond the boundaries of the Arab empires.

Three different kinds of people have been responsible for taking Islam to other countries: (1) traders, (2) teachers, and (3) rulers.

1. *Traders and Merchants:* Muslim traders travelled from the Arab empires to India, China, and south-east Asia by land and sea. Others travelled southwards into Africa across the Sahara deserts, up the Nile, or by the Red Sea to the coasts of East Africa. Wherever Muslims went they practised Islam. They kept the religious law and performed the prayers. Thus they spread Islam among their servants and clients. If they married non-Muslims they spread Islam among their wives' families and relations. If there were a number of Muslim traders in one place they became a Muslim community, and set up their own mosques and schools.

2. *Teachers and Holy Men:* The traders often asked for help and

advice from Muslim teachers and holy men. They interpreted the Law to them, and presided at religious ceremonies. They also taught their children. When local rulers became Muslims, they also used the services of Muslim teachers. Such teachers often came from Arabia, and, in south-east Asia, from India-Pakistan.

3. *Muslim Rulers*: Sometimes a local ruler who had become a Muslim extended his authority over neighbouring territories. As a result other tribes became Muslim. Sometimes such an effort was called a *jihad*, or war undertaken for the spread of Islam (see p. 216).

Through these efforts of traders, teachers, and rulers, Islam spread in three main directions: southwards, northwards, and eastwards.

(a) *Southwards into Africa;* The 'Sudan belt' stretches across Africa from Senegal and Guinea in the west to the Republic of the Sudan in the east. From the earliest times Muslim traders have carried Islam into this part of Africa, and between 1700 and 1900 there were strong Islamic kingdoms in this area. Islam has also come into Africa across the Red Sea and from the east coast.

(b) *Northwards into eastern Europe:* Constantinople was the capital of the Byzantine empire (see p. 168). The Muslim Turks captured it in AD 1453. The Turks spread Islam into eastern Europe.

(c) *Eastwards into Asia:* The Umayyad conquests established Muslim rulers in provinces of what are now Afghanistan and Pakistan. During the centuries which followed, their successors spread Islam throughout north India, along the great valley of the Ganges river. The mountains to the south of the two great rivers, the Indus and the Ganges, prevented the spread of Islam into central and southern India.

Muslim traders travelled in search of goods far into south-east Asia and China. Their efforts were supported by Muslim teachers, and, at a later period, by local rulers who had become Muslims. The growth was greatest between AD 1400 and 1600, and it has continued until modern times. In Malaysia, Islam was greatly strengthened by British rule from about AD 1870 till independence in 1963.

4. ISLAMIC CIVILIZATION

To be a Muslim, a person must keep the Law and perform the Prayer. The Prayer includes recitation of the Qur'an. From the beginning, therefore, Muslims have believed reading and writing to be important, and Muslim states and communities have encouraged education. The mosque and the school have always been the most important buildings in a Muslim community, providing for the study of the Qur'an and of Islam. At the same time, the indigenous peoples of the countries which the Arabs conquered possessed great treasures of literature and of knowledge, and they shared these with their Arab conquerors.

Thus Islamic civilization has been built on three main foundations:

'The mosque and the school have always been the most important buildings in a Muslim community. Islamic civilization enriches the life of Muslim peoples' (p. 202).

In Brunei the Sultan, accompanied by distinguished visitors from abroad, arrives for the opening of a new mosque, built beside an artificial lake to enhance its beauty.

List some of the ways in which religion has enriched and beautified your country.

(1) the religion of Islam which came out of Arabia, (2) the Arabic language and poetry, and (3) the older civilizations of the countries which the Arabs conquered. These were built mainly on the old Greek and Persian civilizations and on Christianity.

During the reigns of the first 'Abbasid Khalifs (AD *c.* 750–900), the one Khalif in Baghdad ruled almost the whole Islamic world. There was great prosperity, and Muslim scholars were free to travel from place to place. Education was available for very many people in all kinds of ways and many books of all kinds were written. A rich and varied culture was built on the foundations listed above.

During the thousand years since the 'Abbasid empire, there have been periods when Islamic civilization has appeared to be tired and stale. There have been other times when there has been a growth of new life. But Islamic civilization remains. It is constantly growing. It has enriched the life of Muslim peoples through the centuries, and has helped them to build stable and humane societies. It enriches them still.

5. MUSLIMS IN THE TWENTIETH CENTURY

Today, Muslims are divided into four main groups:

1. *The Arab Countries:* Most of the people who live in these countries are Muslims, and they hold the place of honour in the Islamic world-community. There are, however, large Christian minorities in Egypt, Jordan, Syria, and Iraq, and smaller groups in other countries. In Lebanon, half of the people are Christians.

2. *The Islamic Nations of Southern Asia:* The Islamic nations of southern Asia speak their own languages, and each of them follows its own independent policy. Modern industry and communications are making very great changes.

The most important of these countries are:

Turkey: 28,000,000 Muslims. Since 1924 Turkey has been a republic organized in secular and European ways. For example, people wear European clothing; Turkish is written in Roman instead of Arabic letters; the Government has reduced the grants which it formerly made to Muslim preachers and mosques.

Iran: 20,000,000 Muslims. Iran has a long history reaching back to the days of Cyrus who died in 530 BC. This long history has always made the Persians a little independent of the main stream of Islam. Most Muslims in Persia are Shi'ites not Sunnis (see pp. 216, 217).

Afghanistan: 14,000,000 Muslims. This is a country which is almost entirely Muslim. It is a very mountainous country, and has been isolated from other countries until recent times.

Pakistan: 44,000,000 Muslims. Pakistan is one of the largest Muslim states in the world. It combines the old Islamic traditions, which reach back to the Arab conquests, with modern industry and development. The main language is Urdu.

Bangladesh: 41,000,000 Muslims. Bangladesh became independent of Pakistan in 1971. Most of its people are peasant farmers, working in the fertile lands of the Ganges delta.

Indonesia: 84,000,000 Muslims. Most people who live in Indonesia are Muslims. Many, however, continue to practise pagan customs together with Islam. Muslim teachers from Arabia and Egypt have been active in recent years, and Islam is gaining a greater hold on the people in many areas. In some areas, however, many Muslims have become Christians.

In these nation-states of southern Asia, Islam is the main religion. It teaches people what to believe about God and the world. It gives them a way of life to rule their behaviour and customs. Islam, however, does not govern the policy of these nations. A person is a Turk, or a Persian, or a Pakistani, and this is often as important to him as being a Muslim.

3. *Africa:* Many African countries south of the Sahara desert have large Muslim communities. In some of them the majority of the people are now Muslims: e.g. Senegal, Mali, Northern Nigeria, Niger, Chad, the Republic of the Sudan, Somalia. In others, there are large numbers of Muslims, but they are not a majority of the population, e.g. Cameroun, Central African Republic, Ethiopia, Kenya, Tanzania, Uganda.

We may say certain things about Islam in these African countries:

(a) Many people in these countries still follow local religions. Both Christianity and Islam are preaching to them. In some areas, Muslims are still growing in number, especially in the towns.

(b) In many places Islam has only a small hold upon people's beliefs and behaviour. Where people have become Muslims in recent times, they often continue to practise traditional customs as well as Islam.

(c) Most African countries have only recently gained their independence. In the work of development and in government, Christians and Muslims work side by side. Their main aim is to build their country, and they do not treat the difference of religion as very important. Islam is, therefore, becoming a matter for personal choice and belief. In some places it is no longer a national or tribal matter.

4. *Muslim Minority Groups in Asia and Eastern Europe:* There are large communities of Muslims living in countries which do not now have Muslim governments, e.g.:

India: 48,000,000 Muslims. The President of India elected in 1967, Zakir Husayn, is a Muslim.

China: 25,000,000 Muslims. The exact numbers are difficult to obtain.

Soviet Russia: 25,000,000 Muslims. These are mostly in the southern provinces. Other large groups are in Yugoslavia, Albania, Poland, and Hungary.

In *Western Europe and America* small groups of Muslims live in many different countries. Some are immigrants who have come from North Africa (to France), Pakistan and India (to Britain), and Indonesia (to Holland). Other groups are university teachers and students, diplomats, and business men. In the United States a large group of negroes have adopted Islam. They call themselves the Black Muslims.

STUDY SUGGESTIONS

WORD STUDY

1. (a) What is the meaning of the Arabic word *Khalif*?
   (b) Who were the Khalifs?

REVIEW OF CONTENT

2. 'Abu Bakr continued the policy which Muhammad had begun' (p. 199).
   (a) What was this policy?
   (b) Who was Abu Bakr, and did his policy develop as he intended?
3. For what chief reasons did Arab armies invade other countries during and after the lifetime of Muhammad?
4. Who were the 'Abbasids and the Umayyads, and what part did they play in the history of Islam?
5. (a) For what reasons did the Islamic empire eventually break up into separate kingdoms?
   (b) Name four of these kingdoms, and say where they were and how long they lasted.
6. What three sorts of people chiefly help to spread Islam beyond the Arab lands?
7. Name two present-day rulers who claim to be directly descended from Muhammad.
8. (a) Into what four main areas are Muslim nations and groups divided today?
   (b) What are the chief differences between them, besides differences of geography?
   (c) Approximately what is the total Muslim population of the world?

DISCUSSION AND RESEARCH

9. Draw a rough map to show the countries which had become part of the Arab empire by AD 720.
10. 'Islam gave the Arab countries courage and determination' (p. 200). What was the reason for this? Which sort of motives are most

likely to make armies fight energetically: religious ones, political ones, or economic ones? Give examples from history to support your answer.

11. On what three foundations has Islamic civilization been built? Compare these with the foundations on which other civilizations known to you have been built.

12. If there are any Muslims in your country, find out how Islam was first brought in, and what sort of people brought it.

13. What is the attitude towards Muslims of other groups in your country? Do Muslims suffer in any way because of their religion?

C. THE TEACHINGS OF ISLAM

There are many millions of Muslims in the world. They do not all believe exactly the same things about God and the world. Just as in other religions, there are differences of opinion between different groups. Some Muslims are well educated in their faith, others have only a little knowledge of it. But most of them share the same basic beliefs about God and the world.

1. WHAT MUSLIMS BELIEVE ABOUT GOD

The Muslim creed (*shahada* in Arabic) begins with the words, 'There is no god except *Allah*'. Allah means 'the one and only God' (see p. 187).

(a) *The Uniqueness of God:* God is unique. He is different from all created things and all creatures. Nothing resembles God. According to Muslim teaching, no thing or person can be associated with Him, or is equal to Him or like Him.

He is God, One,
God the everlasting refuge (or, God is eternal).
He did not beget, nor was He begotten.
No one is equal to Him. (112)

The greatest sin in Islam is 'to associate a partner' with God. It is called *shirk*.

(b) *The Attributes of God:* God is different from all creatures, but it is possible to make certain statements about Him in His relationship with the world; the Qur'an supports these statements:

1. God lives eternally, without beginning or ending. He lives independently of the universe.

2. God knows all things, past, present, and future.

3. God can do all things.

4. All things exist as they are by the will of God.

5. God hears all sounds; yet He has no ear as men have.

6. God sees all things (even the steps of a black ant on a black stone on a dark night!); yet He has no eye as men have.

7. God communicates with men.

There has been much discussion in Muslim theology about these seven attributes. Most Muslims are content to state them as facts without trying to explain *how* the eternal God 'sees' or 'hears', etc.

(c) *The Most Beautiful Names:* Muslims express their beliefs about God by using certain names when speaking about Him. Many of these names are mentioned in the Qur'an. The following examples illustrate the seven attributes of God which are listed above.

1. The One, the Real, the Living, the Secure, the First, the Last.

2. The Wise, the Knower, the One who comprehends (everything).

3. The Great, the Powerful, the Strong, the Mighty.

4. The Agent, the Beginner, the Creator, the King, the Sovereign, the Governor.

5. The Hearer, the Answerer (of prayer).

6. The Watcher, the See-er.

7. The Giver, the Merciful, the Compassionate, the Forgiver, the Generous, the Loving.

2. WHAT MUSLIMS BELIEVE ABOUT THE UNIVERSE

Muhammad preached Islam in Arabia at a time when people knew little about the structure of the universe. The great theologians and writers of past centuries shared the same world-view. Thus both the Qur'an and Muslim theological books describe the universe in traditional, not scientific, ways. They suggest that Heaven is a place beyond the skies in which the planets move. They describe it as a place of cool gardens, with rivers and fruit-trees, in which the blessed will be at rest eternally (47.15; 56.15–22).

Hell also has a place in the Islamic world-view. It is a place of punishment and contains a number of different areas: the wicked are sent to that part of Hell which is suitable for them.

3. WHAT MUSLIMS BELIEVE ABOUT HUMAN BEINGS

Muslims believe that God appointed human beings to be His agents on earth, and gave them the earth with all its resources:

He gave you the earth to live in. He made paths for you in it so that you might be guided aright. He gave you rain from heaven in proper measure, and made a dead land live again. . . . He created all living things, male and female. He gave you ships and beasts to ride upon. When you ride them, then you may recall the graciousness of your Lord and say: 'Praise to Him who gave us these to use, though we were not fit for them: surely we turn to our Lord' (43.10–14).

Because God created them and because God gave them the earth to live in, human beings are the servants of God. A human being can have no higher dignity than to be 'a servant of God', *'abdu llah*. This was a title which Muhammad was proud to use; he was called this when he received the Qur'an and when he was raised to heaven (53.10 and 17.1). Most Muslim families have members whose names are made up of a word for 'servant' like *'abd*, and one of the divine names: e.g. 'Abdullah, 'Abdu l-Baqi, 'Abdu l-Hamid. 'The saints are those who put on the glorious clothes of a servant.'

The Qur'an tells how Satan deceived Adam and his wife. Because of this they were driven out of the Garden. But God in His mercy gave guidance to men. (See 2.30–39.)

4. WHAT MUSLIMS BELIEVE ABOUT REVELATION

God has given to men the guidance which He promised to give.

(a) *Through the natural world:* Because God created the world, men may learn from it about Him. In the Qur'an the good things of the natural world are called 'signs' of God's bounty and mercy (30.46–50).

Similarly men may learn about God from the affairs of human history: He controls these also.

(b) *Through His angels:* The angels are the messengers of God. He sends them to carry out His will. They normally work unseen, and are the constant companions of men. They are sexless and neither eat nor drink. One of the most important is Gabriel, who brought the Qur'an to Muhammad and taught him the prayer-act.

(c) *Through the Scriptures:* Muslims believe that God caused the contents of the Heavenly Book to be revealed to other prophets before Muhammad:

The *Tawrat* (*Torah*), or Law, to Moses;
The *Zabur*, or Psalms, to David;
The *Injil* (*Evangel*), or Gospel, to Jesus.

Finally God revealed the Qur'an to Muhammad. For Muslims the Qur'an replaces all previous Scriptures. They believe that in passages where the Qur'an differs from older Scriptures, the Jews or Christians have wrongly altered the Old and New Testaments.

(d) *Through the Prophets:* God also spoke through the prophets and apostles. He inspired them to speak in His name and to guide their people (see pp. 194, 195).

5. WHAT MUSLIMS BELIEVE ABOUT DESTINY

Muslims believe that God will judge the world. On that day, the angels will bring everyone for judgement. Their deeds will be weighed in the scales. Those who pass the test will be admitted to Paradise; those who fail will be sent to Hell (18.49; 17.13–15).

Muhammad lived and preached in a town where trade was the main business of life, and the Qur'an often refers to God as if He were a great merchant, keeping accounts with men:

Whoever has done the smallest weight of good, shall see it; whoever has done the smallest weight of evil, shall see it. (99.7–8; also 39.10; 2.245)

Islam emphasizes the sovereign power of God. The Qur'an even says in a number of places that those who go astray, do so by the will of God (6.125). At the same time, Islam also teaches that every person is responsible for his own behaviour and his own punishment.

Muslims believe that if Muslims commit great sins and die unrepentant, they will go to Hell. But they also believe that the Prophet will intercede for those Muslims, and that they will eventually pass into Paradise.

D. THE PRACTICE OF ISLAM

1. THE QUR'AN AND THE TRADITIONS

(a) *The Qur'an:* As we have already seen, Muhammad was given passages of the Qur'an on many different occasions to recite to his followers. By the end of his life, all the passages of the Qur'an had been revealed, and they form the sacred Scriptures of Islam (see p. 195). They were all collected together into one standard edition after Muhammad's death, and Zayd ibn Thabit, who had been Muhammad's secretary, did much of the work.

1. In most of the book, the words are words which God, or His angel, addressed directly to Muhammad and others. God addressed Muhammad in this way either to encourage him, to warn and direct him, or so that Muhammad might repeat the words to other people.

2. The Qur'an contains only messages which Muhammad himself believed God gave to him to proclaim. It contains nothing else. Muslims have preserved many Traditions about what Muhammad said on other occasions, but they did not include these in the Qur'an.

3. The present order of the chapters and verses of the Qur'an is not the order in which Muhammad first received them. Some chapters contain verses which were revealed on several different occasions. The first revelations are mostly in the last chapters of the book.

Muslims believe that God gave to Muhammad both the words and the contents of the Qur'an, and they believe that the Qur'an is a faithful copy of the Book which God caused to be written in heaven. They believe that the written or recited Qur'an is identical with the uncreated and eternal word of God: 'What lies between the two covers is the word of God.' They believe that the very language of the Arabic

Qur'an is without an equal, and that no one can write anything as beautiful. Muslims also believe that it is impossible to translate the Qur'an into any other language. Translators of the Qur'an into other languages can never translate the beauty and force of the Arabic. They can only write paraphrases.

Muslims love to recite or to listen to recitations of the Qur'an. They recite it in a particular way which emphasizes the rhythm of the Arabic language and the rhyming which occurs at the end of verses. A person who can recite the whole book by heart is called a *hafiz*, and many boys spend two whole years learning to do this. Muslims use verses from the Qur'an as charms. They hang them in little cases round their necks as a protection against evil and sickness.

(b) *The Traditions:* The Arab conquests raised many problems which Muslims could not answer by a simple reference to the Qur'an. So they asked those who had been the Companions of Muhammad to tell them what they remembered about his actions and his words. They wanted to know:

how Muhammad had behaved in particular circumstances;
what decisions he had made in disputes or law-cases;
what his manners were;
what he had allowed, or forbidden, to be done in his presence;
any particularly striking saying which he had uttered.

The 'customary practice' of the Prophet is called *sunna* in Arabic. Most Muslims are called 'Sunni Muslims', because they follow his example in this way.

The study of the Traditions is a complicated and difficult one because of the great number which were known among Muslims during the first two centuries after Muhammad. Some Traditions mention the words and actions of those who were the Companions of Muhammad, and not those of Muhammad himself.

2. THE SHARI'A: THE LAW OF ISLAM

All Muslims should follow the one path of conduct which is taught by the Qur'an, and by the *sunna* of the Prophet. Muslims call this one path the *shari'a*. (*Shari'a* is an Arabic word meaning 'the road to the watering-place'; stones and other signs marked out such a road and many people used it.) The Shari'a is a path of conduct which is clearly marked and which all Muslims follow.

The Shari'a includes the whole conduct of a person's life: what he does at home and at business; his marriage and his rights of inheritance; his duties to the state, to his neighbours, to his relations and his family. It also includes the religious duties which are referred to in the next section. A Muslim must walk this path in order to obey the Divine Will.

Muslims have never reached complete agreement about the details of the Shari'a law. Many rulers and judges acted on their own, and followed different rules in different parts of the Islamic empire. In the end, it was generally agreed that there are four orthodox versions of the Shari'a law. These four versions only differ from each other in details and Sunni communities may belong to any one of them.

In theory the Shari'a law should govern the life of every Muslim in every respect. In practice, however, this has not been possible. Two other forms of law have also guided the lives of Muslims:

1. *Customary Laws:* Muslims have often followed a pattern of behaviour which has mixed the rules of the Shari'a with local customs. Many African Muslims, for example, keep customary African law as well as the Shari'a.

2. *The Civil and Criminal Laws of Government:* The rulers of Muslim lands, even when themselves Muslims, have often made their own laws to control trade and to deal with crime. This has happened very frequently during the present century. As a result, in many Muslim lands today, modern codes of law have displaced the Shari'a law in the law courts, even in matters of family relationships. Often these codes are based on European law.

Despite this, the Shari'a law remains the ideal pattern for every Muslim. It is the well-marked road along which he must travel if he wishes to do the will of God.

The Shari'a law itself often appears to give women an inferior position in contrast to men. A Muslim husband, for example, is permitted by the Shari'a law to have four wives, in addition to concubines, and he may divorce his wife at his pleasure. But the Shari'a law also lays down that a husband must treat all his wives equally, and it protects women from cruelty and ill-treatment. Muslims claim that their law gives women dignity, and enables them to preserve their modesty easily. In some Muslim countries women are strictly secluded from social life, and may only pass through the streets if they are veiled. Although such customs are permissible according to Shari'a law, they are largely matters of social custom and are not an essential part of Islamic teaching. The Prophet Muhammad contracted many marriages, but he arranged some of them in order to give protection to the widows of important Muslims, and to make peace with great Arabian families. Some of the modern civil law codes in Muslim lands make monogamy compulsory and regulate divorce.

The Shari'a law also permits slavery, but this was a way of life which was customary in Arabia both before and after the time of Muhammad. Owners treated slaves as members of their families, and they were often well looked after. Sometimes slaves held positions of great importance.

3. THE PILLARS OF ISLAM

The Shari'a law lays down certain duties which human beings must perform because they are the servants of God. Muslims call these duties 'the Pillars of Islam'. They are these:

1. Declaration of the Islamic Creed: the *Shahada*.
2. The Prayer-act: the *Salat*.
3. Almsgiving: the *Zakat*.
4. The Fast during the month of Ramadan: the *Sawm*.
5. Pilgrimage to Mecca: the *Hajj*.

These duties are the acts of service, or worship, *'ibadat*, which a Muslim owes to God.

1. *The Declaration of the Creed:* Muslims declare their faith in the simple words: 'I testify that there is no god except God, and that Muhammad is the Apostle of God.' To say this with sincerity makes a person a Muslim. Muslims often place this declaration on the walls of mosques and of private houses, and it is sometimes written on the flags of Islamic states.

2. *The Prayer-Act:* Muslims should perform the prayer-act five times every day:

at dawn, before sunrise;
soon after mid-day;
during the afternoon;
soon after sunset;
before retiring to bed.

All Muslims perform the prayer-act in the same way. They believe that the angel Gabriel taught Muhammad how to perform it.

The Traditions report that Muhammad said: 'the prayer-act is like a stream of sweet water which flows past the door of each one of you. A man plunges into it five times a day. Do you think that anything remains of his uncleanness after doing that?' In performing the prayer-act the Muslim first washes his face, hands, and feet. He then selects a clean piece of ground on which to pray and, if necessary, spreads a mat on the floor. He faces towards Mecca.

There are certain postures which the Muslim must use during the prayer-act, including prostrating himself with his forehead on the ground. The Muslim recites passages from the Qur'an including the *Fatiha* (see p. 189), and he uses prayers many of which are very beautiful.

For example:

My Lord, give my soul its proper piety, and purify it; You are the best one to purify it: You are its guardian and protector.

O God forgive me, have mercy on me, pardon me, preserve me, supply my need, restore me, shield me.

In the mosque, the whole congregation can take an active part in the prayer from beginning to end. Standing behind the leader, who is called the *imam*, they follow his actions, and utter the prayers and praises with him. The senior Muslim present acts as the *imam*, or leader of the act.

The prayer-act has had great influence on Muslims all through the centuries. A modern text-book about it, published in Jordan, says: 'The true practice of the prayer-act illuminates the heart and polishes the soul. It teaches the worshipper the proper practice of worship, and the duties which he owes to God his Lord. It implants in his heart something of the majesty of God and His greatness. It ennobles a man and endows him with the noblest virtues. It directs the one who prays towards God alone, and causes him to wait much upon Him and to fear Him.'

3. *Alms-giving:* Muhammad encouraged Muslims to give money and other goods to the community, and his treaties with the tribes stated the amount of tribute which they were to pay. Muslims thought of these payments as a religious duty, and used the word *zakat*, alms-tax, for it.

The first khalifs developed the system of *zakat*, and made rules for its payment. Muslims should pay the *zakat* each year on their crops and certain kinds of fruit, also on their camels, cattle, sheep, and goats, gold and silver, and merchandise. The amount varies from 10 per cent on crops to 1 per cent or 2 per cent on animals, gold, and silver.

The *zakat* money may only be used for certain purposes as stated in the Qur'an (9.60), and especially for the poor, those in any need, and for travellers.

Muslims often make charitable gifts in addition to the *zakat* tax. The Qur'an contains many verses which exhort people to generosity. The Traditions also record Muhammad's praise of generosity, as well as his disapproval of begging.

4. *Fasting:* Muslims fast between sunrise and sunset during the month of *Ramadan*, as is commanded in the Qur'an (2.183–185 and 187). Muslims keep the fast very strictly. During the daylight hours, they abstain from all kinds of food and drink, as well as from tobacco, the use of perfume, sexual intercourse, and evil speaking. Certain people are excused from fasting, including young children and nursing mothers, the sick, and those on a journey. In some cases, they must fast at other times instead.

'Muhammad said, "the prayer-act is like a stream of sweet water ... A man plunges into it five times a day" ' (p. 213).

Turkish Muslims perform the prayer-act outside a mosque in the suburbs of Istanbul.

Muhammad asked, 'Do you think anything remains of a man's uncleanness after that?' What is your opinion?

Because Ramadan is a month of the Muslim religious calendar it follows the movements of the moon and not of the sun. Ramadan, therefore, takes place at a different time each year. When it comes at the height of summer, it costs Muslims a great deal of effort to keep the fast of Ramadan. But it reminds them of their duty to God, and they accept it as a time of self-discipline and of purification.

One of the two great festivals of the year takes place at the end of Ramadan. Muslims call it *'Idu l-Fitr*, the 'Festival of breaking the fast'. Almost the whole community gathers in the morning at a special open space to pray. Then they visit their friends and relations, and make gifts of alms. Everyone has a time of festivity and rejoicing.

5. *The Pilgrimage:* The annual pilgrimage to Mecca includes some of the customs which pilgrims followed at the Ka'ba in the days before Muhammad preached Islam. It also includes visits to mountains outside Mecca which were places of pilgrimage before Islam.

During all the ceremonies of the pilgrimage, the pilgrims offer prayers and listen to sermons. While they process between the two mountains, 'Arafat and Mina, they continually cry, *'Labbayka, alla humma, labbayka'*: 'We are at your service, O God, we are at your service.' Every Muslim is expected to make the pilgrimage once in his or her lifetime, if able to do so (3.96–97). Each year many Muslims keep the pilgrimage, coming from many different countries to Mecca.

The whole Muslim community throughout the world shares a little in the pilgrimage through the great annual festival of *'Id al-Adha*, 'The Festival of Sacrifice'. This festival begins on the tenth day of the Month of Pilgrimage, at the time when the pilgrims are sacrificing at Mina. It is a time of festivity; every Muslim family offers a sacrifice and gives much of it away to the poor. Muslims sacrifice the animals at the doors of their houses, facing Mecca, and they repeat the name of God while carrying out the sacrifice. (Qur'an 22.26–29.)

6. *The Holy War:* The 'holy war', *jihad*, is not one of the Pillars of Islam, but it is a religious duty. Every male Muslim has a duty to share in the struggle to spread Islam. This was an important duty in the first Muslim community at Medina, and during the Arab conquests. Since that time, however, this Muslim duty has declined in importance. In times of danger, Muslim communities have used this duty to rouse their members to action, and they have done this in particular when nations which are not Muslim have attacked Muslim states in war.

E. GROUPS WITHIN ISLAM

SUNNI MUSLIMS

Most Muslims, perhaps 90 per cent, are called *Sunni* Muslims. They accept the first four Righteous Khalifs (see p. 200). They follow the *sunna* of the Prophet, as recorded in the Traditions (see p. 211). They all belong to one of the four recognized systems of Shari'a law (see p. 212). Within this large group of Muslims there are, however, many differences of opinion and practice. Many are separated from each other by national or social differences.

THE SHI'A

The *Shi'ite* Muslims are the largest group in Islam which broke away from the rest of the community. In many ways, however, they are like Sunni Muslims. They fulfil the religious duties of prayer, fasting, and pilgrimage. They use the Qur'an and follow the example of the Prophet.

Many of the Shi'ites in the early centuries were Persians. Through them and others, ideas from the older religions have entered into the teachings of the Shi'ite Muslims. They differ from the Sunni Muslims in the following ways.

1. The Sunnis believe that the first Muslims were right to elect the Successors to the Prophet Muhammad. The Shi'ites believe that 'Ali should have become the first *Khalif* by inheritance, because he was Muhammad's cousin and had married his daughter Fatima. They believe that 'Ali's sons, Hasan and Husayn, should have become *Khalifs* after 'Ali was assassinated at Kufa in AD 661. Hasan died at Medina, and Husayn was killed by the Umayyad governor at Karbala in 'Iraq in AD 671. The Shi'ites look upon Husayn as a martyr, and commemorate his death each year.

2. The Shi'ites believe that the successors to Husayn have been 'hidden', waiting for the proper time to reveal themselves. They call these successors *Imams*, not *Khalifs*. They believe that the Divine Light which dwelt in Muhammad has passed from him to the *Imam*; and that the *Imam* is therefore both sinless and infallible.

3. The Shi'ites have their own collections of Traditions. Many of them support the claims of 'Ali and his family.

4. They reject the four Sunni law systems, and allow their lawyers to use their own initiative in interpreting the Qur'an. They believe that the infallible and 'hidden' *Imam* guides them in this.

The main Shi'ite sects are:

The *Seveners*, who believe that there were seven Imams: they are in India, the Yemen, and East Africa.

The *Twelvers*, who believe that there were twelve Imams: they are mostly in Iran.

The *'Ibadis*, who believe that the community may elect any suitable Muslim as Imam: they are in Oman.

THE SUFIS

The name *Sufi* comes from the Arabic word *suf*, which means 'wool'. Muslims who practised asceticism wore coarse woollen robes as a sign that they had renounced the world. Thus the word *sufi* came to mean anyone who turned from the world towards religion. The Sufis of Islam may be either Sunni or Shi'i.

The Shari'a law of Islam controls people's outward actions. It says little about the inner attitudes of people's hearts, or about the part which feelings play in religion. The Sufis have tried to direct and to strengthen the inner and hidden lives of Muslim believers. Sufi groups have had considerable influence in the Muslim community from the earliest times until today. The greatest of the Sufi teachers was al-Ghazzali who died in AD 1111. He brought religion back into the study of law and theology. His greatest book was called *the Revival of the Religious Sciences*: this was what he did for Islam.

F. THE MUSLIM

Like all human beings every individual Muslim has his own individual personality. He has his own character, his own virtues, and his own faults. As we have seen, however, there are some things which most Muslims think are important. We can describe the beliefs and practices of ordinary Muslims as follows:

1. Muslims know that they are the servants of God. God has entrusted to each one a certain portion of this world's goods to use in God's service.

2. They believe that God's will controls their whole lives. They express this by using such phrases as 'Thanks be to God', 'What God wills', 'If God wills'.

3. They know that they must give account to God on the Day of Judgement. God will judge them, but they hope that He will be merciful. They believe that Muhammad will intercede for them.

4. They know that they have certain duties towards God. They fulfil them as well as they are able. They keep the prayers at least three times a day, and fast with their families during Ramadan. They all try to make the Pilgrimage once to Mecca, but, if they are poor, they may feel themselves excused by poverty.

5. They are generous in giving alms to the poor. They believe that God will reward them. They give alms with special care on the feast days.

6. They are proud and thankful to be Muslims, and to belong to the community to which Muhammad was God's special messenger. They are loyal to this community and, in times of danger, will fight bravely for it.

7. They follow the Shari'a law, as far as they can, in matters of marriage and inheritance. Men have a position of privilege in comparison with women, but they also recognize and respect the rights of women.

8. In their behaviour Muslims try to follow the example of Muham-mad as far as they know it. They are modest in appearance and manners. They keep promises and guard what is entrusted to them. They bear misfortune with patience. (See 2.172.)

9. They may also follow customs which are not found in the Qur'an or the Traditions. They may, for example, use texts of the Qur'an as charms. They may visit the tombs of holy men in order to seek their help in prayer. They may think of some days as lucky and of others as unlucky.

STUDY SUGGESTIONS

WORD STUDY

1. What is the Arabic word for the Muslim creed?
2. What is the meaning of the Arabic word *Shari'a*, and why is this name given to the Muslim Law of Conduct?
3. Who or what are the following?
   imam   zakat   jihad   hafiz   Sufis   Ramadan

REVIEW OF CONTENT

4. (a) Read again carefully what Muslims believe about God. Compare this with what Jesus taught about God (p. 156). What is the most important difference between these two descriptions of God?
   (b) Choose the one which you think most suitable of the 'Most Beautiful Names' which Muslims use, to illustrate each of the seven attributes of God.
5. What do Muslims believe about 'destiny', i.e. about death, judge-ment, and life after death?
6. In what four different ways do Muslims believe that God gives guidance to human beings?
7. 'Muslims believe that what lies between the two covers of the Qur'an is identical with the word of God' (p. 210).
   (a) What else do they believe about the Qur'an?
   (b) What are some of the differences between the Qur'an and the Bible?
   (c) To which book of the Bible, if any, would you compare the Muslim 'Traditions'?
8. (a) Suggest two ways in which the Jewish *Torah* and the Muslim *Shari'a* are alike, and two ways in which they are unlike.
   (b) What other forms of law besides the *Shari'a* have guided the lives of Muslims?
9. What are the 'Pillars of Islam'? What do you think are the benefits which they give to Muslim communities who practise them?

10. (a) What do Muslims believe about angels?
    (b) Use a Concordance to help you compare this belief with the beliefs of the Jews in Old Testament times, and of Christian writers in the New Testament.
11. Read the following passages in the Qur'an which tell the story of Jesus: 3.33–63; 4.156–159 and 171–174; 5.110–120; 19.16–40. Compare them with the story of the life of Jesus as it is told in the four Gospels of the New Testament.

DISCUSSION AND RESEARCH

12. Compare the Apostles' Creed with what Muslims believe. (Go through the Creed phrase by phrase, and use the passages from the Qur'an listed in Q.11 above.) Underline those parts of the Creed which Muslims could say with Christians.
13. 'The Shari'a law appears to give women an inferior position. . . . But . . . Muslims claim that their law gives women dignity.'
    What is your opinion, (a) from reading this chapter, and (b) from the example of any Muslim family you may know?
14. *Jihad*, the 'holy war', is not one of the Pillars of Islam, but it is a religious duty. In the Middle Ages Christians who fought in the Crusades regarded that as a religious duty. In what circumstances, if any, do you think it is a religious duty (as distinct from a patriotic one) for Christians to take part in war today?
15. Does the description of ordinary Muslims in section F seem to you a correct description of any Muslims whom you know? If not, what would you wish to add or take away from this description?
16. Write a short summary of the religions studied in Part 4 so as to show the differences between them: e.g. what are the teachings of Buddhism, Christianity, and Islam respectively:
    (a) about the Buddha, or Jesus Christ, or Muhammad?
    (b) about the relationship between God and the world?
    (c) about the way in which human beings may find salvation and go to heaven after death?
    (d) about the way their Scriptures were given to them?

PART 5

RELIGIONS IN THE MODERN WORLD

Introduction

The previous chapters of this book have described some of the most widespread religions in the world today. They have also given examples of the religions which guide the lives of people living in smaller communities. These chapters teach us important facts about religion:

1. Religion is a most important part of the life of human beings. We know of very few societies in which there have been no religious beliefs or practices. In almost every human community people have prayed and worshipped. In very many communities people have thought religion to be very important, and some have thought it more important than any other part of life.

2. All religions have much in common with each other, and in Part 1 we discussed 'the characteristics of the religious attitude' (see pp. 10, 11). We have found these characteristics present in some form in all the religions which we have studied. But every religion has grown and developed in its own way. This has happened because people have been isolated from each other by the difficulties of travel and by the barriers of language.

All through the many centuries of human history, the ways in which people live have been changing and developing. In some communities these changes have been greater than in others. The different religions have changed as the lives of their followers have changed. This has been shown in previous chapters. For example:

Shintoism in Japan has passed through many changes. (See chapter 7, section A.)

The story of *Hinduism* is a long story of change and development. (See chapter 8, section C.)

The exile in Babylon had great influence on the prophets of *Judaism*, and brought a new way of thinking to them. (See p. 114.)

Buddhism has changed so much that there are now two distinct forms of Buddhism: Mahayana Buddhism and Theravada Buddhism. (See chapter 11, section F.)

On the other hand the *Maori* religion has almost died out because its former followers have become followers of another religion, Christianity. Many of the *Ga* and *Dinka* are now Christians or Muslims, and in *Korea* more than half the people are Christians, Buddhists, or Confucianists. In *China* most people are communists and do not openly practise any religion.

Human life is changing very rapidly in today's world. In some countries the changes are very great indeed. Change affects the lives of us all, and changes are now taking place more rapidly than they have ever done before. Some communities are facing more changes in the lifetime of one generation than they have had to face previously over the period of thirty or forty generations.

In this world of great and rapid changes, there are important questions which people are asking about religion, and we shall discuss these in this last part of our book. They are these:

1. Will religions survive?

2. Will there be many religions in the future, or will there be only one? We discuss the first question in chapter 14, and the second in chapter 15.

Finally, in chapter 16, we shall discuss the question:

3. What attitude should Christians have towards people of other religions?

Chapter 14
A Changing World

In many communities today there are people who have no religious beliefs and who do not pray or worship. In some countries such people are many more in number than those who are religious in their attitude to life. In the following two sections we examine some of the reasons for this change in attitude.

A. SCIENCE AND TECHNOLOGY

During the past hundred years or so, people have made very great advances in their knowledge about the world (science) and in using their discoveries to improve the ways in which they live (technology). It is said that 90 per cent of all the scientists and technologists who have ever lived are alive and at work today. The difficulties which older people have in understanding the work which their children are doing today show the speed with which new discoveries have been made. Many parents in Europe, especially those who have had little education, find it difficult to understand what their children at secondary school are studying. The same is true of a villager in Asia whose son is a radio engineer or whose daughter is an air hostess; or of an African elder whose son or daughter is doing a science degree in a university.

This growth in knowledge makes people think new thoughts about mankind's place in the universe, and about the existence of God. The universe is now known to be so great, in physical terms, that its dimensions are beyond men's experience and can only be expressed in mathematical formulae. For example, the largest galaxy of our local group of stars, the Andromeda Spiral, is 2,000,000 light years away from earth, and there may be 1,500,000,000,000,000,000,000 stars like our sun, within the known universe. We have to use measurements like these if we wish to have a clear idea of the great universe, in which we live.

We have to think in a new way about *time* as well as *space*. From one point of view, human beings have only lived on earth for a small fraction of the total time it has existed. From another point of view human beings have to look a long way into the future. For example, Sir James Jeans, a great scientist who made many important discoveries, said:

We are living at the very beginning of time. We have come into being in the fresh glory of the dawn. Our descendants of far-off ages, looking down this long vista of time, from the other end, will see our present age as the misty morning of the world's history.

We are learning to think about the planet Earth, our home, in a new and more humble way. We are learning that it is not at the centre of the universe or even of the solar system of which it is a part. We are learning also that our earth's history is only a tiny period in the vast time-span of the universe. We are beginning to realize that there may exist many planets like our own elsewhere in the universe, either at the present time or perhaps in the ages of the past or the future.

There are changes also in the way in which people today make use of their new discoveries about the world. Chemists have discovered new drugs and medicines which can heal the diseases which people used to think were incurable. Today, for example, we no longer fear leprosy or malaria as our ancestors did, because we know how to cure these diseases. Engineers also have discovered wonderful ways in which they can use the resources of the world to build roads and bridges, and to do tasks which former generations could not have attempted. Our governments build hydro-electric power stations and use nuclear power, and in many countries even poor people have electrical power in their homes. Almost everyone in the modern world has the pleasure of listening to people on the other side of the world through the radio. Very many people have watched television or flown in an aeroplane.

All this new knowledge and these new experiences make people ask questions about religion. They ask questions like the following:

1. Can there really be a God who transcends this great universe in which we live, and who has been present through all its long history? (See pp. 1, 2 for the meaning of the word 'transcends'.)

2. If there is a God who transcends this great universe, does he really pay attention to such insignificant creatures as human beings?

3. Because Science can tell us so much that is new about the universe, what is the value of the myths by which people of different religions explain the beginnings of the world? (See p. 15.)

4. Because we can control disease by medicine and medical knowledge, what extra help does prayer give to us? Which is more important, prayer or medicine?

People of all religions have to face questions like these.

B. SECULARISM

Many people today feel that their religion does not help them answer the most important questions of life. They say that the most important questions are not those about God and prayer, but those about politics and society, and the physical needs of men and women. The most important questions, they say, are questions like these: Will there be enough food to feed the growing world population? What is freedom and how can people live in freedom? How can the nations share the wealth of the world more equally? How can development be encouraged in all the countries of the world? How can governments control population growth? How can we prevent people from wasting the earth's resources? How can the United Nations Organization be strong enough to keep peace and enforce justice? Is revolution right or wrong? Is revolution necessary?

Those who spend their lives in searching for answers to questions like these often feel that religion has little to say to help them. They think that religious teachings are old-fashioned and conservative. They become impatient, and no longer pay attention to religious teachers, and they give up praying and worshipping.

Even when people are not concerned with political and economic questions like these, they are often pressed by modern ways of life to give up the practice of religion. People measure success by the amount of material wealth a person possesses, and it is difficult to gain wealth in today's world. Those who wish to succeed have to work very hard, especially in towns and in modern business. Many employers do not care whether their employees are religious or not. They want them to be clever and hard-working, they want them to be skilled at their jobs. In trying to become successful, people find that they have little time left in which to visit the temple, the mosque, or the church.

Life today, especially in the towns, is therefore marked by what is called a 'secularist' approach to life. *Secularism* is a way of thinking and acting which concentrates on the problems which face men and women as they live their natural lives on earth. 'Secularism' comes from a Latin word *saeculum*, which means 'time'. According to secularist thinking, only the problems of man's time on earth are important, not the problems which concern God and eternity. Secularism, therefore, treats religious questions as irrelevant. It is the attitude of many people living in Europe, and is rapidly becoming the attitude of people living in towns and universities in Africa and Asia.

In the teachings of Communism, secularism has become almost a religion for many of the world's peoples. It may seem strange to use the word 'religion' in this way to describe Communism, because Communism teaches that God does not exist. But Communism is like a religion in certain other ways. It aims to teach people a way of life which will enable them to live useful and happy lives. It aims to explain the way in which history develops, and it gives answers to people's questions about life. It makes the building of a new society the goal of life, and so it gives people a purpose to live for. It helps people to fulfil themselves by setting them to work for the fulfilment of this aim. It teaches people to sacrifice themselves for the benefit of society as a whole. The growth of Communism shows that philosophies and attitudes to life which are entirely secular, and in which religion has no place at all, attract very many people today and appear to satisfy them.

225

'Many people today say that the most important questions are not those about God, but those about politics and society' (p. 224).

When Kwame Nkrumah's statue was put up in Accra the inscription said, 'Seek ye first the political kingdom and all other things shall be added to it.'

Who do you think spoke the greater truth, Kwame Nkrumah, or Jesus as recorded in Matthew 6.30–33?

C. RELIGION AND CHANGE

Religious leaders and thinkers often seem slow to respond to the changes which modern science and modern secularist attitudes are making in the ways in which people live today. There are two reasons for this:

1. Religious beliefs are usually expressed in ideas and language which were first used long before the growth of modern science. Moreover, they are associated with sacred Scriptures which were written in times when there was little scientific knowledge. Thus the teachings of a religion sometimes appear to contradict modern ideas about the structure of the universe, or the evolution of living creatures, or human psychology.

2. Religion is one of the activities of life in which people resist change. Religious people do not easily change their ideas or their behaviour. As a result, they find it difficult to understand modern scientific discoveries. They also find it difficult to integrate their beliefs about God with the new facts which modern science has discovered. When religious thinkers try to do this, other teachers often reject them as heretics or dangerous free-thinkers.

At first sight, therefore, it appears that any religion may find it difficult to survive in our modern world which is changing so rapidly. But if we think more carefully, we shall see that there are reasons for believing that people will continue to find comfort and strength from religious beliefs and practices:

1. Religion has always been a part of human life, and as human life has developed and changed so has religion. We may expect that people will grow in their religious beliefs in the same way as they have in their scientific knowledge and their ability to use that knowledge. Some of the greatest teachers of theology are themselves scientists. They will help the people of the different religions to express their beliefs about God in ways which fit the new knowledge which men have about the universe. This does not mean that God changes, or that the most important beliefs about Him will change. But it means that religious teachers will have to improve the language which they use to talk about God and His relationship with the world. It may also mean that some people will have to change their ideas about God so that they think about Him more truly.

2. In the past, religious beliefs often encouraged people to take new ways and to face difficulties with courage and hope. Some people would even say that it was religious beliefs and the practice of worship which made the first men and women human beings and different from the animals. If this is so, then to pray and to worship are essential to human life. Human beings will not stop doing these things in their

new stage of growth and discovery, though they may do them in different ways.

3. Although people who live in modern towns and cities face many urgent problems, their main problems are still the questions: 'What is the meaning of life?' and 'How can I live well?' People will continue to seek the answers to these questions where their forefathers found them, i.e. in their religions.

When the American astronauts in the rocket Apollo XIII, which was nearly wrecked on its way to the moon in September 1970, landed safely in the Pacific, they were picked up by the US aircraft-carrier *Iwojima*. On its deck, in view of the world's television cameras, they bowed their heads while the ship's chaplain said a short prayer of thanksgiving. Many people joined them in their prayer. Their action was important, because it showed that men who are leaders in technology and discovery can still find strength and courage in prayer.

4. Prayer and worship do not simply grow out of the desires and fears of human people. They are the answer which people have given to the great mystery of life which surrounds them on every side. We now know much more about the universe in which we live, but the mystery is still there: the mystery of why things are as they are, the mystery of life, of birth and growth, the mystery of death and our fellowship with the dead, the mystery of our knowledge of what is good and what is bad, of what is beautiful and what is ugly. The mysteries are still there, and people will continue to respond to them in wonder and in prayer. Religion will continue to be the bond which links human beings with the great mystery beyond the universe, which they call God.

5. A person who finds strength and guidance from his belief in God believes that religion will survive for a reason quite different from those discussed above. He believes that God is a living being who seeks to bring men into fellowship with Himself. Religion does not begin in men's hearts, it begins with God's invitation to people that they should worship Him. Religion is the way in which human people respond to God who created them. God is always present in the universe which He created: He is always inviting people to worship Him and to respond to Him. He will continue to do this as long as the world exists, and some people will always respond to His invitation. This is why religious people believe that religion will survive for ever. It is the response of human beings to God who is for ever.

These things show us that religion will survive in the modern world because it answers people's needs in a way that nothing else will do, and because it is the answer which human people give to God's call. But the ways in which people express their religions will change as people's lives change, and religious teachers will learn to express their beliefs in ways more fitting to the modern world.

STUDY SUGGESTIONS

WORD STUDY

1. (a) What is the origin of the word 'secularism'?
(b) What are two chief differences between the secularist attitude to life and the religious attitude?

REVIEW OF CONTENT

2. 'Every religion has grown and developed in its own way' (p. 221). What are the reasons for this?
3. What are two different sorts of ways in which religions can change?
4. 'We have to think in a new way about *time* as well as *space*' (p. 223). Give some examples from everyday life to support this statement.

BIBLE STUDY

5. Read Psalm 10.
(a) Which verses in this Psalm seem to describe a secularist way of thinking?
(b) Which verses show the religious attitude of the writer of the Psalm himself?

DISCUSSION AND RESEARCH

6. (a) Make a list of the five most important changes which have happened in the last ten years:
   (i) to your country;
   (ii) to your town or village;
   (iii) to your work or way of life;
   (iv) to your Church.
(b) How many of these changes have led to greater 'secularism'?
7. Are people today more religious than they were when your father was young, or are they less religious? Do your friends or fellow students agree with you about this? What do you think are the four chief reasons for any changes there have been in people's attitudes?
8 (a) Have you noticed any changes, in recent years, in the ways in which the leaders of your Church teach the meaning of the Gospel? (b) Have you noticed any ways in which the leaders of your Church have *resisted* change in people's ideas or way of life, or have refused to adapt their ways of teaching to changed situations?
9. Discuss with (a) a university student, and (b) a business man, what each thinks about religion.

10. What would be your own answers to the four sample questions on p. 224?
11. From your knowledge of the New Testament discuss the changes in language and ways of thinking which occurred when the Christian Church spread outside of Palestine into the Roman empire.
12. What are the basic beliefs of your Church that will never change?

Chapter 15
One God, Many Religions

A. PLURALISM

Before the discovery of the telegraph in 1837, and before the invention of steam and petrol engines, people living in different parts of the world communicated with each other by using animals and sailing-boats. News and ideas travelled across the world very slowly. Human communities were isolated from each other. Within their own boundaries small groups developed their own languages and their own religions and customs. Examples of such religions are those of the Dinka and the Ga, chapters 3 and 4. Even in larger areas like China, Europe, or the Arab empires, there was usually only one dominant religion.

Sometimes these religions were made up of a number of different elements, as was the case in Japan, where Shinto was mixed with Buddhism, or in China. (See pp. 54 and 89.) Even so, to the ordinary person the religion of his community was one religion and he thought it to be shared by all. Most people had no knowledge of any religion except their own.

Within the last hundred years, however, this situation has changed in many communities: instead of there being only one religion in a community there is now a situation of 'pluralism'. *'Pluralism'* means a situation in which a single community contains different groups of people, sometimes from different races, who practise different religions and have different ways of behaving. Pluralism is an important element in the world today, and it is changing the ways in which people think about religion. We have already noted the fact of 'pluralism' in a number of countries, such as Korea (p. 46), and in Africa (pp. 16, 27). There are many reasons why the inhabitants of a town or country today may include groups of people who follow different religions.

1. *The whole world is becoming one world-community.* Very many people all over the world share the same interests. Air travel makes it possible for national leaders, business men, or sportsmen to travel quickly from their own to other countries throughout the world. The broadcasting services, in most of the world's languages, mention almost the same news items day by day. Television even makes it possible for large numbers of people all over the world to see the same thing at the same time. People of all nations watched American space-men walk on the moon and West German footballers win the World Cup. People of all religions watched the Christian funerals of President Eisenhower and Charles de Gaulle, and the Muslim funeral of 'Abdu l-Nasir. Theoretically, it would be possible for one person to speak to

the whole of mankind at a single moment, either through the radio or through television.

2. *In the universities, colleges, and schools of the modern world students are learning one common scientific attitude* to life through the natural sciences, e.g., physics, chemistry, biology. They often learn history and literature from a nationalist and exclusive point of view, and some countries are unwilling to open their frontiers to a free interchange of news and views. But most modern historians look at things from a world viewpoint, and write their books in this way. Most nations and countries are willing to exchange ideas and information with other countries. As a result, very many people, especially the young, know a good deal about the history and religions of other peoples.

3. *Ordinary people are now able to move about the world* much more easily than in previous generations. Governments often encourage them to do so, because they want to increase tourism, or they want foreigners to work in their universities or development projects. Sometimes governments or business firms encourage the immigration of people from other countries, in order that they may work in special industries, or for other reasons. Thus, for example, there have been many Indian Muslims working in East Africa, and Chinese Buddhists in South-east Asia. Many Muslim immigrants from Pakistan, North Africa, and Indonesia are working in Britain, France, and Holland. The great business corporations now do business in many countries all over the world. They often move their employees from one country to another, and when they do so, they do not pay much attention to the religion which their employees follow.

People who travel to a foreign country in order to find work, or to teach in a university, or to engage in a development project, usually try to fit in with the customs and ways of the country in which they are guests. But if they are many in number, they often try to maintain their own way of life, and their own religion.

We saw in chapter 13 how Muslim merchants carried Islam into Indonesia and China, and how other Muslims did the same in east and west Africa. Today the Islamic Cultural Centres in Europe and America serve large communities of Muslim immigrants and expatriates, and they also attract other people towards Islam. Until a few years ago the communities of European Christians in Africa and Asia also had great influence in spreading the Christian religion.

4. *Missionaries have gone to countries where the inhabitants followed another religion,* in order to convert them to their own religion. Buddhist missionaries long ago took Buddhism from India to many other countries of the Far East (see chapter 11). Buddhist missionary work continues today from centres in Thailand (see p. 142). Christianity has been a missionary religion since its beginning (see chapter 12,

section B), and, during the past 150 years especially, many Christian missionaries have gone from Europe and America into other parts of the world. In the case of Islam, it has mostly been ordinary Muslims who have carried their religion to other peoples, but they have been glad of the help of religious teachers as well (see pp. 201, 202). In recent times, the Ahmadiyya movement has sent out missionaries to Africa and Europe in imitation of modern Christian missionary efforts.

Missionary work of this kind, where it is successful, introduces another religion into a society which before then has in many cases followed only one religion.

For these and other reasons, we live in a world which is marked by pluralism. In almost every important town there are one or more groups of people who follow a different religion from that which most of the inhabitants follow. These small groups may be either Christians, or Muslims, or Buddhists, or members of another religion altogether. In some countries the people who follow a different religion or religions may be a very large number indeed. In India, which is mostly Hindu, there are now 48 million Muslims: in Lebanon the Christians and Muslims are almost equal in numbers. In Egypt, which is mostly Muslim, there are about 3 million Christians, five-sixths of whom are Copts. In many countries in Africa and Asia, where people follow what we have called 'traditional religions', there are growing numbers of Christians or of Muslims (see pp. 16, 27). Even in isolated places where only one religion is practised, people often hear the teachings of other religions through their transistor radios.

Thus very many people in today's world find themselves asking questions like the following: 'Which is the true religion?' 'Are all religions the same?'

B. SIMILARITIES

Some people say that all religions are about God, and that it does not matter which religion a man follows: he can worship God equally well in any of them. Some use the picture of a great mountain to express this. There are many roads up the mountain, but they all lead to the summit; so there are many religions which lead men to God, but they all arrive in the end at the same destination, fellowship with God. Some Hindu thinkers have expressed themselves in this way (see pp. 74, 76).

Those who say this, do so because of the similarities between the religions. We have already noticed many of these, especially in Part 2.

There are very close similarities, for example, between the Dinka, the Ga and the Maori religions, e.g. in the way in which they think of God as being associated with many different powers, in the attention

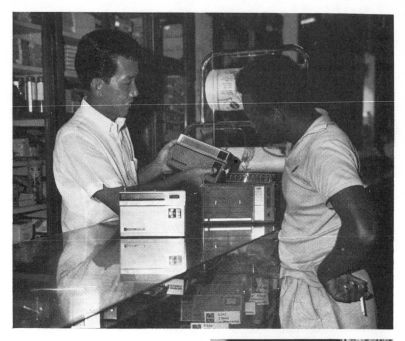

'Today people all over the world can see the same thing at the same time. Even in isolated places people hear the teaching of other religions through their radios' (pp. 231, 233).

In New Guinea a man has come in from a country district to Rabaul to buy a new radio. Melanesian followers of traditional religions often listen to Christian and other religious broadcasts. Japanese schoolchildren are accustomed to TV in their classrooms.

What difference is this likely to make to their ideas about followers of other religions?

which they pay to the spirits of the dead, and in their use of sacrifice. (See chapters 3, 4, and 5.)

Shintoism in Japan has become mixed with Buddhism (see p. 54), and very many Chinese are both Buddhists and also Taoists or Confucianists (see p. 89). Students may also see many resemblances between Christianity and Islam. We might compare, for example, the description of the average Muslim on p. 218 with the description of the average Christian on p. 179, or compare the Muslim daily prayer, *the Fatiha* (p. 189), with the Lord's Prayer of Christianity. Both these prayers begin with the offering of praise to God, the Sovereign Ruler of the world, they then mention the worshippers' need of help, and they finish with a prayer for right guidance. Students might wish to compare these prayers with that of the Dinka spear-master (p. 23), or of the Buddhists in Burma (p. 148).

Why are there so many similarities between the many different religions of the world? Religion is about the relationships between God and human beings, and we find the reasons for the similarities in both these two partners of the religious relationship:

1. Human beings basically are one family. People may differ from each other in the colour of their skins, or in their height, or in their language, but beneath the differences they are all *human* beings. We are learning the truth of this more than ever before. Indeed if the peoples of the world do not realize how much they need each other and act upon this belief, then there will be much unhappiness and conflict. Because all people are members of the one human family, they all practise their religion in ways which are human. Their practices may differ in one way or another, but underneath the differences there will be found one basic pattern common to all. (See chapter 2, section C.)

2. Secondly, there are similarities between the religions because religion is basically the response which human people make to God. God is eternally the same, for He is always Himself, the one living Creator of all that is. Religion is response to His presence in life, and because His presence is always the same, people all over the world respond in ways which are basically like each other. The children of one family may be different one from the other, but because they are children of one father and are influenced by him they will always share some common attitudes towards him. God is the loving Creator-Father, and He looks for love and trust from all His children.

Yet the children of one father do not all respond to him in the same way, nor do they all obey him with the same faithfulness and willingness. Some children may know their father better than others. The father is the same, but the children differ from each other. In the same way there are many differences between the religions. We discuss these in the next section.

C. DIFFERENCES

In this book, we have taken care to emphasize the different circumstances in which the different religions grew and developed. Thus, for example, we saw how Judaism developed during the long history of the Jews; in that history the two great events of the Exodus from Egypt and the Exile into Babylon had great importance on the way that Judaism grew. The Exodus taught the Jews the great power of God, the Exile taught them much about the judgement of God and the importance of obeying Him, as well as helping them to understand that He is present everywhere, even outside Palestine. (See chapter 10, section A.)

The Dinka practised their religion in the swamps of the Sudan, where they were often anxious about the coming of rain and the flow of the river. Because they were very dependent upon their cattle for food and the other necessities of life, they used cattle in prayer and in sacrifice. (See chapter 3.)

Muhammad first preached Islam in the west of Arabia, where life was hard and a strong ruler was needed to control the Bedouin (see pp. 183, 197). Thus Islam is a stern religion, which teaches that obedience and law are very important.

The Maori religion recalls the long voyages which the ancestors of the Maori made in reaching the islands of New Zealand. (See chapter 5.)

In Hinduism we can see the effect of many different events and influences in the long history of the Indian sub-continent. (See chapter 8, section C.)

Thus the different religions of the world closely fit the circumstances in which they are practised. They belong to their own followers in a very special way, and often they are part of the history of one particular nation or country. This is illustrated in the words of an Indian chief in the United States about the religion which his nation had followed before the coming of Christianity:

'In the beginning,' he said, 'God gave to every people a cup of clay, and from this cup they drank from the water of life.'

Many people, many cups: each cup of a special shape and with a special pattern.

But we cannot explain the differences between religions simply by saying that they fit the lives and circumstances of different peoples. If they all said the same thing about God the other differences would not matter. The fact is that they do not all say the same thing. In some things religions are alike, in other important ways, they differ from each other. Let us take some examples.

236

1. On page 235 we compared the Muslim *Fatiha* with the Lord's Prayer of Christianity. In many ways the two prayers are closely alike. But they begin differently. The Muslim prayer begins, 'Praise be to God', while the Christian prayer begins 'Our Father'. The Qur'an forbids the use of the word 'father' when speaking about God, but the difference between the two prayers is not simply that they use different words. Islam teaches that the highest honour which a person can have is to be the servant of God, the Ruler of the Worlds (see p. 209). The Lord Jesus taught that a human being may be born again by God's Spirit to be a child of God, and may live with love and trust in God as 'Our Father in Heaven'. This illustrates the great difference between these two religions.

2. Hindus worship God through the use of idols of all kinds (see p. 81), and in Buddhism the Buddha image is in the centre of the temples, and is an object of worship (see p. 152). Both Judaism (p. 108) and Islam (p. 207) teach that this kind of worship is sinful and call it idolatry. These two faiths teach that God cannot be represented by any image or human picture, because He transcends all human imagining. A Muslim or a Jew (and a Christian also) would find it very difficult to worship in a Hindu or Buddhist temple because of this.

3. There are also many differences between the religions in the ways in which they think about God:

Judaism and Islam teach that God is one living Being independent of the world (pp. 108, 207).

Christianity teaches that God is a Trinity of three persons, one of whom became man (see pp. 177, 178).

Hinduism speaks of the one Supreme Absolute, but Hindu people worship many gods. Some of them, they say, lived among men for a time (pp. 80 and 70).

In some of the traditional religions people worship many gods, and associate some of them with the powers of nature (see pp. 14, 18, 21).

In Shintoism worship is given to any thing or person which is deserving of honour (see p. 56).

Gautama Buddha and Confucius taught little about God and much about life (see pp. 129, 93).

4. Students will also notice the many different ways in which the different religions teach that a person may be rescued from the power of evil. These are not small differences, but differences which affect the way in which people trust in God:

(a) People are rescued or saved from evil by offering sacrifices or gifts. This is the way, for example, of:

    Dinka religion (p. 21);

    Maori religion (pp. 42, 43).

(b) People are rescued or saved from evil by using special prayers or ceremonies in which prayers and cleansing have a part. This is the way, for example, of:

Ga religion (pp. 32, 33);

Shamanism (p. 47);

Shintoism (p. 57).

(c) People are rescued or saved from evil by following a particular way of conduct. This is the way, for example, of:

Confucianism and Taoism (pp. 91, 99);

Buddhism which teaches the Noble Eightfold Path (pp. 128, 129).

(d) People are rescued or saved from evil by fulfilling religious duties or keeping religious law. This is the way, for example, of:

Hinduism (pp. 79, 80);

Judaism (pp. 117–120).

(e) People are rescued or saved from evil by trust in a saviour who has won Enlightenment. This is the way, for example, of:

Mahayana Buddhism (p. 139);

some popular forms of Theravada Buddhism (p. 145).

(f) People are rescued or saved from evil by the will of God. This is the way, for example, of:

Islam (pp. 209, 210).

(g) People are rescued or saved from evil because God Himself overcame evil and defeated it. This is the way of:

Christianity (p. 163).

This short summary emphasizes the differences between the religions in what they teach about salvation. In them all, however, except perhaps Buddhism and the Chinese religions, it is taught that people should trust in God (or the gods) for salvation and healing. This primary trust in God is called *bhakti* in some forms of Hinduism, *islam* in Islam, and *faith* in Christianity (see pp. 70, 71, and 174).

5. Lastly, we should notice that many religions teach beliefs and practices which do not occur elsewhere. Often these beliefs and practices are very important, and make a religion different from others. Notice, for example:

what Hinduism teaches about reincarnation and the law of *karma* (p. 68);

what Christianity teaches about new birth by the Spirit of God (p. 174);

the important place which the town of Mecca has in prayer and pilgrimage for Muslims (pp. 213, 216);

the importance of the Emperor in State Shinto (pp. 54, 55).

The preceding paragraphs show many of the important differences between one religion and another. We may summarize the reasons for them like this:

1. A religion may belong in a special way to one particular country,

nation, or tribe. (This is not true of the international religions described in Part 4.)

2. Every religion has its own special teachings and beliefs.

3. A religion may differ from other religions in some of the things which it teaches about God, or about the way people worship Him, or about the way in which people are delivered from evil.

When people notice the differences between their own religion and the religions of other nations or groups they often say, 'My religion is the true one: the others are wrong or false.' In the past some of these differences led to disputes and to wars. The Old Testament includes records which tell how the Israelites fought with neighbouring tribes and nations in the name of their religion. Muslims and Christians have done the same at different periods of history. In modern times there has been fighting between Muslims and Hindus within India, and between India and neighbouring countries. In many countries of the world there have been clashes of all kinds between different religious communities. Sometimes the struggle has been between two different sects within one religion, when each of the two has claimed to be the only group which taught the religion truly. During the first hundred years and more after the death of Muhammad the Sunni and Shi'ite Muslims fought against each other in battle (see p. 217). At the time of the Reformation, and afterwards, Protestant and Roman Catholic Christians were often bitter enemies.

D. A HIERARCHY OF TRUTHS

The last two sections show that there are two opposite attitudes which people of one religion may have towards other religions:

1. Some people look more at the ways in which religions come close to each other, than at the ways in which they differ from each other. They say that there is a unity between them which lies beneath the differences which appear at first sight. 'Religions are like the colours in a rainbow: they are all parts of one light.'

2. Other people look more at the differences between religions than at the ways in which they come close to each other. They say that these differences are so important that only one of the religions can be the true religion. 'Religions are like the separate colours of a rainbow. Only one is the true colour.'

There are good reasons for both these attitudes. But they do not fit in with each other. Those who take one attitude find it difficult to understand those who take the other.

There is, however, another way of looking at the different religions, which is in between these two attitudes. Those who take this third attitude try to see what true teaching each religion gives about God, and to compare these teachings with each other. This is a difficult thing to do, but it is the only way in which a person can say both that all religions speak truly in some ways about God, and also that there are important differences between them.

Sometimes people speak about 'a hierarchy of truths'. The word 'hierarchy' means a system of authority or government in which each person has his own special place, with greater or less authority. Here are some examples of 'hierarchies'.

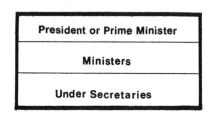

The under secretaries have authority but not so much as the ministers or the prime minister. He has more authority than the ministers.

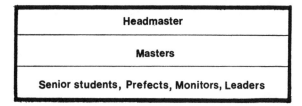

This is the 'hierarchy' of a school.

These examples show us how we can arrange the teachings of the different religions, in what we might call a 'hierarchy of truths'. Some teachings are more true than others, some teachings are more important than others. Some are of basic importance, and clearly true, and we can place these towards the top of the hierarchy. Most of these important beliefs are common to a number of religions, but not all of them. Some beliefs do not matter very much, and we can place these lower in the hierarchy; most of these less important beliefs are teachings which have grown up in one particular place.

It is not possible in this book to outline a hierarchy of truths about God and His relationship with the world. Each reader will do this according to his own beliefs about God, and his own experience of the grace of God. Each person will have his own standard by which to judge the truth, or otherwise, of teachings in religions which are different from his own.

The Christian reader will wish to compare the different teachings with the Bible, as we have been doing all through this book. Above all he will try to weigh up all other teachings in the light of Jesus Christ, in whom he believes that God has revealed Himself in a unique way to men. We return to this theme in the final chapter.

STUDY SUGGESTIONS

WORD STUDY

1. What is the word used to describe a situation where there are many different groups of people practising different religions?

2. (a) Which of the following words could you use instead of 'hierarchies' to describe the two diagrams on p. 240.
   graduations   authorities   gradations   comparisons   dynasties
   orders   rankings
   (b) Give two other examples of hierarchies which exist in everyday life.

REVIEW OF CONTENT

3. Describe some of the reasons why there is religious pluralism in many countries of the world today.

4. (a) List some of the *similarities* between the various religions we have been studying.
   (b) List some of the *differences* between them.

5. Give two chief reasons for similarities between major religions today.

6. In what way does each of the following religions show the country and way of life of its followers?
   Dinka   Maori   Islam

BIBLE STUDY

7. Read James 1.26, 27.
   (a) Which, if any, of the religions we have studied could be called 'pure and undefiled', according to the teaching of this passage?
   (b) Do you agree with this teaching? If not, how would *you* describe 'pure religion'?

DISCUSSION AND RESEARCH

8. (a) What different religions are practised in your country.
   (b) Find out, if you can, when and how each grew up or was brought in.

9. (a) Are the relationships between followers of the different religions practised in your country good or bad?
   (b) In what ways, if any, do the followers of different religions work together?
10. What would be your own answer to the question: 'Will there be many religions in the future, or only one?' Give your reasons.
11. Make a list of the three most important truths about God which you would put at the top of a possible hierarchy. Can you think of any teachings in your own religion which are not of great importance?

Chapter 16
The Christian and Other Religions

A. BIBLE ATTITUDES

In previous chapters we have discussed the different religions in general terms. We have tried to understand them as they are, and to listen to what their followers say about them. In this last chapter we look at other religions from a Christian point of view. We try to understand what attitude the Christian should have to other religions.

If we look for guidance in this matter to the Bible we find that the writers of the Scriptures teach us two points of view. Most of the Biblical writers write as if only the Jewish and afterwards the Christian religions were true ways to God, but a few suggest that other people also may be true worshippers of God.

Most of the Old Testament writers taught that only those who worshipped Yahweh according to the Jewish Law truly worshipped God, and that God was their God in a very special way. Here is an example of this attitude:

Do not fall into the ways of the nations . . .
For the carved images of the nations are a sham, they are nothing but timber cut from the forest, worked with his chisel by a craftsman . . .
They are worth nothing, mere mockeries, which perish when their day of reckoning comes.
God, Jacob's creator, is not like these; for he is the maker of all.
Israel is the people he claims as his own; Yahweh of Hosts is his name. (Jer. 10.2, 3, 15–16)

But the Old Testament writers also looked forward to the day when people of other nations would come to share in the knowledge of God which the people of Israel knew and enjoyed (see, e.g., Isa. 56.3–8).

Some of the prophets, however, taught that God was the God of other people also. Amos rebuked neighbouring nations, together with Israel and Judah, because of their sins, and in Deuteronomy we find the declaration: 'When the Most High parcelled out the nations, when he dispersed all mankind, he laid down the boundaries of every people according to the number of the sons of God; but Yahweh's share was his own people' (Deut. 32.8). Both Rahab of Jericho and Ruth of Moab were among the ancestors of the great King David, and in the story of Jonah the men of Nineveh repented and received the forgiveness of God (Jonah 3.10). In Isaiah 19.23–25, Egypt and Assyria are named together with Israel as the people of God, for they also will know and worship Yahweh.

As we saw in chapter 12, the Lord Jesus declared that He was the Saviour whom God had sent into the world, and that men received God's grace through faith in Him (see p. 159). 'I am the way, and the truth, and the life,' He said, 'no one comes to the Father, but by me' (John 14.6). But at the same time Jesus taught that God gives gifts to all men alike (see p. 156): He healed many who were not Jews and who did not believe in the Jewish religion (Mark 3.7–10; 7.24–30); He tried to make the temple a place in which all nations might pray (Mark 11.17); He welcomed the Greeks who came to Him, and the Roman centurion (John 12.20–26; Matt. 8.5–13).

The apostles proclaimed Christ as the only Saviour: 'There is salvation in no one else,' said the apostle Peter, 'for there is no other name under heaven given among men by which we may receive salvation' (Acts 4.12 NEB). When people asked them what they must do to be saved, they replied, 'Put your trust in the Lord Jesus, and you will be saved, you and your household' (Acts 16.30–31 NEB). But the apostles also recognized that God had given some knowledge of Himself to those who were not Jews and who had not heard of Jesus. This is clear from Paul's words in Romans 1.19–20 and from the account of his speech to the people of Lystra in Acts 14.16–17. According to Luke, it was at Athens where he stated this belief most clearly, when he preached on the hill where there were many temples of the Greek gods:

> The God who created the world and everything in it, and who is Lord of heaven and earth, does not live in shrines made by men. It is not because he lacks anything that he accepts service (worship) at men's hands, for he is himself the universal giver of life and breath and all else. He created every race of men of one stock, to inhabit the whole earth's surface. He fixed the epochs of their history and the limits of their territory. They were to seek God, and, it might be, touch and find him, though indeed he is not far from each one of us, for in him we live and move, in him we exist; as some of your own poets have said, 'We are also his offspring.' (Acts 17.24–28 NEB.)

But the apostles were also careful to emphasize that the knowledge of God which others receive is very different from the knowledge of God which had come to them through Christ. So Paul said to his listeners at Athens, 'What you worship but do not know—this is what I now proclaim' (Acts 17.23 NEB). In the book of Revelation the writer describes a vision in which the whole of creation, animals and birds as well as human people, worship God and Christ (Rev. 4—5).

If a Christian follows the apostles, therefore, he will emphasize the light which he has received through faith in Christ. But he will not think that there is darkness everywhere else. God cares for all men, and His presence gives light.

When a Christian tries to explain the light of God in the world, together with the light of God in Christ, he will find it a help to remember three things:

1. The Coming of God;
2. The Presence of God;
3. The Purpose of God.

B. THE COMING OF GOD

In the long history of the Old Testament it was always God who acted first to help and to bless the people of Israel.

God was the one who called Abraham from Mesopotamia (Gen. 12. 1–2).

God called Moses and sent him to bring the Israelites out of Egypt (Exod. 3.1–10):

God gave the people His Law at Sinai and chose Israel to be His people (Exod. 19 and 20; Deut. 7.6–10):

God brought David to be king in Jerusalem (2 Sam. 5.1–3; 7.4–16):

God chose and sent the prophets to speak His Word to the people (Amos 7.10–15, etc):

God brought judgement upon the people because of their sin, and sent them into exile (Jer. 19, etc.):

God brought back the people of Israel to their own land after the Exile (Isa. 40.1–11, etc.).

We saw in chapter 10 that in the Old Testament God is the God who speaks: again and again He spoke through the events of the history of the Israelites to reveal His will to them and to rescue and restore them.

But the speaking of God was not enough: He spoke in many different ways through the prophets, but men did not listen to them. In the end God came Himself. The Word of God took human form and lived among men as Jesus of Nazareth. The Heavenly Shepherd came down into the world of men, to share their lives and bring them back into the security of the Shepherd's care.

This was the way in which Jesus spoke about God in the picture language which He used to explain what He believed about God's relationship with the world:

God, He said, is like a shepherd who goes in search of one lost sheep;

God is like a housewife who sweeps every corner of her house to find a lost piece of silver;

God is like a king who prepares a feast and sends his servants to bring his guests;

God is like a farmer who sows his seed;

God is like a farmer who engages men to work in his fields;

God is like a father who runs to meet his son when he comes to him in need.

Jesus taught that God is always coming into His world, to help people live good lives. He comes to them with gifts of love and joy so that they may live with joy as His children. He watches over them when they go astray and tries to bring them back into the way of life. Jesus taught that God is the one who comes to men in many different ways: He is the Heavenly Father who gives rain and sun to good and bad alike (see p. 156).

Christians believe that God Himself came into the world of men in the person of Jesus Christ. (See chapter 12, section C. 4.) Jesus is the Son of God; in the words of the Nicene Creed, He is '. . . very God from very God . . . who on account of us men and on account of our salvation came down and was incarnate; He became man . . .' Christians believe that the coming of Jesus was an event which is different from all other events in the whole history of the world. In the birth of Jesus God did not only touch human history, He became part of human history itself. This happening is a great mystery, but Christians believe that it happened once and only once, when Jesus was conceived and born of Mary.

This event is the one event which Christians believe to be unique, and different from all other events in human history ('unique' means 'the only one of its kind'). When Christians say that their religion is different from others, they say so because of this which God did. In many ways the Christian religion is very similar to other religions: Christians pray as others do, Christians read Scriptures as others do, Christians have priests and teachers as others do, Christians teach almost the same things as others do about what is right and wrong. But Christians differ from others in saying that God became man in Jesus Christ. Christians believe that they must witness to this and tell others about it. Christians do not differ from the people of other religions in all the things which they do: nor in all the things which they believe. Many of their beliefs about God and many of the things they do to worship Him are like those of other people. They differ from other people in this: that God has made them witnesses to His one unique coming in Jesus Christ. It is this unique act of God which makes the most important beliefs of Christians about God different from the beliefs of other religions.

C. THE PRESENCE OF GOD

Christians believe that God came into human lives in a unique way in Jesus Christ. But this is not the only way in which God touches

'In the birth of Jesus God became part of human history. When Christians say that their religion is different from others, they say so because of this' (p. 246).

In the town of Bethlehem (above) a priest of the Greek Orthodox Church lights a candle in the church of the Holy Nativity, which is built, according to tradition, on the site of the inn where Jesus was born.

In what ways do you think that Christianity is different from other religions?

the lives of men. Christians share with others the belief that all living creatures live in the presence of God, and that He touches their lives in countless different ways (see p. 156).

Christians are helped to see that God blesses people of other religions in two ways:

1. Christians have the example of the Old Testament to show them how God guides and blesses a nation or a community throughout its history. When they read the Scriptures of the Old Testament they notice all the different ways which God used to teach the Jews what to believe about Him and how to pray. He used all kinds of happenings (earthquakes, famine, defeat in battle, victory, exile), and all kinds of people (kings, priests, prophets, wise men) to do this. But the Jews were not the only people who were precious to God. God loves all men alike, and He spoke to people of other nations in the ways which could help them. Christians can use the Old Testament as a guide, to help them understand the ways in which God has blessed other nations and peoples in the events of their own histories, and through the teachings of their own wise men and prophets, and does so still.

2. Christians believe that the Spirit of God is active among people of all communities to help them worship God in truth. They recall the words of the Lord Jesus to the woman of Samaria: 'The time approaches, indeed it is already here, when those who are real worshippers will worship the Father in spirit and in truth. Such are the worshippers whom the Father wants. God is spirit, and those who worship him must worship in spirit and in truth' (John 4.23–24 NEB). Christians know the power and presence of the Holy Spirit in their Churches, and they believe that God gave the Holy Spirit to them in a special way (see pp. 159, 174). But Christians do not know what are the limits of the activity of the Holy Spirit: He is 'the Lord, the Giver of Life', and as God is present everywhere, so His Spirit is also. He guides and leads all those who respond to His influence and worship God in spirit and in truth.

'No one has ever seen God; but God's only Son, he who is nearest to the Father's heart, he has made him known' (John 1.18). Christians believe that Jesus of Nazareth revealed in Palestine, among His friends and disciples, the character of God. He revealed the eternal love of God in human acts of care and compassion; He revealed the creative power of God in human acts of healing and peace-making; He revealed the holiness of God in human acts of rebuke and forgiveness. Because He revealed the love, the power, and the holiness of God in these human acts, we now understand more clearly what the love, the power, and the holiness of God are like. So Christians are able to recognize the presence of God in people's lives, even when they belong to other religions. They know that a Muslim or a Hindu prays, and they can see God's power working in his life to heal him or to comfort him. They watch a Buddhist boy overcoming temptation and growing into a strong and upright man, and they rejoice because they recognize that God's holiness is helping him. They visit a Dinka, a Maori, or a Shinto home and see that love is there: they recognize that the love of God is present in that home to purify the relationships between parents and children and between man and wife.

A Christian, however, is not content simply to notice the presence of God in other religions. He does two other things as well. First, he takes to himself what he learns about God from other religions. In receiving God's love, power, and holiness, people of other religions learn many things about God. Christians may learn from them, and in doing so enrich their own faith and their own lives. Secondly, a Christian will share with his friends of other religions the story of Jesus, so that they may understand better the love, the power, and the holiness of God. Jesus made these known to men in a unique way. A Christian will try to help others see in Jesus what the love, the power, and the holiness of God are really like. He cannot stop bearing witness to the Lord Jesus, so that others may worship Him also. To worship Him is to see the whole truth of God in all its beauty.

D. THE PURPOSE OF GOD

Christians believe that God intends to bring the whole universe into a unity in Christ (Eph. 1.10; 1 Cor. 15.20–28). The writer of the book of Revelation pictured this unity as a great and lovely city, the new Jerusalem of God. He described his vision in the last two chapters of his book. At the centre of the city would be the throne of God and of Christ: their glory would shine and give light to the whole city. This great city of God would unite together the whole life of the world in Christ. 'The wealth and splendour of the nations shall be brought into it.'

The New Testament writer saw in such a great city the fulfilment of all God's purposes. At the centre would be Christ, but around Him would be all that is good in the whole of human life. We may believe that all the hopes and gifts of God which are good in the religions of the world will be brought into God's Jerusalem. In the end, God will gather into one all the many partial truths about Himself, and all the many ways of prayer which have made human life so rich and beautiful.

Christians also believe that God has done in Christ all that is necessary to bring this great plan to fulfilment. Through the death and resurrection of Jesus Christ God has defeated evil, and opened to men and women the road to eternal life. 'Through Christ God chose to reconcile the whole universe to himself, making peace through the shedding of his blood upon the cross—to reconcile all things, whether on earth or in heaven, through him alone' (Col. 1.20 NEB). God's purpose is to bring all things to a unity in Christ: God is taking His time to complete His purpose, but Christians have no doubt that He will complete it. He has made His victory certain, through the life, death, and resurrection of Jesus Christ.

STUDY SUGGESTIONS

WORD STUDY

1. What is meant by the statement that the coming of Jesus was a *unique* event in the history of the world?

REVIEW OF CONTENT

2. (a) What was the attitude of most Old Testament writers to people of other religions?
   (b) What was the attitude of Jesus to people of other religions?
3. What three things should a Christian remember when he tries to explain to others the belief of the Church about God and Christ?
4. Explain the following picture-language which Jesus used to describe God's relationship with the world.
   God is like:
   (a) a shepherd   (b) a housewife   (c) a king.
5. In what chief ways is the Christian religion different from other religions?
6. (a) In what chief ways does God bless people of other religions?
   (b) How does God enable Christians to recognize His presence in the lives of people of other religions?
7. What do Christians believe about God's purpose for the universe?

BIBLE STUDY

8. What do we learn from Romans 11.9–23; Acts 14.15–17, and Acts 17.24–31 about Paul's attitude towards people of other religions?
9. Study carefully the Bible references set out in this chapter, section by section.

DISCUSSION AND RESEARCH

10. If your answer to Q. 10 on p. 242 was 'only one', which religion do you think that 'one' is most likely to be? Give your reasons.

11. 'God's purpose is to bring all things to a unity in Christ' (p. 249).
   (a) What is God's own part in fulfilling this purpose?
   (b) What is our part as Christians in fulfilling it?
   (c) How far do you think the study of other religions is likely to help you in this task?
12. What is the most important belief in Christianity, which a Christian must place at the top of any 'hierarchy of truths'?

Some Books for Further Reading

Readers may find the following books useful for further study. Most of them are introductions to the particular subjects; those marked with an asterisk are more advanced.

GENERAL

The World's Living Religions, G. Parrinder (Pan)
What World Religions Teach, G. Parrinder (Harrap)
Religion and the Sciences, C .Wilkes (REP)
Secular and Supernatural, F. R. Barry (SCM)
Interreligious Dialogue, Herbert Jai Singh (CISRS, Bangalore)
**The Primal Vision*, J. V. Taylor (SCM)
Glad Encounter, George Appleton (Edinburgh House Press)
God of a Hundred Names, Green and Gollancz (Gollancz)

TRADITIONAL

**African Religions and Philosophy*, John Mbiti (Heinemann)
**Concepts of God in Africa*, John Mbiti (SPCK)
**Biblical Revelation and African Beliefs*, K. Dickson and P. Ellingworth (Lutterworth)
Religion in Africa, G. Parrinder (Penguin)
Ga and Ga-Adangme Peoples, M. Manoukian (International African Institute)
**Divinity and Experience—the Religion of the Dinka*, G. Lienhardt (OUP)
**Pagan Tribes of the Nilotic Sudan*, C. G. and B. Z. Seligman (Routledge)
Shinto, the Fountainhead of Japan, H. Jean (trans.) (Allen and Unwin)
Gods, Ghosts, and Men in Melanesia, P. Lawrence and M. J. Meggitt (OUP)

HINDUISM

Hinduism, A. C. Bouquet (Hutchinson)
India's Religious Frontier: Hinduism, W. Stewart (SCM)
Living Religions of the Indian People, N. Macnicol (YMCA Delhi)
Outlines of Hinduism, T. M. P. Mahadevan (Chetana Publishers, Bombay)

JUDAISM

Faith, a Jewish Approach, L. Jacobs (Valentine Mitchell)
Martin Buber, R. G. Smith (Lutterworth)

A History of the Jewish People, James Parkes (Weidenfeld and Nicolson)
A Short History of the Jewish People, C. Roth (East & West)
Jewish Prayer and Worship, W. W. Simson (SCM)

CONFUCIANISM

Chinese Religion: An Introduction, L. G. Thomson (Prentice Hall)

BUDDHISM

The Buddhist Way of Life, C. Humphreys (Allen and Unwin)
What is Buddhism?, B. Khantipalo (Hurst, Dawson)
*Buddhism, the Religion of Analysis, N. P. Jacobson (Allen and Unwin)
Buddhism, Its origin and spread—in words and pictures, E. Zürcher (Routledge)
What the Buddha Taught, Walpole Rahula (Gordon Fraser)
Buddhist Devotion and Meditation, Pe Maung Tin (SPCK)

ISLAM

The Life and Teaching of the Prophet Muhammad, M. A. Rauf (Longmans)
The People of the Mosque, L. Bevan Jones (BMP Calcutta)
Islam, A. Guillaume (Penguin)
The Teaching of the Qur'an, H. U. W. Stanton (SPCK)
Islamic Philosophy and Theology, W. Montgomery Watt (EUP)
Counsels in Contemporary Islam, K. Cragg (EUP)
A Brief History of Islam, H. Boer (Daystar, Ibadan)

CHRISTIANITY (ESPECIALLY IN RELATION TO OTHER RELIGIONS)

Dogmatics in Outline, K. Barth (SCM)
The Belief of Christendom, J. Burnaby (SPCK)
Why I am a Christian, O. Hallesby (IVF)
What is Christianity?, Robin Boyd (CLS Madras/Lutterworth)
Christianity and Other Religions, Eric James (Hodder)
*Jews and Christians, G. A. F. Knight (Westminster)
Christian Revelation and World Religions, Hans Kung and others (Burns and Oates)
Marxism and Christianity, Alasdair Macintyre (Duckworth)
Buddhism and the Claims of Christ, D. T. Niles (John Knox)
The Church in India, Swami Abishiktananda (CLS Madras/Lutterworth)
Outside the Camp, R. H. Hooker (CLS Madras and ISPCK)
Together to the Truth, Marcus Braybrooke (CLS Madras and ISPCK)
The Impact and the Challenge, T. K. Thomas (CLS Madras)

Key to Study Suggestions

Chapter 1. God
1. See p. 1, last line—p. 2, line 25.
2. See p. 4, numbered paras 1 and 2.
3. See p. 2, lines 3–21.
4. See p. 4, para. 2.
5. See pp. 4 and 6, numbered paras 1–5.
6. Some answers might be: through visions (Abraham), dreams (Isaac and Jacob), and in the events of their lives.
7. (a) Both; (b) transcendence; (c) both; (d) both.
8. That God is a loving Father who knows and cares for all people alike, and steadfastly sustains the universe He has created. See p. 4, para. 4.

Chapter 2. Religions
1. (b) See p. 10, numbered para. 1 and p. 11, numbered para 5.
   (c) A concordance will help you to find an answer. Some examples are: Gen. 16.13; Exod. 8.10; 20.5; 34.6; Lev. 19.2; Deut. 7.9; Ps. 7.11; Isa. 40; Mark 10.7; Luke 5.21; John 4.24; 2 Cor. 1.3; Rev. 1.8.
2. See p. 11, numbered para. 6.
3. See section C, pp. 10 and 11.
4. (a) See p. 8, para. 3.
5. See p. 10, para. 1.
6. (a) See pp. 10 and 11, numbered para. 3.
8. One way to answer this question would be to find which verses in the Psalm could be used to illustrate some or all of the numbered paras on pp. 10 and 11.

Chapter 3. The Dinka
1. See p. 14, last para. and p. 15, lines 1–5.
2. (a) Fables, legends.
   (b) See p. 15, section headed 'Myths'.
   (c) Two examples from the Bible are the story of Adam and Eve, and the story of Noah.
3. (a) See p. 18, numbered paras 2–4 and p. 19, numbered para. 5.
   (b) See p. 19, last para.
4. (a) See especially p. 16, last para. and p. 18, numbered para. 2.
   (b) See especially p. 18, numbered paras 3 and 4 and p. 19, first para
   (c) See especially p. 20, last para.
5. See p. 20, section c.
6. See p. 22, paras (a)—(d).
7. Based on p. 22, last 9 lines and p. 23, lines 1–3.
8. Based on pp. 23 and 24, section E, priests.

Chapter 4. The Ga

1. (a) See p. 27, subsection 1 Naa Nyonmo; p. 28, subsection 4. Other spirit-powers, and para. 5; p. 29, subsection 1. The Wulomo, first para.
3. (a) and (b) see p. 26, para. 4, pp. 27–28, subsections 1–4.
4. (a) See p. 28, para. 2.
   (b) see p. 28, para. 3.
5. See pp. 28, 29, section C.
7. Based on p. 27, subsection 3, first para.
8. See pp. 23 and 24, section E, and pp. 29 and 31, subsection D.
9. See p. 29, subsections 1 and 2, and p. 18, subsections 2, 3, 4.

Chapter 5. The Maori

1. (a) Most people will answer that 'divinities' emphasizes transcendence, i.e. beyond the created universe, and 'powers' emphasizes immanence, i.e. within the created universe.
   (b) Most people will associate 'holy', 'sacred', heavenly', and 'almighty' with divinities, and the other words with powers, though all can be associated with both.
2. See p. 43, para. 3.
3. (a) See p. 36, para. 3.
   (b) See p. 36, para. 4.
4. See p. 37, last 13 lines and p. 38 all except the last para.
6. See p. 40, subsection 3.
7. See p. 43, last 8 lines and p. 44, first 5 lines.
8. See p. 44, lines 6–12.
9. Based on p. 42, subsection 1.
10. Based on p. 18, subsection 2; p. 27, subsection 1; p. 40, subsection 3.
11. Based on p. 19, para. 4; p. 29, paras 2 and 3; p. 39, last para. and p. 40, paras 1–4.

Chapter 6. Shamanism

1. (a) See p. 47, numbered para. 2, line 7.
   (b) See p. 47, numbered para. 2, lines 7–12.
   (c) See p. 47, numbered para. 2, line 4.
2. See p. 48, subsection 2, para. 2.
3. (a) See p. 46, para. 2, lines 3–9.
   (b) See p. 46, para. 3, lines 3–5.
4. (a) See p. 47, section C, line 1.
   (b) See p. 47, section C, lines 2–7.
5. See p. 46, last 5 lines and p. 47, first 3 lines.
6. (a) See p. 48, subsection 2, para. 1.
   (b) See p. 47, last para. and p. 48, first 2 lines.
7. Based on p. 48, subsection 2, para 1.
8. Based on p. 50, example no. 3.
9. (b) See p. 47, lines 1–3 and p. 48, lines 1, 2.

Chapter 7. Shintoism

1. See p. 54, lines 2–6.
2. Ablution—washing; exorcism—expulsion; abstention—refraining.

3. See p. 54, section A, para. 1.
4. See p. 54, section A, para. 2;   p. 55, paras 2 and 3.
5. (a) and (b) see p. 54, section A, paras 3 and 4;   p. 55, paras 1 and 2.
   (c) See p. 55, para. 3, last 3 lines.
6. See p. 54, section A, para. 2;   p. 55, para. 3, lines 3–5.
7. See pp. 55 and 56, numbered paras 1–5.
8. See p. 56, Section B.
9. (a) See p. 57, para. 2, lines 1–5.
   (b) See p. 57, para. 2, lines 6–11.
10. See pp. 57 and 59, section C, subsections 1–3.
12. Based on p. 42, last para. and p. 43, paras 1 and 2;   p. 59, first para. (subsection 2).
14. See p. 19, para. 4;   p. 39, last para. and p. 40, paras 1–4;   p. 57, para. 1.

Chapter 8. Hinduism   Sections A, B

1. See p. 61, para. 5.
2. (a) See p. 61, para. 6, lines 1, 2.
   (b) See p. 61, para. 6, lines 2, 3.
3. (a) See p. 61, para. 5.
   (b) and (c) See p. 61, para. 3.
   (d) See p. 63, subsection 4, para. 2.
   (e) See p. 61, para. 4.
   (f) See p. 63, subsection 4, para. 1.
4. See p. 63, subsection 3, numbered paras 1–3.
5. (a) and (b) See pp. 63 and 64, section B, subsection 1.
6. See p. 64, subsection 2, paras (a)—(d).
7. (a) See p. 65, subsection 4, para. 2.
   (b) See p. 65, subsection 4, para. 3.
8. Based on p. 65, first para. and last para.

Chapter 8. Hinduism   Section C

1. (a) See p. 70, last 2 lines and p. 71 first 2 lines.
   (b) See p. 68, last lines and p. 69, lines 1–7.
   (c) See p. 76, para. (c) lines 2–5.
   (d) See p. 70, para. (b).
2. Based on p. 64, subsection 3, but use a dictionary if you need to.
3. See p. 67, last para. and p. 68 first 2 lines.
4. See p. 66, last 2 lines and p. 67 first 4 lines.
5. See p. 67, subsection 1, lines 1–3;   p. 69, subsection 2, lines 1–7;   p. 70, subsection 3, lines 1, 2;   p. 71, subsection 4, lines 1–3;   p. 74, subsection 5, lines 1–6.
6. See p. 67, para. (a).
7. See p. 69, subsection 2, para. 2;   p. 73, last 4 lines and p. 74, first 3 lines.
8. (a) See p. 70, para. (c) and p. 71, first 6 lines and subsection 4, lines 1–3.
   (b) See p. 70, para. (b).
   (c) See p. 68, para. (d) and p. 69, para. 2.
9. See p. 73, para. (d) and following para.

10. (a) (i) See p. 74, last 13 lines and p. 75, lines 1–24.
  (ii) See p. 74, subsection 5, para. 2.
  (iii) See p. 74, subsection 5, para. 3.
 (b) See p. 74, subsection 5, para. 2, lines 7–12 and para. 5, lines 5, 6; p. 76, para. 3.
11. Based on p. 76, line 4 to end of page.
12. *Puranas:* See p. 71, para. (d).
 Brahmins: See p. 68, para. (c), lines 10, 11.
 Vishnu: See p. 70, last para. (c), line 4.
 Gurus: See p. 76, line 6.
13. (a) See p. 69, subsection 2, paras 1, 3, and 4.

Chapter 8. Hinduism   Sections D, E, F

1. (a) Dasara—a festival; darsana—a world-view.
 (b) See p. 68, last line and p. 69, lines 1–8; p. 79, subsection 1, lines 2, 3.
2. See p. 70, last para. (c); p. 71, para. (d); p. 81, para. 2.
3. (a) See p. 79, subsection 1.
 (b) See p. 79, subsection 2.
4. See p. 80, numbered paras 1, 2, 3.
5. Based on p. 81, subsection 1.
6. (a) See p. 82, subsection 3, paras 2, 3, 4.
 (b) See p. 84, para. 4.
 (c) See p. 84, para. 3.
7. (a) See p. 84, para. 6.
 (b) See p. 82, subsection 3, para. 2, last 4 lines.
 (c) See p. 84, paras 2, 3.
8. See p. 80, subsection 4, paras 1 and 2.
9. Based on p. 79, last 5 lines and p. 80, lines 1, 2.
10. (a) Based on p. 79, para. 1 and p. 80, subsection 4, para. 2.
 (b) Based on p. 68, para. (d) and following paras.

Chapter 9. Confucianism

1. See p. 91, lines 9, 10 and line 15, and use a dictionary if you need to.
2. See p. 90, para. 5, and the list of five titles which follow. The answer is meaning (c).
3. (a) See p. 90, para. 1 and para. 3, lines 6 and 7.
 (b) See p. 90, paras 2 and 3.
4. (a) See p. 90, para. 5.
 (b) See p. 90, last 5 lines and p. 91, lines 1–10.
 (c) See p. 90, para. 5 and p. 91, lines 11–21.
5. (a) Based on p. 92, paras 2–5.
 (b) Based on p. 92, last para. and p. 93, paras 1–3.
6. (a) See p. 94, para. 3.
 (b) See p. 94, paras 3 and 4.
7. See p. 29, paras 3–4; p. 39 last 4 lines and p. 40, paras 1–4; p. 94 last 8 lines and p. 96, paras 1, 2.
8. See p. 93, paras 1–3.
9. Based on p. 91, last 10 lines and p. 92, lines 1–11 and paras 4, 5.

10. Based on pp. 91, 92, subsection on The Meaning of Benevolence.
11. Based on p. 89.
12. Based on p. 93, paras 1–3 and pp. 68, 69, para. (d), following para. and summary.
14. Based on p. 93, para. 4, p. 94, para. 5.

Chapter 9. Taoism
1. See pp. 98–100, section B: nothingness, struggle, competition.
2. (a) See p. 98, para. 1.
   (b) See p. 98, para. 2.
3. See p. 89, para. 3.
4. See p. 98, last para.
5. See p. 100, paras 3–6.
6. Based on pp. 99, 10 numbered paras 1–3.
7. See p. 99, lines 10, 11 and italic headings to numbered paras 1–3.

Chapter 10. Judaism   Sections A, B, C
1. (a) Use a dictionary if you need to.
   (b) See p. 104, section A, subsection 1, para. 3 and p. 105, subsection 4.
2. Torah—see p. 111, para 3.
   Yahweh—see p. 108, para. (a).
3. Canaanites—see p. 104, para. 4.
   Philistines—see p. 104, para. 4.
   Maccabees—see p. 105, subsection 5, lines 3–5.
   Ba'al—see p. 110, subsection 2, para. 1.
   Assyrians—see p. 105, subsection 3, para. 2.
   Herods—see p. 105, subsection 5, lines 7–9.
   Jamnia—see p. 111, para. 3.
   Hyksos—see p. 104, para. 2.
4. Antiochus Epiphanes—see p. 105, subsection 5, lines 1–3.
   Solomon—see p. 104, last para.
   Cyrus—see p. 105, subsection 4, para. 2.
   David—see p. 104, last para.
   Hitler—see p. 104, subsection 7, lines 3–5.
   Joshua—see p. 110, line 2.
   Moses—see p. 104, para. 3;   p. 109, last line and p. 110, lines 1, 2.
5. See pp. 108, 109, paras (a)—(e).
6. See p. 109, last para., lines 1–3;   p. 110, paras 3 and 5.
7. See p. 111, para. 3.
8. Based on p. 108, paras (c) and (d).

Chapter 10. Judaism   Sections D, E, F
1. See p. 116, last 4 lines and p. 117, lines 1–7.
2. (a) See pp. 113–115, subsection 2.
3. See pp. 112, 113, subsection 1.
4. See p. 114, para. 3.
5. (a) See p. 115, para. 4, lines 1–5.
   (b) See p. 115, last 2 paras and p. 116, para. 1.

(c) See p. 115, para. 4, last 2 lines.
6. See p. 82, para. 3, lines 4–6 and p. 117, para. 2.
7. *Rosh Hashanah*—see p. 117, para. 4.
   The Talmud—see p. 119, subsection 2, para. 2, lines 3–5.
   Pharisees—see p. 119, subsection 2, para. 2, lines 1, 2.
   The Sabbath—see p. 115, para. 6 and p. 119, lines 1, 2.
8. (a) See p. 117, section F, para. 1, line 1.
   (b) See p. 119, section F, para. 1, lines 2–5;   para. 2, and p. 119, sub-section 2, para. 1.
   (c) See p. 112, subsection 1, para. 1, lines 4–6 and p. 113, the Yigdal hymn.
9. A summary of Jesus's teaching might be that His followers must obey all God's commandments as given to Moses, but that they must do so in the Spirit of Love rather than according to the letter of the Law.
10. (b) The Christian interpretation is that these verses foretell the coming of Jesus.

Chapter 11. Buddism   Sections A, B
1. Knowledge, insight, illumination, liberation, serenity.
2. Some possible translations are:
   Dukkha—suffering.
   Nirvana—an experience of bliss in freedom from bodily existence.
   Karma—the law of cause and effect.
   Samsara—the cycle of birth and rebirth according to Hindu and Buddhist doctrine.
3. Use a dictionary if you need to.
4. Based on p. 123, paras 3 and 4.
5. (a) See p. 123, last 2 paras.
   (b) One example is St Francis of Assisi.
6. See p. 123, para. 4.
7. (a) See p. 125, para. 5, last 3 lines.
   (b) See p. 126, para. 2.
8. (a) See p. 126, last 3 lines and p. 127, paras 1 and 2.
   (b) See p. 127, paras 3–6.
9. See p. 130, last para. and p. 131, para. 1.
10. See pp. 132, 133, subsection 5, para. 1 and numbered paras 1–4.
11. Based on pp. 128, 129, numbered para. 4.
12. Based on p. 132, paras 2, 3.
13. Based on p. 131, last para.
14. (a) Based on pp. 130, 131, subsection 3.
15. Based on p. 131, last 5 lines.
16. Based on pp. 132, 133, subsection 5.

Chapter 11. Buddhism   Sections C, D, E, F
1. See p. 137, last 2 paras and p. 138, para. 1.
2. See p. 141, para. 4, lines 6–8.
3. (a) Based on p. 135, and p. 136, lines 1–7.
   (b) See p. 135, para. 2, last 3 lines.

(c) See p. 136, lines 3–7.
4. (a) See p. 138, paras 2 and 3.
   (b) See p. 138, last para. lines 1, 2.
5. See p. 138, subsection 1, paras 3–4.
6. See p. 137, last 3 paras and p. 138, para. 1.
7. See p. 136, section D, paras 1, 3.
8. Tantrism—see p. 137, para. 3.
   Zen—see p. 141, para. 3.
   Dhammapadda—see p. 138, subsection 1, last para.
9. See p. 139, last para; p. 140, para. 1 first 2 lines and last 4 lines; p. 141, last 3 lines.
10. See answer to Q. 9 and p. 94, para. 5.
11. Amitabha Buddha—see p. 140, para. 2.
    Kuan Yin—see p. 141, para. 2.
    Bodhidarma—see p. 141, para. 5.
12. See p. 135, paras 3–8 and p. 136, paras 1–3.
13. Based on p. 139, last para.; p. 140; and p. 141, lines 1–3.
14. Based on p. 139, last para. and p. 140, lines 1–4.

Chapter 11. Buddhism   Sections G, H, I
1. See p. 145, last para.
2. (a) See p. 146, subsection 1, lines 1–6.
   (b) See p. 146, subsection 1, lines 6–20.
3. See p. 148, subsection 4.
4. (a) See p. 149, subsection 6, and p. 150, lines 1, 2.
   (b) See p. 150, paras 2–4.
5. See p. 150, last 4 lines and p. 151, lines 1–5.
6. See p. 151, para. 2; p. 151, para. 5; p. 151, last para. and p. 153, lines 1–10.
9. See p. 135, para. 1.

Chapter 12. Christianity   Section A
1. See p. 159, para. 6.
2. (a) and (b) Use a dictionary to check your answers.
3. Most people will answer: teacher, founder, witness, messenger.
5. See pp. 156–159, italic lines (a), (b), (c), (d).
6. (a) See p. 160, subsection 3.
   (b) See p. 161, paras (a)—(c).
7. (a) See p. 162, lines 1–6.
   (b) See p. 162, lines 7, 8.
   (c) See p. 162, line 9.
   (d) See p. 162, lines 10–12.
   (e) See p. 162, lines 13, 14.
8. Matt. 5.43–48: God's love is for *all* human beings alike.
   Matt. 6.25–34: God's love upholds and sustains all created things.
   Luke 6.35, 36: God's love is steadfast even for people who disobey and reject Him.
9. Mark 8.27–38: He brought deliverance by His readiness to suffer for others.

Luke 4.1–21: He brought deliverance by overcoming temptation, and so preaching freedom to the people.
John 6.15: He brought deliverance by choosing the way of humility, refusing to be made king.

Chapter 12. Christianity   Section B

1. See p. 166, para. 1.
2. See p. 169, last 4 lines.
3. See p. 166, last para.; p. 168, last para.; and p. 169, paras 1, 2.
4. (a) See 166, last 2 paras;   p. 167, para. 1.
   (b) See p. 167, para. 1, last 3 lines.
5. (a) See p. 167, paras 2 and 3.
   (b) See p. 167, para. 2, last 5 lines.
   (c) See p. 167, para. 5.
6. (a) See p. 167, last 2 paras and p. 168, para. 1.
   (b) See p. 168, para. 3.
7. (a) See p. 168, para. 7.
   (b) See p. 168, para. 5.
   (c) See p. 168, paras 5, 6.
8. (a) See p. 169, subsection 3 (a).
   (b) See p. 169, subsection 3 (b).
   (c) See p. 171, para. (c).
   (d) See p. 171, para. (d).
   (e) See p. 171, para. (e).
9. See p. 169, para. 3.

Chapter 12. Christianity   Sections C, D

1. (a) See p. 175, para. 4.
   (b) See p. 177, para. 4.
2. (a) See p. 99, numbered para. 1, last 2 lines.
   (b) See pp. 99, 100, subsection 'Human Virtue' and pp. 173, 174, subsection 1. 'The Way and the Spirit'.
3. See p. 100, paras 1 and 2.
4. (a) See p. 174, subsection 2, para. 2, lines 2–6.
   (b) See p. 174, subsection 2, para. 3.
   (c) See p. 174, last 6 lines and p. 175, line 1.
5. (a) See p. 175, heading to subsection 3.
   (b) and (c) See p. 175, para. 5.
6. See p. 175, last 8 lines and p. 177, paras 1 and 2.
7. See p. 177, para. 4.
8. See p. 177, last 2 paras and p. 178, first 3 paras.
9. Based on p. 178, last 2 paras.
14. See p. 174, para. 2.

Chapter 13. Islam   Section A (1)

1. See p. 187, subsection 3 (b), para. 2.
2. See p. 182, para. 1.
3. (a) See p. 187, subsection 3 (a), para. 2.
   (b) See p. 182, para. 3.

4. Oases: see p. 182, subsection 1 (a), para. 2.
   Bedouin: see p. 182, subsection 1 (a), para. 1.
   Hanifs: see p. 187, subsection 3 (b), para. 2, last 7 lines.
   The Ka'ba: see p. 184, subsection 2 (a), para. 2.
5. (a) See p. 184, subsection 2, para. (b).
   (b) See p. 184, subsection 2 (a), para. 3.
   (c) See p. 184, subsection 2 (b), para. 2.
6. See p. 38, last para. and p. 40 last para.;   p. 183, para. (d) 1 and 2 and
   2 following paras and p. 187, subsection 3 (b), para. 2, lines 4–8. Some
   likenesses are:
   Belief in many deities or powers.
   Association of deities with natural objects.
   Belief in the protective power of deities.
   Belief in a 'High God' above and beyond other deities.
7. Based on pp. 119, 120 and pp. 187–190. You will find similar sayings, for
   example, about: death and judgement, dependence on God, kindness and
   compassion, keeping God's law, God as Creator, modesty and humility.
8. See p. 186, last 17 lines and p. 187, lines 1–10.
9. (a) See p. 110, subsection 2, paras 2 and 3.
   (b) See p. 190, numbered paras 1–3 and following para.
10. Based on p. 191, numbered para. 1 and 2 following paras.

Chapter 13. Islam   Section A (2)

1. (a) See p. 193, subsection 4, para. 3.
   (b) See p. 193, subsection 4, para. (a) and para. 3.
2. (a) and (b) See p. 187, subsection 3 (a), para. 2, and p. 195, para. (c).
3. (a) See p. 193, subsection 4, paras 2 and 3.
   (b) See p. 196, subsection 5, para. 1.
4. See p. 194, paras 1–4.
5. (a) See p. 194, para. (b) and following paras and p. 195, first 8 lines.
   (b) See p. 195, lines 9–12.
6. (a) See p. 195, para. (c).
   (b) See p. 195, numbered paras 1–4.
7. (a) See p. 195, numbered para. 3, 2 following paras, and p. 196, para. (a)
   and following para.
   (b) See p. 196, subsection 5 (a), para. 3.
8. (a) See p. 196, para. (b).
9. (a) See p. 197, final para. with subparas 1–3.
   (b) Based on p. 162, lines 1–17;   p. 197, last 13 lines and p. 180, first·
   5 lines.
   (c) See p. 196, para. (b).
10. (a) Some examples are:
    Guidance on social responsibility: Exod. 21.1–11.
    Lending money: Exod. 22.25–27.
    Punishment for offences: Exod. 21.12–end.
12. (a) See p. 166, subsection 1, both paras.

Chapter 13. Islam   Section B

1. (a) and (b) See p. 200, para. 3.

2. (a) See p. 199, section B.1, paras 2–4.
   (b) See p. 199, section B.1, para. 1.
3. See p. 200, para. 1.
4. See p. 200, paras 3–5 and p. 201, lines 1–5.
5. (a) See p. 201, lines 6–18.
   (b) See p. 201, lines 19–27.
6. See p. 201, subsection 3, paras 1, 2.
7. See p. 200, para. 3, last 3 lines.
8. (a), (b), and (c) See pp. 204, 205, and p. 206, first 5 lines.
10. See p. 200, para. 1, last 4 lines.
11. See p. 202, last line, and p. 204, lines 1–4.

Chapter 13. Islam   Sections C, D, E, F
1. See p. 213, line 6.
2. See p. 211, subsection 2, para. 1.
3. Imam—see p. 214, para. 2.
   Zakat—see p. 214, numbered para. 3.
   Jihad—see p. 216, numbered para. 6.
   Hafiz—see p. 211, para. 2.
   Sufis—see p. 217, last 2 lines and p. 218, paras 1 and 2.
   Ramadan—see p. 214, numbered para. 4.
4. (a) See p. 207, subsection 1 and p. 208, lines 1–19.
5. See pp. 209, 210, subsection 5.
6. See p. 209, subsection 4, paras (a)—(d).
7. (a) See p. 209, para. (c); p. 210, last para. and p. 211 lines 1–5.
   (b) Some differences are:
   The Qur'an is the work of one man only, the Bible is the work of many.
   The Qur'an was written in one man's lifetime, the Bible was written over many centuries.
8. (a) Likenesses: both Books contains Laws for human behaviour; both were the result of direct 'revelation' by God to a prophet.
   Unlikenesses: The Qur'an is a single book, the Torah is five separate books, written at different times and by different people.
   (b) See p. 212, numbered paras 1 and 2.
9. See p. 213, subsection C, para. 1, and explanation on pp. 213, 214, 216.
10. (a) See p. 209, subsection 4 (c).

Chapter 14. A Changing World
1. (a) and (b) See p. 224, para. 3 and numbered questions 1–4 and p. 225, para. 4.
2. See p. 221, numbered para. 2 and following para.
3. See p. 228, last para.

Chapter 15. One God, Many Religions
1. See p. 231, para. 3.
2. (a) Gradations, orders, rankings.
3. See pp. 231 and 232, numbered paras 1–4.
4. (a) See p. 233, last para. and p. 235 paras 1 and 2.
   (b) See pp. 237, 238.

5. See p. 235, numbered paras 1–2.
6. Dinka: see p. 236, para. 2.
   Maori: see p. 236, para. 4.
   Islam: see p. 236, para. 3.

Chapter 16. The Christian and Other Religions

1. See p. 246, para. 4, lines 1–4.
2. (a) See p. 243, para. 3.
   (b) See p. 244, para. 1.
3. See p. 245, lines 6–8.
4. Based on p. 245, last 9 lines.
5. See p. 246, para. 4.
6. (a) See p. 248, numbered paras 1 and 2.
   (b) See p. 248, last para. and p. 249, lines 1–7.
7. See p. 249, section D, para. 1.
8. See p. 244, para. 2, lines 6–10.

Index

References in bold type show where a full definition or description is to be found in the text.